Teaching Salinger's NINE STORIES

Teaching Salinger's NINE STORIES

by

Brad McDuffie

Nyack College

2011
New Street Communications, LLC
Wickford, RI

newstreetcommunications.com

© 2011 by Brad McDuffie.
Please see the conclusion of the book for additional copyright information.

All rights reserved under International and Pan-American Copyright Conventions. Except for brief quotations for review purposes, no part of this book may be reproduced in any form without the permission of New Street Communications, LLC.

Published 2011
New Street Communications, LLC
Wickford, Rhode Island

newstreetcommunications.com

For

Richard Allan Davison

and

Donald Junkins

Contents

Part I:

Teaching Salinger's *Nine Stories*

Preface / 1

Nine Stories as a Short Story Cycle / 8

A Perfect Day for Bananafish / 18

Uncle Wiggily in Connecticut / 45

Just Before the War with the Eskimos / 69

The Laughing Man / 87

Down at the Dinghy / 106

For Esmé, With Love and Squalor / 123

Pretty Mouth and Green My Eyes / 145

De Daumier-Smith's Blue Period / 160

Teddy / 181

Part II:

Nine Essays

The View from Shore:
Seymour Glass in *The Waste Land* / 210

Uncle Wiggily's Haunted House / 230

From York to Lexington: A Pilgrimage Through Allusions
in "Just Before the War with the Eskimos" / 259

Salinger Criticism and "The Laughing Man": A Case of
Arrested Development / 285

"the old ship is steady again": Empathy and *The Divine
Comedy* in "Down at the Dinghy" / 316

Esmé's Kind of Squalor / 334

The Necessity of Art in
"Pretty Mouth and Green My Eyes" / 351

Salinger and Sincerity:
"De Daumier-Smith's Blue Period" / 364

"One Little Genius Among the Missing": Loss, Human
Communion, and the Negative Way in "Teddy" / 393

1111

J.D. Salinger

NINE STORIES

BY THE AUTHOR OF
The Catcher in the Rye

W.D.Niller

A SIGNET BOOK
Complete and Unabridged

Part I

Teaching Salinger's *Nine Stories*

Teaching Salinger's Nine Stories

Preface

In a 1945 letter to Ernest Hemingway, Jerry Salinger, as he was then known, explained to the older writer that his first book of short stories had collapsed, but, he added, that it was actually a good thing because of the flaws in his prose and he felt that seeing his name on a dust jacket would interfere with his development as a writer. Salinger had landed a number of stories in *The Saturday Evening Post* and other magazines and journals, but his fiction was about to take a major step forward, a fact that seems to be directly connected to his conversations with Hemingway during the war. **(E1)** The best evidence for this can be found in the economy and precision of Salinger's post-war fiction beginning with, "A Perfect Day for Bananafish," "Uncle Wiggily in Connecticut," and "Just Before the War with the Eskimos," the first three stories of what would become *Nine Stories*, in *The New Yorker*.

Though Salinger would make his name and ultimately retire on the success of *The Catcher in the Rye*, *Nine Stories* might very well be his masterpiece. Since its publication in 1953, critics have struggled to come to terms with the collection. Was it, many wondered, a proper story collection? Was it meant to be read as some sort of experimental novel? Few critics have addressed the collection as a whole, choosing to focus on what they see as the more successful stories; and only one book-length study, John Wenke's *J. D. Salinger: A Study of the Short Fiction*, focuses solely upon Salinger's command of the short form. Many other critics have written about *Nine Stories* including Warren French, Paul Kirschner, Ruth Prigozy, Frederick L. Gwynn, Joseph Blotner and, most recently, Christine Kerr; yet, much of this criticism gives little more than a cursory overview of the stories and fails to engage the thematic depth and unity of *Nine Stories*.

One reason for the critical neglect and oversight of *Nine Stories* could be the fact that Salinger criticism has suffered for years now from what we might term an idealization of the adolescent. It is almost impossible to ignore the tension that Salinger creates between the adolescent and adult worlds in *Nine Stories*; and this tension is likely why many critics have ignored the stories in the collection that address this theme. In rebuttal to such notions, Lillian Ross' postscript in *The New Yorker*, "Bearable," written after Salinger's death, refutes years of wrongheaded thinking about adolescents in Salinger's fiction. Ross writes: "He loved children with no holds barred, but never with the sentimental fakery of admiring their 'purity.'" Ross was a close friend of Salinger, and her postscript offers a unique glimpse behind the scenes of his fiction and a glimpse of the often overlooked complexity of his writing and thinking about the world. It is my hope, in this light, that this book will help in part to move Salinger's readership and criticism beyond "the easy labels" (to borrow a phrase from Hemingway's Jake Barnes) attached to him and his fiction through the years.

Since Salinger's death, friends such as Ross, who respected his request for privacy throughout his life, have finally felt at liberty to open up and share their stories about him. These stories, in addition to the letters that have begun to surface, have already helped to debunk a number of myths surrounding Salinger's life and work. In an interview not long after Salinger's death, Ross spoke of Salinger's relevance and importance: "I just think he [Salinger] is one of the greatest. In my opinion, the two writers who will be remembered for the Twentieth Century in literature are Hemingway and Salinger." Only time will tell how correct Ross is in her appraisal, but this book in part attempts to display why Salinger is worthy of such praise.

With Salinger gone now, perhaps readers will be allowed to get out from under the shadow of his myth and appreciate the short fiction for what it is: intense, exquisite, and groundbreaking. Often viewed as inaccessible for high school students and too remedial for university classrooms, for the contributors to this book *Nine Stories* is a masterwork the reading of which signals a deep devotion to Salinger's writing. (You see someone reading it on the subway or a park bench and you think, "Ah, they're in on it. They know.")

Teaching Salinger's NINE STORIES addresses not only each individual story but also the way the collection works as a short-story cycle.

Because a number of the recent publications on Salinger recycle well-known and well-worn essays, I have made it a point to incorporate eight new original essays in the second half of the book. Also included is Richard Davison's seminal 1981 essay, "Salinger Criticism and 'The Laughing Man': A Case of Arrested Development," which has not lost any of its power and charm.

One of the highlights of the 2009 South Atlantic Modern Language Association Convention in Atlanta (where the idea for this book began with three panels exploring *Nine Stories* that I co-chaired with William Boyle) was Davison's reading from "The Laughing Man," as well as a conversational reappraisal of his essay. Davison and Donald Junkins (whose essay "Esmé's Kind of Squalor" is also included here) were our honorary keynote presenters on those panels, and we were thrilled when they told stories about the energy and excitement that surrounded Salinger's fiction in the 1950s and early 1960s.

They helped to conceptualize the heartfelt seriousness surrounding "authenticity" and "phoniness" in those times, and they described how lines stretched out from newsstands to buy copies of *The New Yorker* when Salinger's stories were published. It would be an understatement to say that their presence at the conference, and their support of this project, has been a major influence upon this book as a whole, and I would like to acknowledge my debt to them as scholars and dedicate this book to them.

I would further like to acknowledge with profound gratitude and appreciation all of the work that my two good friends William Boyle and Alex Shakespeare have done in helping me write and edit this book. *Teaching Salinger's NINE STORIES* truly would not have been possible without their help and support. The primary idea for taking a pedagogical approach to the book came from Bill, but in true Max Fischer fashion he shared it with me and allowed me to see it through to the end. I can only hope that I have done justice to the book and will be forever grateful to him for backing me through the entire process. Bill not only helped as a reader, but made considerable contributions to the first couple of chapters.

For his part, Alex's generous advice and honest insight as a reader for the drafts of the book (in addition to his advice on several essays) was instrumental to the successful completion of the project. Alex also made contributions to the first couple of chapters and has a keen eye as an editor that is something akin to "the quantity x itself." I'm thankful that he was willing to devote so much time and energy. Both Bill and Alex are talented writers, as their fine essays on "Teddy" and "De Daumier-Smith's Blue Period" display, and I am really honored by their contributions.

I would also like to thank all of the students from my classes at Nyack College who have read *Nine Stories* with me over the years-especially those eighty or so students from the Spring 2011 semester (and my assistant Christina Carelli-Schulz) who allowed me to immerse them in all things Salinger as I wrote this book. At last, I thank my beautiful wife Rachel (who always knows when to send her father's watch to a broken soul) for her unwavering support and our three wonderful children, Anna, Jonah and Micah, for their boundless love. As Salinger once wrote to Ross, "If your child likes-loves-you, the very love he bears you tears your heart out about once a day or once every other day."

-*Brad McDuffie*, Nyack College

Endnote:

See my essay in the spring 2011 edition of *The Hemingway Review*, "For Ernest, With Love and Squalor: The Influence of Ernest Hemingway on the Life and Work of J. D. Salinger."

Bibliography:

Ross, Lillian. "Bearable." *The New Yorker*. Feb. 2010. 22-23.

---. (2010, August 30). "A Reporting Life." Podcast. New York, NY: *The New Yorker Out Loud*. Retrieved May 6, 2011 from iTunes.

Salinger, J. D. *Raise High the Roof Beam, Carpenters and Seymour an Introduction*. Boston: Little Brown, 1991.

Nine Stories as a Short Story Cycle

Nine Stories has never been seriously considered as a short-story cycle. One of the most recent essays, Ruth Prigozy's "*Nine Stories*, J. D. Salinger's Linked Mysteries," -from J. Gerald Kennedy's, *Modern American Short Story Sequences: Composite Fictions and Fictive Communities* -investigates the cycle (or links) within the book but concludes, "No attempt to explain *Nine Stories* can erase its mysteries" (130). Prigozy's supposition follows the trend of Salinger criticism in acknowledging the genius of *Nine Stories* on one hand, while calling it impenetrable (as a cycle of stories) on the other. Other books such as James Nagel's *The Contemporary American Short Story Cycle* and Susan Garland Mann's *The Short Story Cycle: A Genre Companion and Reference Guide* make no reference to it. Yet aside from Sherwood Anderson's *Winesburg, Ohio* and Ernest Hemingway's *In Our Time*, - two works that directly influenced Salinger in the 1940's-it would be difficult to name a collection of stories more representative of the American short-story cycle than *Nine Stories*.

Nagel argues that Anderson and Hemingway were not consciously aware they were the progenitors of an important new form in modern letters, but he also stresses the significance of the fact that each wrote volumes of stories "with unifying characters and themes" (1). Nagel's observation helps to establish the impact of *In Our Time* and *Winesburg, Ohio* on writers like Salinger. In *Nine Stories*, Salinger makes new the lessons he learns from Hemingway and Anderson by composing a short-story cycle unified by both theme and a cast of related characters. Though each story in *Nine Stories* can be read and analyzed independently of the others, Salinger clearly intended it to be read as a short-story cycle. And Salinger's fiction seems to build off of *Nine Stories* (which he writes congruently with *The Catcher in the Rye*). Understanding the principles he establishes in the cycle opens the door to reading his overall body of work. Thus, the importance of *Nine Stories* in Salinger's canon cannot be overstated.

The thematic cohesion of *Nine Stories* comes principally from the tension he builds between the sacred and the secular throughout the work; indeed, as Dennis L. O'Connor points out, "religious concerns are, in fact, the key to Salinger's fiction" (182). In John Wenke's estimation, *Nine Stories* functions "as a progression based upon the slow painful achievement of spiritual enlightenment, something like what the Christian believer experiences upon passing through the ritual of the Stations of the Cross" or the "successive stages that a soul would pass through according to Vedantic teachings" (63). The religious vision of the book is established by the Zen koan that serves as the epigraph to the collection:

Teaching Salinger's Nine Stories
10

We know the sound of two hands clapping.

But what is the sound of one hand clapping?

The koan provides the central juxtaposition of the sacred and secular throughout *Nine Stories*. The collection follows the pattern of the koan; early on in the collection the sound of one hand clapping, or the spiritual, appears far removed from the events in the stories. However, by the final story, a sense of enlightenment into the sound of one hand clapping is offered in "Teddy." Salinger presents the riddle of the koan in terms of East and West as Teddy states, "it's very hard to meditate and live a spiritual life in America. People think you're a freak if you try to" (188).

In terms of the cycle, Teddy's statement sheds light on how distant the sound of one hand clapping is within the early stories of the collection, but it also provides insight into the events that occur within those stories. Thus, this study will explore how Salinger uses both allusions and teachings from the Christian, Buddhist and Hindu religions, respectfully-though most of the central allusions within the cycle come from the Judeo-Christian tradition- to unify the collection, which comes as a direct result of many years invested in teaching the collection as a short-story cycle.

One might consider how the Zen koan, for instance, informs the collection as a whole. A koan, in Alan Watts's words, presents "the central problem of life in an intensified form" (qtd. in Prigozy); in *Nine Stories*, the mysterious sound of one hand clapping echoes in each of the problems of life experienced by the characters of each story. Prigozy sees the central problem of Salinger's book as "the path from spiritual death to spiritual enlightenment," but she rejects the idea of "imposing any pattern, though logical analysis, on this random collection of fiction" (116). Prigozy thus borrows Teddy's philosophy of "getting rid of the apple of logic" to explain away any logical pattern in *Nine Stories*; but Prigozy neglects that, in order to rid oneself of the apple of logic, a person has to recognize she has taken a bite of that apple. Logic is necessary to understand the difference between one and two hands clapping. Salinger's Teddy reinforces its necessity by his use of logical examples-examples drawn from secular reality-to illustrate spiritual concepts. Salinger's fiction, (indeed, nearly all fiction except the most fantastical) depends on logical analysis, on any recognizable patterns. *Nine Stories* follows the pattern established by its epigraph-the koan that juxtaposes a logical reality (two hands clapping) with an illogical concept (one hand clapping).

D.T. Suzuki, in an essay on "The Reason of Unreason: The Koan Exercise," writes:

> *Technically speaking, the koan given to the uninitiated*

> [Zen Buddhist monk] *is intended to 'destroy the root of life,' 'to make the calculating mind die' ... etc. This may sound murderous but the ultimate intent is to go beyond the limits of intellection, and these limits can be crossed over only by exhausting oneself once and for all, by using up all the psychic powers at one's command ... What could not be solved on the plane of empirical consciousness is now transferred to the deeper recesses of the mind.* (164-165)

But, Suzuki adds, "once solved the koan is compared to a piece of brick used to knock at a gate; when the gate is open the brick is thrown away" (165). The koan is only an *exercise*, "useful only as long as the mental doors are closed, but when they are opened it may be forgotten. What one sees after the opening will be something quite unexpected, something that has never before entered even into one's imagination" (165).

Prigozy is undoubtedly right that "No attempt to explain *Nine Stories* can erase its mysteries," and that it is "as fresh today as it was on publication" (130). But the mystery that cannot be erased in *Nine Stories* has less to do with any *explication de texte* than with Salinger's extended contemplation of how and where the secular and the sacred meet.

"What is the sound of one hand clapping?" is a useful starting-place for a literature teacher. Bernice and Sanford Goldstein write in Heinrich Dumoulin's *History of Zen*

Buddhism about the originator of the 'sound-of-one-hand' koan: Hakuin (1685-1768), called the greatest of the Japanese Zen masters. When he was an old man, Dumoulin notes, he devised this koan as a "problem which he believed would penetrate into one's consciousness with incomparable sharpness and would readily lead to the awakening of doubt and to progress in the exercises" (82).

They add:

"If someone claps his hands, one hears a sound at once. Listen now to the sound of a single hand!" What the "solution" to the koan means, continues Dumoulin, is that "He who lifts one hand and while listening quietly can hear a sound which no ears hear, can surpass all conscious knowledge. He can leave the world of distinctions behind him; he may cross the ocean of the karma of rebirths, and he may break through the darkness of ignorance. In the enlightenment he attains to unlimited freedom." (82)

In light of Dumoulin's "solution" to the koan, one might say that each of Salinger's nine stories makes a sound that can be heard at once; but only by listening in quietude will the reader be surprised beyond conscious knowledge and see how these stories, taken together, may open a door in the mind.

Salinger must have understood that his "religious concerns" would alienate some of his readers, or at least that some of his readers would not take those concerns seriously. But as teachers (and responsible readers) Salinger's religion matters no less than Albert Camus's atheism matters. *Nine Stories* is unified by a universalistic vision in which Salinger believes that everyone is at a different stage of what Teddy calls "spiritual advancement" (188). In *Nine Stories*, "everybody is a nun,"- a philosophy that Salinger will continue to visit in *Franny & Zooey* when Zooey says "There isn't anyone out there who isn't Seymour's Fat Lady" (201), or when he says that the "secret" is "It's Christ Himself. Christ Himself, buddy" (202).

Salinger receives this philosophy (as Bryan and other critics have noted) from Sherwood Anderson's story "The Philosopher" (part of *Winesburg, Ohio*), in which Dr. Parcival tells the young George Willard: "The idea is very simple, so simple that if you are not careful you will forget it. It is this-that everyone in the world is Christ and they are all crucified" (Anderson 39). With Dr. Parcival's philosophy in mind, Salinger seems to use Zooey's reflection on Christ to offer further insight into the one hand clapping koan: "'Jesus realized there is no separation from God.' Zooey here clapped his hands together-only once, and not loud, and very probably in spite of himself" (*F&Z* 170). Zooey's actions reveal-through the sound of two hands clapping-that oneness with God comes through a realization (or epiphany) that "there is no separation from God." The paradox here-two hands clapping to illustrate the sound of one hand clapping-provides yet another example of how Salinger conveys an illogical concept through a logical pattern.

One final point that needs to be made concerns Salinger's use of language. As with his use of the koan, Salinger delights in the division between secular and sacred to framework his character's use of curse words, specifically blasphemy, in the cycle. James E. Bryan points out that apparent blaspheme such as "Chissake" can be also read as "for Christ's sake" (228); and later, in "Seymour an Introduction," Salinger refers to blasphemy, through Seymour, as "a low form of prayer" (*Raise High* 154). Language, thus, becomes another means by which Salinger inverts high and low and challenges his reader to think beyond conventional interpretations.

In the following chapters, as *Nine Stories* is explored as a short-story cycle, it is with the understanding that "religious concerns are, in fact, the key to Salinger's fiction" (O'Connor 182). Only by examining these structures can readers (students and teachers alike) begin to unravel the themes that connect the stories. In teaching the collection over the years, I have asked students to be free thinkers and open their minds to consider both the sound of two hands clapping as well as the more difficult sound of one hand clapping-asked them to enter into a dialogue respectful of both aspects of the koan, respectful to both the material and spiritual ways of being-and it is my hope that you will enter into this dialogue with us.

Bibliography:

Anderson, Sherwood. *Winesburg, Ohio*. New York: Modern Library, 1999.

The Bible. King James Version.

Bryan, James E. "The Fat Lady and the Chicken Sandwich." *College English* 23.3 (1961): 226-229.

O'Connor, Dennis L. "J. D. Salinger: Writing as Religion." *The Wilson Quarterly* 4.2 (1980): 182-190.

Prigozy, Ruth. "*Nine Stories*: J. D. Salinger's Linked Mysteries." *Modern American Short Story Sequences: Composite Fictions and Fictive Communities*. Ed. J. Gerald Kennedy. New York: Cambridge, 1995. 114-132.

Salinger, J. D. *Franny and Zooey*. Boston: Little Brown, 1991.

---. *Nine Stories*. Boston: Little Brown, 1991.

---. *Raise High the Roof Beam, Carpenters and Seymour An Introduction*. Boston: Little Brown, 1991.

Suzuki, D. T. *Zen Buddhism: Selected Writings*. New York: Random House, 1996.

Wenke, John. *J. D. Salinger: A Study of the Short Fiction.* Ed. Gordon Weaver. 26 vols. Boston: Twayne, 1991.

Suggestions for Further Reading:

Alsen, Eberhard. *Salinger's Glass Stories as a Composite Novel.* Troy, NY: Whitson, 1983.

Blotner, Joseph L. and Gwynn, Frederick L. *The Fiction of J. D. Salinger.* Pittsburgh: Pittsburgh UP, 1958.

Cotter, James Finn. "Religious Symbols in Salinger's Shorter Fiction." *Studies in Short Fiction* 15 (1978): 121-132.

Smith, Dominic. "Salinger's *Nine Stories*: Fifty Years Later." *The Antioch Review* 61.4 (2003): 639-649.

A Perfect Day for Bananfish

Overview

The first part of "A Perfect Day for Bananafish" revolves around a phone conversation between Muriel Glass and her mother. In the second part, the primary action follows Seymour Glass and his discussion with a young girl named Sybil Carpenter. In the first section, Salinger centers the conversation on material things; in the second, Seymour's parable of the bananafish reflects more of a spiritual focus. In the closing section, the material and spiritual concerns of the story come together in Seymour's suicide.

Salinger establishes the materialistic thrust of Muriel's telephone conversation with her mother in the opening sentence: "There were ninety-seven New York advertising men in the hotel, and, the way they were monopolizing the long-distance lines, the girl in 507 had to wait till almost two-thirty to get her call through" (3). When the operator finally puts Muriel's call through, the conversation with her mother mostly concerns Seymour's state of mind and clothing fashions during the New York vacation season in Florida. Among the important details Muriel shares about Seymour are: 1) that he sent her a book of poems "by the only great poet of the century" (6) from Germany; and 2) that he has "played the piano both nights we've been here" in "the Ocean Room" (7).

Furthermore, Muriel's mother makes a number of elliptical claims about Seymour's erratic behavior: "The trees. That business with the window. Those horrible things he said to Granny about her plans for passing away. What he did with all those lovely pictures from Bermuda-everything" (6). Muriel also reveals that she is "so sunburned" she "can hardly move" even though she used the "jar of Bronze" (7) her mother gave her.

In contrast to the matter-of-fact materialism that opened the story, the spiritual and imaginative concerns of the second section open with the words of Sybil Carpenter: "See more glass" she says, "Did you see more glass?" (10). Sybil's mother puts sun-tan oil on her and sets her loose on the beach as she returns to the hotel. Sybil runs down the beach and finds Seymour. Seymour and Sybil engage in small talk about her father arriving on "a nairiplane" (11) and Muriel-"the lady" (12)-before Sybil begins talking about another little girl named Sharon Libschutz. From this point on, the conversation turns to trying to "catch a bananafish" (13) and the story of "'Little Black Sambo'" (14). Once in the water, Seymour pushes Sybil on a float out "to the horizon" (16) until a wave washes over the top of them and Sybil exclaims that she has seen a bananafish. At this point, Seymour kisses Sybil's foot and brings the fishing expedition to an abrupt halt.

In the final section of the story, Seymour returns to the hotel and accuses a woman on the elevator of looking at his feet. He says, "If you want to look at my feet, say so [...] But don't be a God-damned sneak about it" (17). Seymour gets off at the fifth floor and enters room 507 (the room he shares with Muriel), and takes out an "Ortgies calibre 7.65 automatic" (18), then he "looked at the girl, aimed the pistol, and fired a bullet through his right temple" (18).

Analysis

In the first paragraph of the story Salinger disorients the reader with a reference to New York, withholding that the story will take place in Florida. The beachside setting will provide an ironic counterpoint to the title, since this perfect day "is the hottest day they've had in Florida in-" (4). And Florida itself suggests a failed materialistic paradise that seems more like hell (as hinted at by Muriel's debilitating burn) than heaven. Indeed, Muriel is reading "an article in a woman's pocket-size magazine, called 'Sex is Fun-or Hell'" (3), and many of the fun pleasures of the story, such as drinking and sun bathing, are associated with hell. This subversion of expectations-in which "paradise" is hellish-sets the scene (and the background) for Seymour's suicide.

Muriel and her mother's discussion of clothing fashions and social class in Florida ("You should see what sits next to us in the dining room," she says to her mother [9]) is an almost exaggerated depiction of their materialism-their less than healthy obsession with the "meaning" of material things. People's clothing becomes a means of caricature and criticism. Muriel says of the wife of the psychiatrist Dr. Rieser that she "was horrible" because of an "awful dinner dress" that was "all hips" (8). And later, her mother asks Muriel, "How's your blue coat?" (8). The absurd personification of Muriel's coat dramatizes the absurdity that Salinger sees in a culture obsessed with appearances.

Salinger sees this overwrought materialism embodied in psychiatry (specifically 1940's Freudian psychotherapy), as well and his satire of modern psychotherapy is made clear in the story (and this satirical stance towards psychotherapy will continue throughout *Nine Stories*). Muriel's mother, in particular, seems to value the opinions of psychiatrists above all others. She urges Muriel, time and again, to get Dr. Rieser's advice, (though one might doubt his expertise after Muriel states, "[he's] in the bar *all day long*" [8]). Her limited materialist view of the world, which she imposes on Muriel (and on Seymour), is one that takes into account status symbols-not only fashionable clothing but the fashionable and expensive practice of psychotherapy-to the exclusion of everything non-material, non-social, and non-logical.

Muriel's reflections on psychotherapy are key to the structure of "Bananafish," especially with regards to the adult/child themes. Muriel says the doctor could not diagnose Seymour's behavior because, "He had to have more facts, Mother. They have to know about your childhood-all that stuff. I told you, we could hardly talk, it was so noisy in there" (8). In her conversation with her mother, Muriel ironically implies facts about her childhood and why she seems to value her blue coat over the book of poems Seymour sent her from the war. Salinger seems to reinforce this through the counterpoint of his transition to the second part of the story and the brief conversation between Sybil Carpenter and her mother. Consider, for instance, that Mrs. Carpenter is "putting sun-tan oil" on the back of her child. Like the bottle of bronze that burns Muriel, the sun-tan oil will provide Sybil with no protection from the Florida sun. In spite of the fact that Sybil is only four years old, her mother leaves her unsupervised on the beach while she goes "up to the hotel [to] have a Martini" (11).

Because the instruction of children is a central theme throughout *Nine Stories*, we should also consider how, when the story shifts from the first to the second section, Sybil says, "See more glass" (10). She then asks her mother, "Did you see more glass?" (10). Mrs. Carpenter does not listen to Sybil; instead, she tells her to "stop saying that. It's driving Mommy absolutely crazy" (10). When Sybil asks the question again, Salinger draws parallels between Sybil and Muriel's conversation about fashions. Sybil's mother ignores her question about "See more glass" and instead listens to her friend describe how to tie what was "really just an ordinary silk handkerchief-you could see when you got up close" in a "really darling" manner (10-11). The contrast Salinger makes here is between what Sybil learns to see "up close" from her mother and her friend and from Seymour Glass, who will teach her to "see more."

Sybil's question to her mother also invites the reader into the text -suddenly we are forced to make sense of the text, to use our own imaginations rather than merely confronting and absorbing a barrage of numbers and facts. In contrast to the cool third-perspective eye that documents the conversation between Muriel and her mother, we are invited to see beyond the supposedly "adult" world of facts and fashions, much as Seymour invites Sybil to see the bananafish below the glass of the ocean water. One of the central ways that Salinger invites the reader to "see more" in "Bananafish" is through the allusions he makes to T. S. Eliot's poem, *The Waste Land*. **(E1)** One of the first direct allusions to *The Waste Land* comes through Mrs. Hubbel's statement about seeing "an ordinary silk handkerchief" (10). In the third section of *The Waste Land*, "The Fire Sermon," Eliot cites the "Silk handkerchiefs, cardboard boxes, cigarette ends / Or other testimony of summer nights" (11). The silk handkerchiefs, or used condoms in *The Waste Land* are meant to illustrate a state of moral decay in which the sexual act between humans becomes little more than the "automatic" (14) **(E2)** copulation of animals (a theme Salinger will return to in "Pretty Mouth and Green My Eyes"). **(E3)**

Another central allusion to Eliot's poem comes through Sybil's name. According to Michael North, the epigraph to *The Waste Land* comes from Petronius Arbiter's *Satyricon*: "For I once saw with my own eyes the Cumean Sibyl hanging in a jar, and when the boys asked her, 'Sibyl, what do you want?' she answered, 'I want to die'" (qtd. in Eliot 3). "The Sybil, one of a number of prophetic figures so named in ancient times, is confined to a jar because her body threatens to deliquesce," North explains: "Granted a wish by Apollo, she had asked for as many year of life as there are grains in a handful of sand, but she forgot to ask for eternal youth as well" (3). With this in mind, in "Bananafish," Sybil Carpenter's name could be interpreted in several ways. A possible clue comes through the fact that she walks "in the direction of Fisherman's Pavilion" and stops "only to sink a foot in a soggy, collapsed castle" (11).

Here Salinger is most likely alluding Eliot's use of "the Grail legend" (51) and "the Fisher King" (56). By distancing Seymour from the hotel as he lies on the beach by "Fisherman's Pavilion," Salinger appears to associate Seymour with the Fisher King of Eliot's poem. According to Jesse L. Weston, "the key to the puzzle" of the Fisher King "is to be found in the rightful understanding of the Fish-Fisher symbolism" (38). And Weston adds later, "that the Fish is a Life symbol of immemorial antiquity, and the title of Fisher has, from the earliest ages, been associated with Deities who were held to be specially connected with the origin and preservation of life" (qtd. in Eliot 38). Finally, in the wasteland of "Bananafish," Seymour's actions might be understood in terms of the "The Grail Quest" Eliot employs in *The Waste Land*.

"The story postulates a close connection between the vitality of a certain King, and the prosperity of his kingdom," Weston explains, "the forces of the ruler being weakened or destroyed, by wound, sickness, old age, or death, the land becomes Waste, and the task of the hero is that of restoration" (36). Thus, as Salinger depicts Seymour out beyond the hotel and "a soggy, collapsed castle," Eliot's lines from "The Fire Sermon" come to mind: "By the waters of Leman I sat down and wept" (44). This line, which is an allusion to Psalm 137, is echoed at the end of *The Waste Land* in section V, "What the Thunder Said":

> *I sat upon the shore*
>
> *Fishing, with the arid plain behind me*
>
> *Shall I at least set my lands in order?* (51)

The fact that Seymour is literally estranged from the rest of the people in the hotel throughout the story is notable here. It is also worth noting that Psalm 137 occurs during the Israelites time within Babylonian captivity and they weep when "they remembered Zion" (137.1). Later the Psalmist writes, "How shall we sing the Lord's song in a strange land? If I forget this, O Jerusalem, let my right hand forget her cunning" (137.4-5).

Not only is Seymour a stranger in a strange land, but it seems that he has not forgotten Jerusalem and his right hand has not forgotten its cunning, as implied when he fires the "bullet through his right temple" (18). At last, the Psalmist writes, "Remember, O Lord, the children of Edom in the day of Jerusalem; who said, Rase it, rase it, even to the foundation therof. O daughter of Babylon, who art to be destroyed; happy shall he be, that rewardeth thee as thou has served us" (137.7-8). In the context "Bananafish", it appears that Seymour reveals to Sybil how to endure the destruction of the Babylonian type excess that will lead to her spiritual destruction. With *The Waste Land* as a subtext, it is also worth noting that as Seymour shows Sybil Carpenter how to fish he is showing her how to die, at least in Christian and Buddhist terms of denying the world.

After seeing the bananafish, Sybil, a type of "daughter of Babylon," runs "without regret in the direction of the hotel" (17). Because she has, like Seymour, seen more, her destruction will ironically, as the Psalmist says, lead to her happiness-ironically following the same path that appears to lead Seymour to his "salvation." Therefore, Seymour might be said to "set his lands in order" through Sybil, as he implies when he first sees her: "I was waiting for you" (11).

When Seymour quotes *The Waste Land* to Sybil, he quotes from section I, "The Burial of the Dead." The allusion comes after Sybil has said the name of another little girl in the hotel, Sharon Lipschutz, three times. **(E4)** "Ah, Sharon Lipschutz," Seymour states, "How that name comes up. Mixing memory and desire" (13). The name Sharon Lipschutz might have direct bearing on Seymour's quoting of *The Waste Land*. For one, the name Sharon, which means forest, might be an allusion to a fertile plain called Sharon on the shore of Israel. In addition, the Jewish name Lipschutz also seems to indicate part of Seymour's lamentation "mixing memory with desire" in light of the events of the Holocaust (a theme Salinger will return to throughout *Nine Stories*).

The fact that Seymour quotes *The Waste Land* after Sybil tells him he should have pushed Sharon Lipschutz off the piano bench has significance here. Sybil's innocence is not idealized, and Seymour indicates that he saw her poking a "little dog with balloon sticks" (15). Thus, when Seymour, the Fisher King, teaches Sybil not to be "mean or unkind" (15) through his parable of the bananafish, he might be seen as instructing Sybil in how to be a proverbial fisher of men (Matt 4.19). Furthermore, as the Fisher King, Seymour's parable of the bananafish reveals the division between the spiritual and material worlds in the story. When Seymour and Sybil go beneath the wave and Sybil sees "A bananafish," the scene represents an archetypal baptism for Sybil who, like Seymour, "sees more" (16).

Because baptism represents a symbolic death, burial and resurrection, **(E5)** the scene casts Seymour's quote from "The Burial of the Dead" in a new light. If she has truly been baptized and seen through the glass, Sybil's vision of the bananafish will cause her to shift her memories and desires through a symbolic death. In Sybil's death by water, to borrow from section IV of *The Waste Land*, Seymour's parable parallels Christ's words to his disciples, "For whosoever will save his life shall lose it: and whosoever will lose his life for my sake shall find it" (Matt 16.25). With this in mind, perhaps the best way to understand the conclusion of "Bananafish" is by first quoting the final lines of *The Waste Land*:

> *These fragments I have shored against my ruins*
>
> *Why then Ile fit you. Hieronymo's mad againe.*
>
> *Datta. Dayadhvam. Damyata.*
>
> *Shantih shantih shantih* (51)

With Sybil, Seymour has shored up his "fragments" and ascends the elevator of the hotel (or hell) into his "ruins" (51). Eliot's allusion to King Hieronymo in *The*

Spanish Tragedy appears to disclose a number of clues within "Bananafish." Hieronymo reveals that when he was younger he gave his mind to poetry that was "passing pleasing to the world," but later he wrote a "Tragedie" in which he suggests, "Each one of us must act his parte / In unknowne languages" (qtd. in Eliot 64-65).

The irony behind King Hieronymo's tragedy is that he has the actors play their parts because he is mad with grief over the murder of his son. Shakespeare's play turns into a metafiction in which the actors are acting out their own tragic fates, and in the final, act Hieronymo literally kills the murderers and then himself. In "Bananafish" Salinger essentially does the same thing through Seymour, who has also 'given his mind to poetry.' The tragedy that Seymour tells Sybil is about the life of the bananafish, which also serves as a metafictional parable within the story. Having told his "tragedy," Seymour acts it out by walking back into the hotel where he appears to be in the midst of the living dead who have swum into the bananafish hole; there amongst the dead, he dies. The complexity of Seymour's suicide is perhaps best communicated through the final line of "The Burial of the Dead" when Eliot quotes from Baudelaire: "You! hypocrite lecteur!-mon semblable,-mon frere!" ("Hypocrite reader! -my likeness -my brother! [Eliot 7]). Seymour does not judge Muriel but, instead, joins her in the room, a kinship Salinger may be pointing to when he sits upon the "twin bed" (18).

From another point of view, like King Hieronymo, Seymour seems to be "mad" with grief for the living dead in the waste land around him, namely Muriel. His madness is displayed through his rebuke of the woman in the elevator for looking at his feet. Like Eliot, Salinger juxtaposes Seymour's madness with what Eliot terms "Datta. Dayadhvam. Damyata" ("Give. Sympathize. Control" [20, 25]). Throughout the story, Seymour gives and sympathizes within the waste land and ultimately he controls his destiny-though his control works in contrast to how others view him, "[he] may completely lose control of himself" (6). In this way, his death, as with the Fisher King, might be said to be performed with what Eliot translates from "a formal ending to an Upanishad" as, "The Peace which passeth understanding"-"Shantih" (26).

This peace comes through the "tragic life" (15) of the bananafish, which for Seymour represents the division between the material and spiritual worlds. From a material point of view, the bananafish signifies a death in life, an inability to see beyond this world. From a spiritual point of view, the bananafish can be seen as redemptive. For instance, Christ's tragic life leads to epiphany rather than despair. In the end, though, Seymour's actions are disquieting and it would seem that this is the point. The disquiet is meant to wake up Muriel (and the reader) to the material and spiritual wasteland of the modern world. "HURRY UP PLEASE ITS TIME," Eliot writes in *The Waste Land* (10). It is a refrain throughout the closing lines of the second section ("A Game of Chess")-in which a nameless woman tells her friend Lil how she should improve her appearance for her husband when he returns home from the war. The refrain serves as a last call, "HURRY UP PLEASE ITS TIME"; yet, one might say that Seymour hears it differently in the Ocean Room than Muriel or Dr. Reiser do in the bar, and this refrain, "HURRY UP PLEASE ITS TIME," echoes throughout *Nine Stories*. **(E6)**

Tying "Bananafish" into the Cycle

When Sybil sees the bananafish (16), **(E7)** her experience of seeing *beyond* the surface of the water -and the surfaces of the material world-reverberates throughout the nine stories. The surface of the ocean and the horizon becomes a defining line between the material and spiritual worlds. As Seymour tells the parable of the bananafish to Sybil, he "edged" "the float and its passenger a foot closer to the horizon" (16) -an image that Salinger will take up again in "Down at the Dinghy" when Boo Boo Tenenbaum (née Glass) looks out at the horizon. (She may, as will be explored in the chapter on "Down at the Dinghy," be remembering Seymour as she looks out and salutes the opposite shore.)

But after Seymour explains the tragic fate of the bananafish and a wave breaks over Sybil and her float, the horizon vanishes for a moment, and Sybil momentarily passes under the surface of the water, and she exclaims "I just saw one" -she has seen a bananafish. Sybil's epiphany anticipates Seymour's suicide. When Seymour sits "on the unoccupied twin bed" and fires "a bullet through his right temple" (18), both he and Muriel can be seen as bananafish. In the terms Seymour defines in the parable, both he and Muriel are bananafish and they both lead tragic lives, but the distinction between them comes in the division Salinger draws between the material and spiritual worlds.

Salinger accentuates the difference between Muriel and Seymour by contrasting the settings of the first and second parts of the story. While Muriel is depicted within the "hole" of the hotel (a type of hell) where she is "burned," Seymour is outside on the beach near the ocean. Even when he is inside the hotel, Seymour is in the "Ocean Room" (7) a room surrounded by glass. Far from burnt, Seymour is "pale" and "won't take his bathrobe off" (10) despite the fact that Muriel says, "this is the hottest day they've had in Florida" (4). Seemingly unaffected by the heat, Salinger even suggests that Seymour might be cold as he pulls on "the lapels of his terry-cloth robe" (11) and he states, "Wow! It's cold" (15) as he wades into the ocean. Unlike Sybil, Seymour appears to see the bananafish in the hotel rather than the ocean, and Salinger indicates that Seymour has already begun to transcend the material world in the way that he "sees more" than those around him.

This is subtly shown when Seymour mistakes the color of Sybil's swimsuit for "blue" instead of "yellow" (12).

Seymour's vision beyond the material world is important to consider because he appears to already have transcended its boundaries when he is completely "released" (18) by firing the bullet through his temple. Another clue comes through Muriel when she tells her mother that Seymour will not take off his robe because he "doesn't want a lot of fools looking at his tattoo" (10). **(E8)** Here Salinger/Seymour seem to be referring to tattoo as "the signal for soldiers or sailors to retire for the night, given by a prolonged continuous drum-beating or by a bugle call" ("Tattoo"). **(E9)** The one time that Seymour does take off his robe comes when he takes Sybil into the ocean to "see if we can catch a bananafish" (13).

Salinger could be revealing how Seymour's physical condition literally indicates that he is about to retire, through the glass, to the spiritual world. Seymour's condition might be best illustrated through his statement that he is a "Capricorn" (12), which comes as he takes "both of Sybil's ankles in his hands" (12). Capricorn is sometimes referred to as a sea-goat and in some myths about him he is portrayed as a goat above the surface of the water and a fish below it. **(E10)** From this point of view, Sibyl would be seeing Seymour's feet/fish below the surface of the water, a detail that might further illuminate Seymour's words to the woman on the elevator since she is not looking at his feet through the surface of the water (or glass).

As with the demarcation of glass, the paradox of Seymour's suicide is a succinct illustration of the riddle of "one hand clapping" in *Nine Stories*. From a materialistic point of view (two hands clapping), Seymour's death is tragic and might be explained away by a psychologist as a type of war trauma or some lingering fact about his childhood, all of which the story offers little to no support. In contrast, by seeing the final action from a spiritual perspective, the story opens the door to the mystery that is "the sound of one hand clapping." Does Seymour's final action indicate a Christ-like martyrdom? Salinger subtly indicates this possibility by having Seymour's death fall sometime after 2:00 on Friday afternoon, which would correspond with a perfect/Good Friday. This theme will come full circle in "Teddy," when Teddy states that people are "afraid to die" and that "all you do is get the heck out of your body when you die" (193). Teddy also says that people "want new bodies all the time, instead of stopping and staying with God, where it's really nice" (191). Teddy's words illuminate the primary theme of *Nine Stories* through the tension created between the seen and unseen worlds.

There is also another revealing detail through which Salinger seems to establish Seymour as the Fisher King in *Nine Stories*. In the story that follows "Bananafish," "Uncle Wiggily in Connecticut," Salinger employs an important allusion to Lloyd C. Douglas' *The Robe*, which is a novel based upon one of the Roman centurions at Christ's crucifixion. The centurion, Marcellus, wins Christ's robe by casting lots for it, and over the course of the novel, he eventually converts to Christianity. **(E11)** Salinger appears to foreshadow the allusion to *The Robe* through the close attention he pays to "the robe" that Seymour is wearing on the beach along with his "royal blue" swimming trunks (13). **(E12)** When Seymour takes his "key out of his robe pocket" and then fires a bullet through his "right temple" (18), his actions might indicate that he has the *key* to the Kingdom-in addition to paralleling Christ's prophecy that he would "destroy the temple of God" and "build it in three days" (Matt 26.61). Here the key also might provide another important link to *The Waste Land*. In the final section, "What the Thunder Said," Eliot writes,

> *Dayadhvam: I have heard the key*
>
> *Turn in the door once and turn once only*
>
> *We think of the key, each in his prison*
>
> *Thinking of the key, each confirms a prison*
>
> *Only at nightfall, aethereal rumors*
>
> *Revive for a moment a broken Coriolanus*
>
> *Da*

The lines capture the isolation of Seymour throughout "Bananafish" as well as his "thinking of the key" and entry into his "prison" with Muriel. But Eliot's allusion to

Coriolanus could provide us with an insight into the depth of Salinger's allusions to *The Waste Land* in "Bananafish." Coriolanus was a Roman war hero who lost his life leading an army against Rome (see Eliot 19). **(E13)** Eliot's use of the allusion as an example of what the Thunder (or God) said, "Dayadhvam" ("Sympathize"), seems to connect Coriolanus death to Christ's sympathetic death at the hands of the Roman soldiers and by his own people. In this way, Seymour's death might be connected with both Coriolanus and Christ. Salinger also appears to reveal this through the fact that, like Marcellus (a Roman soldier), Seymour seems to feel the tattoo of the robe he wears.

It is also worth noting that at the conclusion of *The Robe* Marcellus and his wife choose to become martyrs in order to enter "a better Kingdom" and "meet their King!" (508). As they walk to their deaths, they give Christ's robe to their servant to comfort him and tell him that their deaths are "For the Big Fisherman" (508). In the greater context of *Nine Stories*, the allusion to *The Robe* provides the clearest indication of Seymour's final actions as a type of martyrdom with a peace that passeth all understanding in the material world. Within the cycle of *Nine Stories*, Seymour's suicide should be understood as a wake up call to "see more."

The horrific violence of Seymour's death, as with Christ's, leaves those who witness it with questions and doubts, many of which Salinger does not address until the final story, "Teddy." But in "Teddy," Salinger confronts readers with a doctrine of death and belief in God through the resurrected/ reincarnated body of Teddy McArdle that brings us full circle to "Bananafish." In this cyclic pattern, Salinger parallels the path to spiritual enlightenment. Like the believer who "sees more" in the journey between life and death, the reader will "see more" as they read and re-read the collection and get rid of the "conscious knowledge" (197), as Teddy puts it, of the logical divisions between life and death.

Endnotes:

E1: James Finn Cotter and other critics have argued that that the book of poems that Seymour gives Muriel (and which she misplaces) might be by the German poet Rainer Maria Rilke. Cotter makes a convincing argument that Rilke's *Voices* provides a subtext for *Nine Stories* and that one poem from the sequence, "The Song of Suicide," has a particular bearing on Seymour's suicide. Aside from Cotter's analysis, it is important to note that the poem that Salinger alludes to throughout "Bananafish" (and *Nine Stories*) is *The Waste Land*, the great poem of the 20th Century, and that the opening section, "The Burial of the Dead," is set primarily in Germany.

E2: At the center of "The Fire Sermon" is a sex scene which might be described as "Fun-or Hell."

E3: Eliot seems to clarify his use of the "automatic" sexual encounter to his essay on Baudelaire when he writes: *What distinguishes the relations of man and woman from the copulation of beasts is the knowledge of Good and Evil (of moral Good and Evil which are not natural Good and Bad or puritan Right and Wrong). Having an imperfect, vague romantic conception of Good, [Baudelaire] was at least able to understand that the sexual act as evil is more dignified, less boring, than as the natural, "life-giving," cheery automatism of the modern world . . . So far as we do evil or good, we are human; and it is better, in a paradoxical way, to do evil than to do nothing; at least, we exist.* (qtd. in Eliot 186) "The last statement is highly important for understanding *The Waste Land*" Cleanth Brooks adds when citing this passage, "The fact that men have lost the knowledge of good and evil, keeps them from being alive, and is the justification for viewing the modern waste land as a realm in which people do not even exist" (qtd. in Eliot 186).

E4: The name *Lipchutz* has several possible origins including the Czech town in Bohemia, Liebeschitz, and the German city of Leipzig (taken from the Slavic word Lipsk), which has been defined as a settlement where lime trees stand. The cryptic allusion and the association of Sharon's name with trees might offer a clue into Seymour's "funny business with the trees" (5). "Olives and wax," Seymour tells Sybil, "I never go anyplace without 'em" (15). In the book of Revelation it states, "These are the two olive trees, and the two candlesticks standing before the God of the earth" (11.4). If indeed Salinger is alluding to the book of Revelation here, the impending sense of doom and the coming Kingdom of God that are referenced in eleventh chapter of Revelation provide further insight into the unfolding events of "Bananafish."

E5: Romans 6.4: "Therefore we are buried with him by baptism into death: that like as Christ was raised up from the dead by the glory of the Father, even so we also should walk in newness of life."

E6: Salinger especially seems to echo this phrase in "De Daumier-Smith's Blue Period" and "Teddy." In "Blue Period" he writes, "With her right hand raised overhead, she was frantically signaling to someone-her child, perhaps, or her husband, or possibly the viewer-to drop everything and hurry over" (149). In "Teddy" there is a sense throughout his conversation with Nicholson that Teddy needs to hurry to his swimming lesson to, as he tells Nicholson, "wake up."

E7: Guercino's painting "The Cumaean Sibyl with a Putto" might shed some light on the role of Sybil in the story. In Guercino's painting, the Cumaean Sibyl foretells Christ's birth and his death upon the cross.

E8: Tattoo derives from "doe het tap toe" or "do the tap to; that is, shut it up; a signal for closing public houses" ("Tattoo"). There might be another parallel with Eliot's use of the refrain, "HURRY UP PLEASE ITS TIME" (10) in Salinger's use of tattoo, which doubles as a closing time for a pub and a wake up call to get out of the waste land. Yet another might come from Eloise (right after she "wakes up") when she tells Lew, "Why don't you boys form a platoon and march home? You can say that hut-hope-hoop-hoop business" (Salinger 35).

E9: The events that lead up to Seymour's death and Salinger's use of tattoo come full circle in "Down at the Dinghy" when Salinger writes that Boo Boo makes "something like a bugle call" (81), which is "a peculiar amalgamation of 'Taps' and 'Reveille' before she "saluted the opposite shoreline" (82). Boo Boo is thinking about Seymour, among others, and parallels specific details from "Bananafish" such as the fact that she is on the "pier edge" looking out at the "petty horizon" (82). Finally, Boo Boo's son Lionel picks up Seymour's "underwater goggles" with the toes of his *foot* and throws them in the water (84).

E10: According to Mary Ellen Snodgrass, Capricorns "traditionally thrive in the past. Their keen interest in genealogy, tradition and past events and heroes gives them a toehold in the present where they apply what they have learned about human tendencies and accomplishments" (185). "On the negative side," Snodgrass adds, "the type epitomizes self-discipline and embodies the stodgy, humorless grind characterized in English slang as the goat, a pejorative referring to the expendable person sacrificed for the good of the group" (185). In "Bananafish" the "sacrifice" of Seymour as a goat and a fish seems to serve the dual purpose between the sacred and the secular, especially if we consider the voracious appetite of a goat. Also worth noting is the fact that "Art depicts Capricorn as a curved arc of bright stars, the sacred token of the moon goddess called Cybele" (Snodgrass 187). At last, Snodgrass writes: *A fanciful Greek myth depicts Capricorn with a fishtail. The story of Pan, a male Arcadian god named for the Greek for all, describes how, during a war with giants, he repeatedly changed into animal shapes to elude the monster Typhon. Just as Pan leaped into the Nile River, his upper half changed into a goat; his lower half became a fish and swam out of Typhon's reach.* (184) The myth only seems to enhance the reading of Seymour as Fisher King when he guides Sybil into the water.

E11: See "Uncle Wiggily" chapter for a thorough discussion of this allusion.

E12: The royal blue of Seymour's swim trunks might be an allusion to the priestly garments described in the book of Exodus: And thou shalt make the robe of the ephod all of blue. (28.31) And he made the robe of the ephod of woven work, all of blue. (39.22)

E13: Eliot wrote a poem on Coriolanus, "Coriolan," which contains the following lines: "At the still point of the turning world. O hidden. / Now they go up to the temple. Then the sacrifice" (*Complete Poems and Plays* 86). In addition to their bearing on "Bananafish," the lines recall Eliot's *Four Quartets* and the search for God, or the still point of the turning world. Also worth noting is that fact that Eliot famously claims in his essay, "Hamlet and His Problems," that *Coriolanus* was Shakespeare's most successful work as an artist.

Bibliography:

Bible. King James Version.

Cotter, James Finn. "A Source For Seymour's Suicide: Rilke's *Voices* and *Nine Stories*." *Papers on Language and Literature* 25.1 (1989): 83-98.

Douglas, Lloyd C. *The Robe*. New York: Mariner, 1999.

Eliot, T. S. *The Waste Land*. Ed. Michael North. New York: Norton, 2001.

---. *The Complete Poems and Plays: 1909-1950*. New York: Harcourt, 1980.

Salinger, J. D. *Nine Stories*. Boston: Little Brown, 1991.

Snodgrass, Mary Ellen. *Signs of the Zodiac: A Reference Guide to Historical, Mythological, and Cultural Associations*. Westport, CT: Greenwood Press, 1997.

"Tattoo." Def. 1. *Webster's Universal Dictionary*. 1st ed. 1936.

Suggestions for Further Reading:

Lane, Gary. "Seymour's Suicide Again: A New Reading of J. D. Salinger's 'A Perfect Day for Bananafish.'" *Studies in Short Fiction* 10.1 (Winter 1973): 27-34.

Wiegand, William. "J. D. Salinger: Seventy-Eight Bananas." *J. D. Salinger.* Ed. Harold Bloom. New York: Chelsea House Publishers, 1987.

Discussion Questions and Possible Essay Topics:

1. Compare and contrast Muriel's conversation with her mother with that of Sybil and Mrs. Carpenter. What is Salinger trying to imply through the parallels in the conversations?

2. What is Salinger trying to convey through the use of the settings of the first and second parts of the story? What significance might the reader draw from the final scene taking place inside the hotel?

3. Compare Seymour's actions with what is said or implied about him.

4. Discuss the possible interpretations of "banana fever" based upon the details given in the story.

5. What significance do numbers have in the story?

6. How does Salinger use italics here? To what effect?

7. When Seymour compliments Sybil on her bathing suit, he pretends that it is blue. She insists that it's yellow, which it is. Why does Seymour do this? Is he merely having fun with her or is something more meaningful happening here?

8. Write an essay comparing and contrasting Salinger's use of the material and the spiritual, using Seymour's parable of the bananafish as a guide.

Uncle Wiggily in Connecticut

Overview

At the beginning of "Uncle Wiggily," Mary Jane arrives two hours late for a lunch date with Eloise Wengler, her college roommate. Salinger notes that while she waits for Mary Jane, "Eloise turned up the collar of her camel's hair coat" and "put her back to the wind" (19). When they go inside, they proceed to discuss the latest gossip about their old college friends while drinking highballs in the living room. Eloise makes several comments about the ineptitude of her maid, Grace, and complains when she has to get up to refresh their drinks herself. Although Mary Jane tries to stop drinking so she can drive home, Eloise insists she stay. When Eloise's daughter Ramona walks into the house, Mary Jane says that she is "dying to see her" and asks "How're her eyes now?" (24). Eloise dismisses the question casually and says that Ramona is "lousy with secrets" (25). Ramona tells Mary Jane about her imaginary friend Jimmy Jimmereeno and Eloise reveals the fact that "there are no little boys in the neighborhood. No children at all" (27). Ramona then asks if she can go back outside (in spite of the cold) to get Jimmy's sword.

After Ramona leaves, Eloise begins to talk about her old boyfriend, Walt. She tells Mary Jane about how she fell down one time and hurt her ankle and Walt "said, Poor Uncle Wiggily" (29) as he consoled her. Mary Jane attempts to compare Walt with Lew, Eloise's husband, but Eloise dismisses her and says that husbands do not want to hear the truth about other men their wives once dated. She then tells Mary Jane that she married Lew because he said he liked Jane Austen's novels, although she learned later that he had never read them. Eloise proceeds to tell a couple of other stories about Walt and eventually confesses her secret about how he died accidentally in the war. Eloise begins to cry and Mary Jane goes into the kitchen to attend to Ramona. When Mary Jane comes back out of the kitchen with Ramona in tow, she reveals that Jimmy Jimmereeno "got runned over and killed" (34). Eloise tells her that she is feverish and sends her to bed.

Eloise wakes up a few hours later when Lew calls and asks her to pick him up from the train station. She lies to him and says she cannot find her keys and tells him to find his own way home. After she hangs up the phone, Grace enters into the dining room and asks if her husband can stay the night, but Eloise refuses her request and stumbles upstairs to check on Ramona. Eloise wakes Ramona up and asks her why she is making room for Jimmy Jimmereeno in her bed if he died. Ramona tells her that she does not want to "hurt" Mickey Mickeranno, her new beau (37). In a fit of frustration, Eloise drags Ramona into the middle of the bed and tells her to "go to sleep" (37). As she leaves the room, Eloise pauses in the doorway before rushing back into the room, picking up Ramona's glasses and repeating Walter's words, "Poor Uncle Wiggily" (37). She kisses Ramona awkwardly and goes back downstairs to wake up Mary Jane to ask her about their freshman year in college when Miriam Ball made fun of her dress. "'I was a nice girl,' she pleaded, 'wasn't I?'" (38).

Analysis

When Mary Jane arrives late after getting lost when she turns off the Merritt Parkway (which she mispronounces as "Merrick") **(E1)** at the beginning of "Uncle Wiggily," Salinger relates that she gets lost in spite of the fact that she "had found the house twice before" and arrives "looking upset, even fouled" (19). Mary Jane's poor sense of direction and "fouled" appearance establish a parallel with Eloise, who compares her own looks to "a cocker spaniel" and has lost her way within her own home. Throughout the story, Salinger undercuts Eloise's air of superiority-her supposedly matter-of-fact statements-with dramatic irony. (For example, she tells Mary Jane that she does not have to worry about getting a hernia (20) when in fact some forms of hernias occur more often in women than in men.)

Salinger draws other parallels between the two women's lives when he writes that they both dropped out of college in 1942 for soldiers. While Mary Jane has a disastrous three-month marriage to "an aviation cadet" (two of which he spends "in jail for stabbing an M.P."), Eloise leaves after she gets "caught with a soldier in a closed elevator on the third floor of her residence hall" (20). Salinger hints that Eloise left school to be with Walt, a detail that might be confirmed later when she describes waiting "for him at the bus stop, right outside the PX" (the Army Post Exchange; 29).

Salinger also implies, throughout the story, that Mary Jane has the tendency to follow Eloise and idealizes her life. In addition to leaving school after Eloise ("same year, same class, almost the same month" [20]), Mary Jane's visit marks the third time she has come to visit Eloise in Connecticut. Indeed, she goes out of her way to visit Eloise in Connecticut passing the home of her boss, Mr. Weyinburg, in Larchmont on the way. Also, as Eloise points out, Mary Jane calls to see if she can come visit (22), and she seems to know and care about Ramona and Lew more than Eloise. When Ramona enters the room later in the story, Mary Jane asks about "her eyes" and whether or not she can see without her glasses "if she gets up in the night to go to the john or something?" (25).

Mary Jane's comments reveal more than a passing knowledge about the seriousness of Ramona's myopia and intimates, perhaps, that Eloise was not always so cold about her daughter. As things are, though, Eloise responds to Mary Jane's query about Ramona's eyes with a dismissive, "God! Not that I know of" (25), a statement that reveals both Eloise's lack of empathy and myopia concerning Ramona. Mary Jane has an equal concern for Eloise's happiness with Lew and when Eloise continues to idealize her relationship with Walt, Mary Jane defends Lew. At one point Mary Jane asks Eloise if Lew has a sense of humor the way that Walt did, Eloise repeats her words about Ramona's eyes, "Oh, God! Who knows?" (29).

Here Eloise's words are essentially a confession and they lead directly to her epiphany at the conclusion of the story. The first indication of this comes when Salinger writes that Eloise crosses her legs "at the ankles" (20). The crossing of the legs at the ankles is a motif that Salinger repeats in many of the nine stories to adumbrate a character's spiritual epiphany. Crossing one's legs at the ankles is, in effect, a secular correlative for Salinger's spiritual vision, adapted from Sherwood Anderson, in which "everyone in the world is Christ and they are all crucified" (Anderson 39). The allusion to ankles and feet calls to mind countless depictions of Christ's crucifixion as well as Christ's call that his disciples "ought to wash one another's feet" (John 13.14). **(E2)** Salinger continues the crucifixion motif in "Uncle Wiggily" in the character of Eloise's maid, Grace, whom Eloise mocks constantly (even though she left her own family to serve the Wengler's in Connecticut).

The first reference to Grace comes when Eloise calls her a "dopey maid" for not filling the cigarette container.

When Grace does not come into the living room to refresh their drinks, Eloise again demeans her, "Honestly, that *dope*. I did everything but get Lew to make love to her to get her to come out here with us" (21). Eloise reveals her dependence on Grace to serve her; though, she does not reveal any sense of gratitude or compassion for Grace's dislocation from her own home to come live with the Wengler's. Salinger foreshadows Eloise's spiritual epiphany through the third reference to Grace when Eloise complains that she is "sitting on her big, black butt reading 'The Robe'" (22).

As previously mentioned, *The Robe* is a novel by Lloyd C. Douglas that explores the quest of a Roman soldier named Marcellus. **(E3)** In the novel, Marcellus is the centurion who wins the robe of Christ (Mark 15.24), and at a party that is held after the crucifixion he is encouraged to wear it. As the novel progresses, Marcellus journeys to the places that Christ did and talks to those who knew him until he converts to Christianity. Fittingly, Salinger contrasts Grace's immersion in *The Robe*, with Eloise's disparaging remarks about her "sitting on her big, black butt" (22). Salinger ties a number of central themes of the story into the allusion to *The Robe*. For instance, as Eloise bemoans Grace's lack of servitude, she is distracted by the "cameo brooch" Mary Jane wears "at her throat" (21). Mary Jane tells her that she "had it at school, for goodness sake" and that it was her "Mother's" (21). "God," Eloise exclaims upon seeing it, "I don't have one damn thing holy to wear"

(21). The scene is important because as the story progresses, Salinger reveals how much Eloise has failed to notice about her past. Even more, Salinger appears to show how Eloise's material luxury has damned her and that she will need to put on the proverbial Robe of Christ (the "suffering servant"). Thus, Salinger juxtaposes Eloise and Grace's roles in the story.

Perhaps the most telling example of the contrast between Eloise and Grace comes when Ramona walks into the room and Eloise tells her to "go out in the kitchen and let Grace take your galoshes off" (24). Here Salinger parallels Eloise's trip into the kitchen with Ramona's, and we are meant to understand that when Grace takes off the galoshes she is still reading *The Robe*. From this point on, Salinger seems to triangulate Eloise, Grace and Ramona throughout the story. While Grace reads a fictionalized story about a man who learns to follow Christ, Ramona tells Mary Jane about Jimmy Jimmereeno, her imaginary "beau" (26). What becomes increasingly clear is that Jimmy Jimmereeno is Ramona's version of Walt, Eloise's own "imaginary" beau. Though Eloise mocks both Jimmy Jimmereeno and *The Robe*, she treats her own story about her courtship with Walt and his accidental death as if it were sacred. Yet while both Eloise and Ramona's stories about their "beaus" are self-serving, Grace's story explores the nature of denying oneself and serving others by following Christ. Salinger confronts Eloise with the role of the servant the second time Ramona comes into the house and Eloise again tells her to "Go out and tell Grace to take your galoshes off" (34). When Ramona tells her that Grace is "in the lavatory" (presumably reading *The Robe*), Eloise has to get down on her knees and, one might say, gracelessly take off Ramona's galoshes.

As Eloise struggles with the galoshes, Ramona tries twice to tell her how Jimmy Jimmereeno died-though Eloise does not really listen to what she is saying and interrupts her before she can finish. The inherent irony in the situation comes through the fact that Eloise has just told Mary Jane about how Walt died. The two deaths, once again, are drawn in contrast with Grace's story about how Christ died. Notably, the death of Jimmy Jimmereeno is most likely a direct result of Eloise's words and offers insight into just how much Ramona desires her mother's attention and affection. For example, it appears the last thing that Ramona hears before she puts her galoshes back on and returns outside to play is Eloise's statement to Mary Jane to tell her boss that she was "killed" and to "Say you're dead" (28).

Eloise's words are only in partial jest. In fact, all of her words and actions seem to indicate that she is spiritually dead throughout the story. When Ramona comes back into the house, she seems to think that by saying Jimmy is dead that Eloise will listen to her and perhaps console her. But Eloise only thinks she is "feverish" and says, "Go tell Grace you're to have your dinner upstairs. Then you're to go straight to bed" (34). **(E4)** At last, Salinger brings all three stories together at the end after Eloise wakes up as "Grace appeared in the dining-room light" (35). Salinger portrays Grace between the light of the dining room and the darkness of the living room and writes that she "didn't come forward" (35). The scene is important because of the attention that Salinger pays to Grace standing in the light looking at Eloise in the darkness, which appears to lead directly to Eloise's epiphany.

The epiphany begins with Eloise denying Grace's request for her husband to stay the night because "it's so bad out" (36). Eloise tells her, "I'm not running a hotel" (36). Eloise then goes up to Ramona's room and violently wakes her up and states, "I thought you told me Jimmy Jimmereeno was run over and killed" (36). Eloise's statement comes not out of empathy but out of annoyance at the fact that Ramona seems to be making room in her bed for Jimmy to sleep (a possible parallel to where Eloise sleeps in relation to Lew).

When Ramona tells her that she is doing it for a new imaginary friend, Mickey Mickeranno, Salinger writes, "Eloise grabbed Ramona's ankles and half lifted and half pulled her over to the middle of the bed. Ramona neither struggled nor cried; she let herself be moved without actually submitting to it" (37). Salinger's portrayal of Ramona in the scene has subtle parallels with the crucifixion of Christ that are highlighted when he situates Eloise standing, like Grace, "for a long time in the doorway" (37) between the darkness and the light. In this way, Salinger proverbially ties Eloise's epiphany to seeing through the eyes of Grace. Thus, as Eloise rushes back into the room, she appears to see beyond her own pain for the first time in the story and empathize with both Grace and Ramona.

Moreover, as she states "Poor Uncle Wiggily . . . . over and over again" (36), Salinger seems to indicate that she connects her story with their stories because she is "too full of purpose to feel pain" (37). Along these lines, Salinger creates another interesting parallel with *The Robe* that comes thorough the endings of both works, respectively. At the conclusion of *The Robe*, Marcellus is condemned to die because he chooses the Kingdom of God over the Kingdom of Rome. Caligula (Gaius Julius Caesar Augustus Germanius) mocks his wife Diana for stating that she wants to go with Marcellus after she proclaims that she is a Christian: "your love will do you no good-when he's dead" (507). But Diana counters his claim by declaring, "we will live together-always-in a Kingdom of love" (507). As they walk to their deaths, Douglas writes, "the procession marched briskly the length of the corridor, and down the marble steps into the congested plaza," and Diana tosses the Robe to Old Marcipor (their servant), and the novel concludes with her words to him, "For the Big Fisherman!" (508).

As in *The Robe*, Eloise descends the stairs and seems to be experiencing a spiritual death (or awakening) as she wakes Mary Jane up and asks her to remember their freshman year when she wore a "brown-and-yellow dress" and Miriam Ball mocked her because "nobody wore those kind of dresses in New York" (38). "I was a nice girl" she pleads, "wasn't I?" (38). Salinger appears to indicate that Eloise needs to put on Christ's robe of grace in order to "be a nice girl." Another way to interpret this final passage is to connect Eloise's malaise with living a past life through a dead man. To proverbially rise from the dead, Eloise must put on *the Robe* to transcend death through Christ. The final scene also alludes to the fact that by waking up herself she might help Mary Jane to wake up instead of leading her into a drunken blindness. As Eloise pleads with Mary Jane to tell her she "was a nice girl," she appears to recognize that she has been living in a past life that she created in her imagination and that she does not really know the girl she once was. In order to put on the Robe of Christ, Eloise needs to follow Walt's example and advance in society "in a different direction from everybody else" (30) and to deny the myopia of her material existence for one that *sees more*.

Tying "Uncle Wiggily" into the Cycle

In "Uncle Wiggily," Salinger brings Seymour's parable of the bananafish to life in the depiction of Eloise and Mary Jane drinking to the point where Eloise imposes her own spiritual condition on Mary Jane: "Say you're dead" (28). And, in Eloise's grief over Walter Glass' death, Salinger offers a glimpse into how Muriel will struggle to reconcile herself to Seymour's suicide. Yet Salinger seems to provide a similar resolution for both Muriel and Eloise to see beyond the material world, as he conveys when Seymour takes off "the robe" (13) he is wearing before he enters the ocean. Salinger connects these first two stories through a series of common details: both stories are set in the winter and depict a similar state of *ennui* (even with the shift of climate and geography).

There are a number of parallels between the mother daughter relationships in the stories as well (and many close readers will remember that Sybil tells Seymour she lives in "Whirly Wood, Connecticut" [14]). Of course, Sybil makes up the name in order to pretend that she knows where she lives because Sharon Lipschutz "knows where she lives and she's only three and a half" (14). Salinger's juxtaposition of Miami with Connecticut shows how the characters suffer from the same spiritual conditions in spite of the physical settings of the stories. He conveys this in corresponding details such as Muriel's being so "burned" she can hardly move while in a tropical haven, and the drunk/blind stasis of Eloise and Mary Jane in Connecticut. Mary Jane's difficulty in finding where Eloise lives only seems to highlight this dislocation of spiritual and physical state of being. Later in the story "Pretty Mouth and Green My Eyes," Arthur will attempt to cure his wife Joan's infidelity by moving her from New York to Connecticut: "What I think maybe we'll do, if everything goes along all right, we'll get ourselves a little place in

Connecticut maybe. Not too far out, necessarily, but far enough that we can lead a normal goddam life. I mean she's crazy about plants and all that stuff. She'd probably go mad if she had her own goddam garden and stuff. Know what I mean?" (129).

In Mary Jane's own attempt to escape New York City she gets lost along the way, which possibly reflects her spiritual condition. And rather than being content with her life, Eloise wallows in misery, idealizing the past and even Mary Jane's life over her own: "At least, you have a job. I mean at least you-" (32). Eloise's discontent is echoed throughout *Nine Stories* in characters who seek happiness in some material relocation that they feel will cure their spiritual disconnect.

Along these lines, the sound of one hand clapping in "Uncle Wiggily" comes through an accretion of intertwined glass images. The first examples of these glass images are illustrated through Eloise filling up their *empty glasses* and Mary Jane looking out the window. Salinger writes, "She drew aside the curtain and leaned her wrist on one of the crosspieces between panes, but, feeling grit, she removed it, rubbed it clean with her other hand, and stood more erectly" (22). The symbolic leaning on the "crosspiece" between the "two panes" of glass appears to parallel both Eloise and Mary Jane's pain with the highball glasses. Thus, Salinger indicates that they need to "lean" on the cross in order to cure their two pains.

This continues as Mary Jane passes the bookcase "without glancing at any of the titles" (22). Ironically, Grace, the "dopey maid," is the one who seeks to cure her pain through a book about a man's journey to Christ while Eloise and Mary Jane drink to the point where they are blind and can hardly stand on their own power-a point Salinger seems to punctuate when he writes that after leaning on the crosspiece Mary Jane "stood up more erectly" (22). The grit and the "filthy slush" outside the window that "was visibly turning to ice" are oblique indicators of how Mary Jane is made aware of her "fouled" condition and leads her to open her mirror and "look at her teeth" (22). Salinger employs the "grit" and the "filthy snow" as objective correlatives to convey how Mary Jane attempts to make sure her teeth are clean, as the external conditions become reflective of the internal conditions (both physically and spiritually) throughout the story. When Eloise reenters the room with "a fresh drink in each hand," she pretends that her fingers are guns and states, "Don't nobody move. I got the whole damn place surrounded" (22). Her statement coincides with how the drinks inside the glasses will deaden both her and Mary Jane's pain to the point where they can hardly move. Appropriately, Eloise then reveals to Mary Jane that Grace is reading *The Robe*.

Furthermore, Salinger parallels the dead condition that Mary Jane observes from the Wengler's window as she looks through Ramona's glasses. When she "enthusiastically" questions Ramona about her "beau," Salinger writes, "Ramona's eyes, behind thick, counter-myopia lenses, did not reflect even the smallest part of Mary Jane's enthusiasm" (25). Ramona's lack of "enthusiasm," a word that means "to be possessed by god" ("Enthusiasm"), reflects how the truth about Eloise's own beau is only revealed once the alcohol from her glass leads her to confess her own lack of enthusiasm. Salinger seems to contrast Ramona's lack of enthusiasm with Eloise's memory of Walt holding his hand on her stomach (seemingly as a way of touching her unborn child) and saying "he wished some officer would come up and order him to stick his other hand through the window" (30).

In accordance with Salinger's use of glass, Walt's words connect Ramona with the world beyond the glass. While Eloise and Mary Jane remain inside all day to avoid the cold, Ramona prefers to go outside and play. Here Seymour's words about marriage and children-which Salinger relates in *Raise High the Roof Beam, Carpenters and Seymour an Introduction*-are at least worth considering in the context of "Uncle Wiggily": "Marriage partners are to serve each other. Elevate, help, teach, strengthen each other, but above all, *serve*. Raise their children honorable, lovingly, and with detachment. A child is a guest in the house, to be loved and respected-never possessed, since he belongs to God" (*Raise High* 91). **(E5)** Seymour describes precisely what is lacking in Eloise's life, approaching her marriage with a sense of servitude and loving and respecting Ramona as a gift of God. The servitude that Seymour speaks of is not a sexist servitude, but of an equal serving of "each other." If Eloise were to take on this attitude she might get beyond the romantic notions about marriage that she has from Jane Austen novels (which is the absurd and ironic reason she cites for marrying Lew). **(E6)**

The next notable use of glass comes later on after Eloise has at last made her confession about how Walt died and clutches her "empty glass" (33) to her chest. The scene begins with Eloise waking up to the ringing phone "from the window seat" (35). Instead of following her own instructions to Mary Jane, she does not tell Lew that she's "dead" on the phone; rather, she lies and tells him she cannot find her key to the car to avoid telling him that she is drunk. She then goes back over to the "window seat" and attempts to take away the pain of her lie by drinking off the Scotch she pours "into her glass" (35). Grace appears in the dining room but does not "come forward" into the darkness where Eloise is sitting. Though Salinger portrays Eloise on the window seat, a seat that is enclosed in glass, it is dark outside and she is drunk, thus she cannot see through the glass on two levels. Instead, she can only see Grace in the light. This pattern continues as she goes up the stairs into Ramona's room and turns "on the light" and holds on to the switch, "as if for support" (36). Here Salinger literally implies that Eloise needs to lean on the light of grace for support. Later, when Eloise reenters the room in the darkness "full of purpose" and picks "up Ramona's glasses" (37), Salinger portrays how she sees spiritually rather than physically for the first time in the story because she does not depend upon the light and does not focus on her own pain. As she lays Ramona's glasses "lenses down" on the table, the action, from a material point of view, might illustrate how she has scarred her daughter's view of the world. Yet now that she has identified Ramona's pain with her own, "Poor Uncle Wiggily" (37), they both might *see more* and transcend it through the light of grace.

Endnotes:

E1: Mary Jane's mispronouncing Merritt as Merrick might indicate that she is from Long Island. Other than the trace of an accent that can be heard by pronouncing (or mispronouncing) the two words, Salinger could be drawing attention to Merrick, New York because it was an early colony for Puritans coming to the New World, and it was also a popular cite for Methodists' annual religious meetings (often drawing thousands of people) in the 1800's.

E2: In "Uncle Wiggily" in particular, Salinger might also be making an allusion to Paul's first letter to Timothy when addressing the "good works" of widows: "if she have brought up children, if she have lodged strangers, if she have washed the saints' feet, if she have relieved the afflicted" (5.10). While Salinger never indicates that Eloise was married to Walt, she certainly hoped to marry him and grieves him throughout the story as a widow would her husband.

E3: While *The Robe* might be the predominant allusion in "Uncle Wiggily," Salinger also informs the story through three cryptic allusions to actor Akim Tamiroff. The first reference to Tamiroff comes from Eloise after Mary Jane asks "You know who I saw last week? On the main floor of Lord & Taylor's?" (23). Eloise responds, "Akim Tamiroff," and then explains to the baffled Mary Jane that "Akim Tamiroff" is "in the movies" (23). A little bit later she tells Mary Jane that Ramona looks like "Akim Tamiroff." Comparing Ramona's looks to Tamiroff, and then saying Ramona looks like Lew and Lew's mother, seems both cruel and indicative of the fact that they are all, along with Eloise ("I'm not funny . . . . it's just my face") physically unattractive. The allusions to Tamiroff seem to be an allusion to the obscure 1939 film *Disputed Passage* that was based upon another Lloyd C. Douglas novel with the same title. Set in war torn China, Tamiroff plays the role of Dr. Milton (Tubby) Forrester, a scientist whose pragmatism contrasts with the humanistic ideals of Dr. Cunningham. According to Fred Camper, "The salvation of the characters in . . . . *Disputed Passage* is not specifically through love, but rather in, an entire spiritual system" (339). "There are the true believers, those who without ostentation know the truth," Camper explains, adding, "this kind of spirituality gives one a strong feeling of one's own position and place in the world, as well as great knowledge and wisdom .... love itself is a spiritual state which makes itself apparent through a shield of surface appearances" (340). There are a number of obvious links between "Uncle Wiggily" and *Disputed Passage*. When Eloise states that she likes Tamiroff/Dr. Forrester and by associating him with Ramona and then with Lew, Salinger might be indicating her lack of love for her family and her need to see beyond surface appearances in order know and love them. Also, because the film is set in China, the dichotomy between religious beliefs between East and West is also a central theme. Because Walt died in Japan, the contrasts between life and death from scientific and spiritual points of view, especially within the context of the Glass family's Eastern predilections, seems relevant to the story, as well.

Moreover the allusion also might be to Tamiroff's appearance in the adaptation of *For Whom the Bell Tolls*. The ringing of the phone that wakes Eloise up before she goes up the stairs to Ramona's room seems to indicate that the bell is tolling for Eloise. But the allusion to Tamiroff might also be a nod to the 1936 film *The General Dies at Dawn*. The plot of the film, which also seems to echo "The Laughing Man" in places, concerns a mercenary played by Gary Cooper who has a brief love affair with a woman (played by Madeline Caroll) in war torn China. The film actually has a number of parallels with *For Whom the Bell Tolls*, and it employs an innovative stylistic technique ahead of its time by creating a picture within a picture to make revelations to the viewer when characters are discussing plot points. The stylistic innovation would have certainly appealed to Salinger, and he uses the same metafictional storytelling method throughout *Nine Stories*. In relation to "Uncle Wiggily," the film seems tied to Eloise's statement that Walt once told her "he was advancing in the Army, but in a different direction from everybody else. He said that when he'd get his first promotion, instead of getting stripes he'd have his sleeves taken away from him. He said when he'd get to be a general, he'd be stark naked" (30). Eloise does not share Walt's lack of concern for rank, appearances or upward advancement and is embarrassed to tell anyone that he died in an accident. Another tie between the film and the story comes through Eloise's memory of riding on the train with Walt, "right after he was drafted," from "Trenton to New York" (29). The scene has distinct parallels with a *The General Dies at Dawn* because the brief and conflicted love affair that takes place between Cooper and Caroll takes place on a train. Thus, the film seems to elliptically convey how when Walt dies, through his sacrifice, he has advanced to the position of general but in the opposite direction of "everybody else" (30). Another way that Salinger might use the film comes through the type of split screen that is created between Eloise and Ramona. Salinger offers clues about Eloise through Ramona and about Ramona through Eloise. One example of this comes when Ramona tells Mary Jane that Jimmy Jimmereeno has "No mommy and no daddy" (26). On the one hand, Ramona's statement seems to depict the world that she lives in; yet, on the other hand, Ramona might be revealing that Eloise does not have any parents. Eloise does not mention her parents throughout the story, and when she admires the "cameo brooch" that belonged to Mary Jane's mother, she states that she does not have "one damn thing holy to wear" (21). She then adds, "If Lew's mother ever dies-ha, ha-she'll probably leave me some old monogrammed icepick or something" (21). Though she mentions Lew's mother repeatedly, she never mentions her own mother or father.

E4: Eloise's command here echoes the last words of "The Laughing Man." Salinger seems to parallel the Laughing Man's death with Jimmy Jimmereeno and the corresponding spiritual undertones (note especially the Laughing Man's sacrificial death against a tree) in both stories.

E5: Another interesting connection between *Raise High the Roof Beam Carpenters* and "Uncle Wiggily" comes early on in the story when Buddy Glass, the narrator, describes his company commander as "a bookish man by his own confession, whose favorite author, as luck had it, happened to be my favorite author-L. Manning Vines" (10). Because Buddy meets his company commander in 1942, there is at least the possibility that he is Lew. Eloise states that Lew's favorite author is the apparently fictional author L. Manning Vines. At the least, the detail seems to provide more evidence that Lew is not as unintelligent as Eloise makes him out to be. The irony of Eloise's claims about Walt and Lew is that they are often more similar than dissimilar. Perhaps the best example of this comes when Eloise belittles Lew by saying that he laughs at "cartoons and stuff" (29), but goes on and on about how nice Walt was because he called her ankle, "Poor Uncle Wiggily" (29), a cartoon character.

E6: The irony of Eloise's statement about marrying Lew because he told her "he loved Jane Austen" is that she does not find out "that he hadn't even read one of her books" until after they are married (32). The fact that Eloise doesn't discover that Lew was lying until after they are married indicates that she never actually discussed Jane Austen's works with Lew and possibly that she has never read them herself. Salinger seems to employ the allusion to Austen to show that Eloise has not considered her marriage wisely and has not married out of love. The allusion to Austen also could be a social satire on the limitations placed upon women in post-World War II America.

Bibliography:

The Bible. King James Version.

Camper, Fred. "*Disputed Passage.*" *Movies and Methods: Volume I*. Ed. Bill Nichols. Berkley: California UP, 1976. 339-44.

Douglas, Lloyd C. *The Robe*. New York: Mariner, 1999.

"Enthusiasm." Def. 1. *Webster's Universal Dictionary*. 1st ed. 1936.

Salinger, J. D. *Nine Stories*. Boston: Little Brown, 1991.

---. *Raise High the Roof Beam, Carpenters and Seymour an Introduction*. Boston: Little Brown, 1991.

Discussion Questions and Possible Essay Topics:

1. Compare and contrast Eloise and Ramona's "beaus," Walt and Jimmy Jimmereeno, and discuss their replacements Lew and Mickey Mickeranno.

2. What significance does Salinger pay to the various rooms in the house and the things that occur in them throughout the story.

3. Discuss what Eloise reveals about Walt with what she reveals about Lew. What are the major similarities and differences between them?

4. Explore the role of Grace in the story.

5. What is the role of imagination in the story? Does it have positive or negative implications?

6. Eloise indicates that she is from Idaho in the final paragraph of the story. What else do we know about her past. What clues does Salinger provide about the kind of girl she used to be? Does this shed light on her character?

7. Examine some of Salinger's pop culture allusions-Bela Lugosi, *The Robe*, Donald Duck, Uncle Wiggily, Akim Tamiroff, Jane Austen-and how they inform the story.

8. Compare and contrast Walt's "Uncle Wiggily" with Seymour's "bananafish."

Just Before the War with the Eskimos

Overview

"Just Before the War with the Eskimos" begins with Ginnie Mannox and Selena Graff riding home together in a taxicab after playing tennis together at the East Side Courts. Ginnie considers Selena to be "the biggest drip" in her school and confronts her about "getting stuck-every single time-for the whole cab fare" (39), even though Selena brings the tennis balls every week. The two girls argue about the cab fare until Ginnie insists that Selena give her the money so she can "go to the movies," even though it requires Selena to "go upstairs and get it from [her] mother" (41). Ginnie waits in the living room while Selena goes to get the money from her mother, and while she waits Selena's brother, Franklin, walks into the room. Franklin tells Ginnie that he has cut his finger and to stick around because he might need a "transfusion" (43).

When Franklin learns that her full name is Virginia Mannox, he tells her he knows her sister, "Joan the snob" (44). They argue about whether or not Joan is a snob until Ginnie reveals that Joan is engaged and Franklin changes the subject back to the cut on his finger and the best way to clean it. Franklin then offers Ginnie "half a chicken sandwich," but Ginnie declines his offer. Franklin starts talking about Joan again and asks about the guy she is marrying. When Ginnie tells him that he is "a lieutenant commander in the Navy," Franklin responds, "Big deal" (46). A little later Franklin reveals that he wrote Joan "eight goddam letters," but "She didn't answer one of 'em" (47).

Franklin's revelation leads to another revelation-that he worked in an "airplane factory" (48) during the war because he has a heart condition. Franklin eventually goes to the window and looks down at the "fools" on the street and says they are all going to the draft board to sign up to "fight the Eskimos" (48). Ginnie does not understand but tells him he "wouldn't have to go, anyway" before realizing "she was saying the wrong thing" (49). Shortly after this, Franklin leaves the room and brings back the sandwich and tells Ginnie to eat it. Ginnie forces a bite of the sandwich down, and Franklin leaves the room. Ginnie attempts to throw the sandwich out, but she puts it in her pocket when Franklin's friend, Eric, walks in the room.

Eric begins to talk with Ginnie while he waits for Franklin to finish shaving. He tells Ginnie that he has been sharing his apartment with a writer who just robbed him. Eric also reveals that he worked with Franklin during the war and that they are going to see "Cocteau's 'Beauty and the Beast'" (53). When Selena reenters the room, Ginnie tells her she does not want the money and asks if she can come over later. They talk about Franklin briefly before Ginnie leaves and considers dropping the sandwich in the street before she puts it back in her pocket. Salinger compares this final action to the way she once found an "Easter chick" in her "wastebasket" and kept it for three days.

Analysis

Early on in "Just Before the War with the Eskimos," Salinger establishes the tone of the story when he writes, "Ginnie had conjured up a vision of dinner over at the Graffs'; it involved a perfect servant coming around to everyone's left with, instead of a glass of tomato juice, a can of tennis balls" (39). From this point on, Salinger begins a process of converting Ginnie's "vision" from a girl who is "existing on four-fifty a week" (and insists upon collecting the "dollar ninety" Selena owes her), to one who forgives her debt and remembers the faith that she had "A few years before" (55). Salinger draws attention to the flaw in Ginnie's vision of the Graff family when she meets their supposed "perfect servant," "a colored maid with whom Selena didn't seem to be on speaking terms" (42). The passing glimpse that Salinger offers of the servant accentuates just how narrow-minded Ginnie's vision of the Graff family was. Even more, when Selena confronts her with the pettiness of her actions-"I never in my life would've thought you could be so small about anything"- Ginnie is unfazed, "Now you know" (42).

When Franklin walks into the room, as James E. Bryan has noted, Salinger draws direct parallels between him and Ginnie's vision of the Graff's perfect servant (Bryan 228). As Franklin walks across the room, he is "cradling" his hand next to his chest because of the cut on his "goddam finger" (42). Recalling Ginnie's vision, Franklin's cut contrasts with the symbolism of the servant bringing "a can of tennis balls" rather than "a glass of tomato juice" (39). The significance of Ginnie's vision comes through the fact that she gets to use the Graff family's tennis balls every week for free, and through Franklin (who is carrying his cut in place of the tennis balls or tomato juice), Salinger invokes the "perfect servant," Christ.

In this way, Salinger juxtaposes Franklin's cut, "in the goddam wastebasket" (43), with the Christian theology of Christ's death upon the cross-as the Apostle Paul writes: "who gave himself for our sins, that he might deliver us from this present evil world" (Gal. 1.4). Franklin tells Ginnie he is "bleedin' to death" and "Stick around. I may need a goddam transfusion" (43). Through the coded religious inflections of Franklin's speech, Salinger implies that Ginnie needs a "transfusion" from the blood of the perfect servant. This theme is furthered when Franklin offers her what Bryan calls "a symbolic prop, a chicken sandwich suggestive of the Eucharist" (227). The fact that Franklin offers Ginnie "half a chicken sandwich" may be significant since the partaking of bread at the Lord's

Supper is representative of Christ's "body, which is broken for you" (1 Cor. 11.24).

Ginnie, though, rejects the sandwich the first time Franklin offers it to her. Salinger then seems to parallel Franklin's war experience with Christ's earthly ministry. For example, when Ginnie asks how long Franklin worked in the "airplane factory," he responds, "I don't know, for Chrissake. Thirty-seven months" (48). Having made this statement, Franklin looks into the street, calls the people below "Goddam fools," and then states, "We're gonna fight the Eskimos next" (48). As she watches him, Ginnie tells him that his "finger'll start bleeding more if [he] holds it *down* that way" (48). The blood that Franklin will shed on the people on the street down below is meant to connect with the fact that he cut his finger while looking for something *down* in the wastebasket.

Franklin's words are probably a reflection of the guilt he feels over the people who died from the bombs dropped by airplanes he built during the war. But from the point of view of Ginnie's vision of the perfect servant in the Graff home, Franklin's meditation may also be heard in light of Christ's ministry-as Salinger might indicate when Franklin commands Ginnie, "Open your ears, for Chrissake" (49). In this way, the cut on Franklin's hand being connected with the deaths of the people down below seems to recall the Apostle Paul's letter to the Phillipians, "And being found in fashion as a man, he humbled himself, and became obedient unto death, even the death of the cross" (2.8).

After making this speech to Ginnie,-who has come up from her place with the fools down below into the house of the "perfect servant"-Franklin offers her the half of his chicken sandwich, "Take it, for Chrissake" (50). As Bryan explains, "Franklin means for Christ's sake" (228), and after Ginnie swallows "with difficulty" ("Eskimos" 50), Franklin says, "Jesus! There's the bell" (50) before he exits the room. An important distinction to note when analyzing the story, though, concerns the direct parallels Salinger makes between Franklin and Christ and the fact that these parallels come through Ginnie's vision of "a perfect servant" at the Graff house and not because Franklin is meant to uniquely embody a Christ figure. Central to spiritual epiphany in Salinger's work is the ability to, as Zooey Glass puts it, see *everybody* as Christ (*Franny and Zooey* 202).

After Franklin leaves the room, Salinger displays the manner in which Ginnie's vision begins to shift throughout the rest of the story. In fact, it is because of Eric's entry into the room that Ginnie has to put the chicken sandwich in her pocket before she can find a place to dispose of it, and our knowledge of the sandwich in her pocket provides a subtext for her interaction with Eric. Thus, in introducing Eric, Salinger points out that his "regular features, his short haircut, the cut of his suit, the pattern of his foulard necktie gave out no really final information" about him (50). In spite of this, Eric has been the object of numerous critical attacks. For instance, John Wenke states that "The story's implied drama suggests that Franklin's inability to participate in conventionally masculine domains are leading him toward homosexuality" (42).

Gwynn and Blotner on the other hand imply that Ginnie needs to save Franklin from the "clutches of the mannered, effeminate Eric" (24). Contrary to this harsh critical appraisal of Eric, it seems clear that Ginnie needs to see him through the eyes of the "perfect servant" embodied by Franklin-by judging or condemning Eric the reader becomes as superficial as Ginnie appears to be at the start of the story. The first clue Salinger provides into how Ginnie's vision needs to be altered comes through Eric's name, which means "eternal ruler." Salinger combines this with the fact that Eric sits in a "red damask chair" and "rubbed his closed eyes with the tips of his extended fingers" (51). The precise detail Salinger offers about the type of chair Eric sits in is revelatory when we consider that the word "damask" means "originating at, or pertaining to Damascus" ("Damask"). In conjunction with Eric's closed eyes, the allusion recalls the conversion of Saul/Paul of Tarsus on the road from Damascus (Acts 9).

In the story, God speaks to Saul/Paul and blinds him for three days. When Saul/Paul's sight is restored, he sees Christ and becomes one of his disciples. Yet another clue that Salinger offers comes when Eric says he is the "original Good Samaritan" (52). In the parable of the Good

Samaritan, a Samaritan helps a Jew who has been beaten and left for dead on the side of the road. After telling the parable, Christ says to "Go, and do thou likewise" (Luke 10.37). It is worth noting that both biblical allusions are concerned with showing mercy to one's enemies by following the words of Christ and clue the reader into the literal change in Ginnie's vision towards the Graffs through the "perfect servant," Christ.

At last, Eric tells Ginnie that they are "going to see Cocteau's 'Beauty and the Beast' and it's the one film where you really should get there on time" (53). Other than the obvious allusion to Franklin as a type of Beast, Cocteau's film begins with the following epigraph:

Children believe what we tell them. They have complete faith in us. They believe that a rose plucked from a garden can bring drama to a family. They believe that the hands of a human beast will smoke when he slays a victim and that the beast will be ashamed when confronted by a young girl. They believe a thousand other simple things. I ask of you a little of this childlike simplicity. And to bring us luck let me speak four truly magic words, childhood's open sesame, *"Once upon a time."* (Beauty and the Beast)

The quote could serve as a second epigraph to *Nine Stories*; Salinger could just as easily say that children believe in bananafish, and in imaginary friends, and the Laughing Man and that the adults need to see the world as they did when they were children. Salinger, though, seems to tie the quote directly to Ginnie's transformation at the end of the story. For instance, when Selena reenters the room, Ginnie says she does "not want the money" any longer and says she would like to "come over" later (54). Salinger appears to bring Ginnie's vision of the "perfect servant" at the Graff's full circle when she considers throwing the "sandwich in the street" but, instead, puts it back in her pocket. Salinger writes, "A few years before, it had taken her three days to dispose of the Easter chick she had found dead on the sawdust in the bottom of her wastebasket" (55). Here Salinger connects Ginnie's belief with Franklin's cut from the wastebasket, his condemnation of the fools in the street, and her childlike faith in the Easter story about the death and resurrection of Christ. **(E1)**

The fact that Ginnie keeps the sandwich seems to speak for itself in terms of how her vision has changed throughout the course of the story, but there is one other detail worth considering. According to Shlomo Deshen, on Yom Kippur, the Jewish Day of Atonement, the ritual of Kapparot calls for a chicken (or sometimes a fish) to be sacrificed in order to be granted atonement. "The custom calls for a fowl (usually a rooster for a male and hen for a female) to be swung around the head of the penitent after he recited certain biblical verses and the following formula: 'This is my substitute, this is my change, this is my redemption. This rooster will go to its death, and I shall be admitted a good and peaceful life.' The fowl is then slaughtered, and it (or its value) is given to the poor" (130). When Franklin gives Ginnie the chicken it might be a symbolic act of atonement (bought in a "goddam delicatessen" [50]) that Salinger draws attention to when he sets the story on Saturday. Yet, with the final allusion to Easter (otherwise known as resurrection Sunday), Salinger symbolically recognizes the shift from the ritualistic sacrifice of animals under the law to the sacrifice made by Christ, who Christians recognize as the "perfect servant," for the atonement of sins. **(E2)**

Tying "Eskimos" into the Cycle

"Eskimos" picks up where "Uncle Wiggily" left off with Eloise pleading for assurance from Mary Jane that she was "a nice girl" (38). Ginnie's view of Selena as "the biggest drip" in her school (which is "ostensibly bounding with fair-sized drips" [39]), recalls much of Eloise and Mary Jane's early gossip in "Uncle Wiggily" and the fact that Eloise is, as Mary Jane states, "getting hard as nails" (23). It seems clear that Ginnie is in danger of becoming "hard as nails" throughout "Eskimos," which makes her transformative epiphany at the conclusion of the story all the more dramatic. In addition, the epiphanic visions of both Ginnie and Eloise come through the idea of a "perfect servant" leading them back to "grace." Salinger also appears to connect Franklin with Walt. Like Walt, who tells Eloise that he is advancing in the Army, "but in a different direction from everybody else" (30), Franklin's war service "advances" him in the opposite direction of other soldiers. Franklin fights in the proverbial "war with the Eskimos" while he works an airplane factory for three years during the war. When he learns that Ginnie's sister Joan is engaged to "a lieutenant commander in the Navy," he responds, "Big deal" (46). Franklin's response may reflect his bitterness over not being able to fight in the war and the fact that Joan apparently scorns him for a man who has a higher rank. Salinger also might offer an explanation of Walt's statement that he is going to advance in the opposite direction until he is "stark naked" -through the way Franklin is dressed, "pajamas and no slippers" (42). Salinger also draws parallels between Walt and Franklin's idiomatic expressions and the way they allow others to see the world (like Seymour) from a different perspective. Another detail worth noting is that Franklin tells Ginnie he sent Joan "eight goddam letters" while he was stationed in Ohio, and "She didn't answer *one* of 'em" (47). The letters Franklin sends to Joan seem to be juxtaposed with the ones Walt sent to Eloise. It is clear Franklin was attracted to Joan to the point he continued to write her letters in spite of the fact that she never replied. Salinger provides another clue concerning Franklin's intimacy with Joan when he recognizes who Ginnie is right away, "You Ginnie Mannox?" (43). While Eloise's pain is evinced through the letters Walt writes her from the war, Franklin's pain comes through his rejection from both the Army and subsequently, it would appear, from Joan's affection.

Another connection with "Uncle Wiggily" comes through Lew's favorite author, "L. Manning Vines," who writes "a book about four men that starved to death in Alaska" (32). Eloise mocks Lew because "He isn't even honest enough to come right out and say he liked it because it was about four guys that starved to death in an igloo or something. He has to say it was beautifully written" (32). The irony of Eloise statement is that it is unwittingly self-reflective. She is not honest enough with herself or Lew to say that the reason she really idealizes Walt is because he died during the war; instead, she has to say that "the best thing about it was that [Walt] didn't even try to be funny-he just *was* funny" (28-29). In addition, Eloise's description of the book also parallels her day inside the house with Mary Jane while the "filthy slush" outside is "visibly turning to ice" (22) and they proceed to "starve to death" as they drink themselves into oblivion. Through parallels with Eloise and Mary Jane's igloo like hermitage in Connecticut, Salinger portrays Franklin's "war with the Eskimos" as a type of spiritual malaise in which the living are dead and moving without any meaningful sense of purpose through the world.

Concerning the sound of one hand clapping in "Eskimos," Salinger symbolically illustrates the division between the spiritual and material through glasses Franklin wears and the window that he looks through when he describes the war with the Eskimos. The glasses Franklin wears might indicate that he has seen beyond the superficial routines of those fighting the war with the Eskimos. Franklin's insight seems to make Ginnie aware of her own superficiality and, in turn, leads her back to the Graff house. Salinger could be implying that the war that has led Franklin to a state of physical and spiritual stasis might be overcome through his interaction with Ginnie. We might consider that while Franklin helps Ginnie to overcome her own war with Selena, Ginnie might be able to help Franklin through his war by accepting his gift and returning to talk to him, something her sister never did. When Franklin begins discussing the war with the Eskimos, Salinger draws specific symbolic attention to Franklin's hands. The scene begins when Franklin "two fingered out a cigarette" from his "pajama pocket" (46). A little later, Franklin smokes the cigarette as he looks out the window at the people down below. Salinger juxtaposes the horizontal and vertical movements throughout the scene. For example, after Ginnie tells Franklin his finger will bleed if he holds it down towards the street, Salinger writes, "He heard her. He put his left foot up on the window seat and rested his injured hand on the horizontal thigh" (48). Here we should note that Franklin transfers his "injured hand" from the vertical position to the horizontal position. In this way, Salinger parallels his wound with the "fools" down below. Because he has his foot on the "window seat," a window that protrudes over the people below, the image of Franklin might be correlated to a gun turret in an old bomber, which were enclosed in glass, dropping a bomb on the people below. Salinger subsequently connects Franklin's horizontal wound with the fools below when he "raised the window slightly and snapped his cigarette streetward" (49).

On the one hand, the cigarette may parallel Franklin's sense of guilt for all the people he has helped to kill during the war, yet, the action also appears to correspond with the spiritual planes-both a horizontal and vertical-of the story. When Franklin opens the window, he symbolically removes the division between the material and spiritual worlds (or life and death) as he tosses the cigarette "streetward" (49). Salinger then connects the horizontal and the vertical when Franklin offers Ginnie the chicken sandwich. When Ginnie puts the sandwich into "her pocket" instead of tossing it into the street-an inversion of the cigarette that Franklin takes from his pocket and tosses in the street-Salinger connects the sandwich with "the Easter chick [Ginnie] had found dead" (55). Franklin, therefore, appears to make Ginnie aware of the fact that by fighting the war with the Eskimos ("existing on four-fifty week") she was a spiritually dead "fool," but her faith can be renewed if she remembers the faith she once had in the resurrection of the dead when she was a child. **(E3)**

Endnotes:

E1: Salinger appears to be connecting "Bananafish" and "Eskimos" through Ginnie's decent back down to the street on the elevator. The action preceding Seymour's death (taking the elevator to the fifth floor) resonates in Ginnie's ascent and descent on the elevator in the story. Another significant connection comes through the wastebasket-an obvious allusion to *The Waste Land* throughout the story. Finally, the symbolic connection between the sandwich in Ginnie's coat pocket and the dead Easter chick in the wastebasket recalls the key in Seymour's robe as he dies in the waste land of the hotel.

E2: When writing about the link between Jew and Gentile, the Apostle Paul refers to it as a grafting in of the Gentiles to the family tree of God's chosen people: "And they also, if they abide not still in unbelief, shall be grafted in: for God is able to graft them in again" (Rom. 11.23). Salinger might be punning off of the Graff family name through Ginnie's transformation throughout the story. While at first she mocks the Graff family and their "perfect servant," once she visits their home her belief might be said to be renewed and she is "grafted" into the family.

E3: The closing lines of the story have mystified critics and scholars for years. Part of this mystery might be attributed to Salinger's apparent use of an intricate theological idea revolving around the allusion to Easter. Because the story most likely takes place in 1946 or '47

(Franklin was at a Christmas party in 1942 with Joan and away in Ohio for three years), the Easter (or Passover) holiday would have taken place in April. Salinger tells us that the girls had played tennis for five straight Saturdays and that it is warm Saturday in May. Thus, Easter has recently passed and the day of Pentecost (which takes place fifty days after Easter/Passover) is either approaching or upon them. The celebration of Pentecost is important because it represents God's pouring out of the Holy Ghost upon the earth (see Acts 3). In Matthew 12.31 Jesus famously states, "All manner of sin and blasphemy shall be forgiven unto men: but the blasphemy against the Holy Ghost shall not be forgiven unto men." Salinger seems to use this verse in "Eskimos" and throughout the cycle as a means of distinguishing belief from unbelief (and possibly damnation). The blasphemy of the Holy Ghost that Christ speaks of here has nothing to do with words and everything to do with belief. As "Eskimos" concludes, the shift between Ginnie keeping the Easter chick and keeping the chicken sandwich, might indicate that she has been affected by the Holy Ghost (from within). This would also correspond with the transition between the material and spiritual in the story. Of course, Christ states that it is easier for "a camel to go through the eye of a needle, than for a rich man to enter into the kingdom of God" (Matt. 19.24)-a verse Salinger seems to use with regards to Ginnie's camel hair coat. Furthermore, after he answers Thomas' doubts about his physical resurrection from the dead, Christ states, "blessed are they that have not seen, and yet have believed" (John 20.29).

Bibliography:

Beauty and the Beast. Dir. Jean Cocteau. Perf. Marcel Andre, Michel Auclair, Noel Blin, Josette Day, Janice Felty. Criterion, 1998.

Bible. King James Version.

"Damask." Def. 2. *Webster's Universal Dictionary.* 1st ed. 1936.

Deshen, Shlomo. "The Kol Nidre Enigma: An Anthropological View of the Day of Atonement Liturgy." *Ethnology.* 18.2 (1979): 121-133.

Salinger, J. D. *Nine Stories.* Boston: Little Brown, 1991.

---. *Franny and Zooey.* Boston: Little Brown, 1991.

Wenke, John. *J. D. Salinger: A Study of the Short Fiction.* Ed. Gordon Weaver. 26 vols. Boston: Twayne, 1991.

Discussion Questions and Possible Essay Topics:

1. Explore Salinger's allusions to war in the story and the possible meanings of Franklin's "war with the Eskimos."

2. How might the allusion to Jean Cocteau's "Beauty and the Beast" be applied throughout the story?

3. Examine Salinger's portrayal of Franklin Graff as a "boy, or man." What is the significance of the fact that Franklin seems to be caught between being a boy and becoming a man?

4. Explore Ginnie's transformation throughout the story. Would she have kept the chicken sandwich in her coat pocket in the beginning of the story? What are some of the reasons she might keep it at the end instead of throwing it into the street.

5. Compare and contrast Ginnie with Eloise Wengler in "Uncle Wiggily." Is Ginnie in danger of becoming a "snob" like her sister?

6. Salinger pays close attention to Franklin's cut. What significance might be applied to the various ways his cut is described throughout the story?

7. Compare Franklin with Eric and how Ginnie interacts with them both.

The Laughing Man

Overview

"The Laughing Man," as Gwynn and Blotner observe, "is a complete change in theme and technique" from the first three stories in the collection, and "it turns out to be one of the most sophisticated and intricate of all of Salinger's tales" (24). The rite-of-passage story is told by an unnamed narrator who reflects on his boyhood experiences as part of a group of twenty-five boys called the Comanche Club. The leader of the Comanches, John Gedsudski, "the Chief," takes care of them "every schoolday afternoon" and on "Saturdays and most national holidays" (56). As the narrator relates, at the end of their days together, "we Comanches relied heavily and selfishly on the Chief's talent for storytelling" (58). The Chief's story, which is also titled "The Laughing Man," relates the adventures of "The only son of a wealthy missionary couple" who was kidnapped by Chinese bandits who permanently deform him by putting his "head in a carpenter's vise" and giving it "several turns to the right" (58). The Comanche's devotion to the story is such that they consider themselves "legitimate living descendants of the Laughing Man" (62).

The story shifts when the Chief begins dating a girl named Mary Hudson, interrupting the "general men-only dăcor" of the Chief's bus and the Comanche's world. At first the Comanches tolerate Mary, but they protest when she attempts to participate in their baseball game. But once she talks herself into the game she proves her worth as a hitter, though "Her fielding couldn't have been worse." When the story shifts, something goes awry in the Chief and Mary Hudson's relationship that has a direct effect upon the events of the final two installments of "The Laughing Man" the Chief tells the Comanches. Mary comes to one final baseball game, but she does not play and the narrator realizes that "Mary Hudson had permanently dropped out of the Comanche lineup" (70). The breakup with Mary appears to have a profound effect on the Chief because in his final telling of "The Laughing Man" serial, the Laughing Man dies and the story ends, "never to be revived" (73).

Analysis

In "The Laughing Man" **(E1)** Salinger playfully constructs a metafictional framework as a means of distinguishing the narrator of "The Laughing Man" from John Gedsudski's story, "The Laughing Man." Salinger will experiment with this technique throughout his fiction, as he does with the narrator of "For Esmé, With Love and Squalor," who states, "I've disguised myself so cunningly that even the cleverest reader will fail to recognize me"

(103). Thus, the narrator's telling of "The Laughing Man" to the reader doubles with the Chief's telling of "The Laughing Man" to the Comanches so that the two stories blend. Salinger effectively demonstrates how the two stories run parallel to each other when the narrator states, "'The Laughing Man' was just the right story for a Comanche. It may even have had classic dimensions. It was a story that tended to sprawl all over the place, and yet it remained essentially portable. You could always take it home with you and reflect on it while sitting, say, in the outgoing water in the bathtub" (58). Though the narrator is now an adult, he tells the story of the events that happened when he was a boy living in New York in 1928. Therefore, the narrator (and Salinger) invites "you" to read the story of "The Laughing Man" through the eyes of a child, or a Comanche.

In the beginning of the story, the narrator distinguishes childhood perception from adult perception when he tells us that "if wishes were inches" the Comanches would have had John Gedsudski "a giant in no time" (57). "The way things go, though," he adds, "he was a stocky five three or four" with a "large and fleshy" nose and a torso "as long as his legs were" (57). Yet, to punctuate the hyperbole of his childhood imagination, the narrator states that as a boy, "it seemed to me that in the Chief all the most photogenic features of Buck Jones, Ken Maynard, and Tom Mix had been smoothly amalgamated" (58). The way the Comanches view the Chief reflects the way they see the Laughing Man, but Salinger juxtaposes the narrator's childlike perceptions with those of Gedsudski, who apparently creates the Laughing Man in his own image. As the story progresses, most of the clues concerning what goes awry in Gedsudski's relationship with Mary Hudson come through his telling of "The Laughing Man." "I had no idea what was going on between the Chief and Mary Hudson," the narrator confesses before adding parenthetically, "(and still haven't, in any but a fairly low, intuitive sense)" (70). The importance of narrator's statement comes through the fact that he connects what he knew as a child with what he knows as an adult. Just as Salinger is always seeking the meridian between child and adult in *Nine Stories*, he invites us to read and interpret "The Laughing Man" from both perspectives. These dual perspectives might best be understood as Gedsudski tells the final installment of "The Laughing Man" and the narrator states, "The story ended there, of course. (Never to be revived)" (73). In fact, the narrator revives the story in his own telling of "The Laughing Man" implying that a story can never die and that by reading it we too have become part of the story.

One of the ways that Salinger illustrates the dual perceptions of childhood and adulthood in "The Laughing Man" comes through his use of baseball. Throughout the story Salinger employs the games of baseball to suggestively hint at the sexual nature of Mary Hudson's relationship with the Chief. For example, after the narrator tells us how the Comanches did not want Mary to play and that she was a terrible fielder, he conveys how she came to bat and earned her place in the game. "She swung mightily at the first ball pitched to her and hit it over the left fielder's head," he states, adding, "It was good for an ordinary double, but Mary Hudson got to third on it-standing up" (66). The narrator continues,

> When my astonishment had worn off, and then my awe, and then my delight, I looked over at the Chief. He didn't so much seem to be standing behind the pitcher as floating over him. He was a completely happy man. Over on third base, Mary Hudson waved to me. I waved back. I couldn't have stopped myself even if I'd wanted to. Her stickwork aside, she happened to be a girl who knew how to wave to somebody from third base.
>
> The rest of the game, she got on base every time she came to bat. For some reason, she seemed to hate first base; there was no holding her there. At least three times, she stole second. (66)

Salinger carefully crafts the baseball scenes so they can be read from two perspectives. From the point of view of the narrator and the Comanches the scene reads innocently, but from an adult's point of view, the fact that Mary hates to stay on first base hints at her sexual experience, which leaves the Chief "floating" (66). Notably, when the narrator states that Mary "happened to be a girl who know how to wave to somebody from third base" (66), her playful jesting with the him turns serious as the mood of the game shifts in the second baseball scene Salinger describes in the story.

Salinger foreshadows this shift and the breakup of the Chief and Mary's relationship when the narrator tells us that when she first comes on the field to play the Comanches all have a "some-girls-just-don't-know-when-to-go-home look" (64) on their faces. Once the game begins, Salinger constantly distances Mary from home plate. As the second baseball scene unfolds, the narrator asks Mary if she would like to come to his home and tells her that the Chief came over "a lot" (70), but Mary rejects his offer telling him to leave her "alone" (70). Perhaps drawing a further contrast between the Chief and Mary domestically, in addition to going over to the narrator's house "a lot," Salinger repeatedly pictures the Chief with the other Comanches at "home" (71). The final time Mary Hudson and the Chief are pictured together in the story Salinger draws attention to the different paths they take:

The last good look I had at Mary Hudson, she was over near third base crying. The Chief had hold of the sleeve of her beaver coat, but she got away from him. She ran off the field onto the cement path and kept running till I couldn't see her any more. The Chief didn't go after her. He just stood watching her disappear. Then he turned around and walked down to home plate and picked up our two bats; we always left the bats for him to carry. (70-71)

The passage suggests the difference between the Chief and Mary's feelings towards getting married and having children. Salinger also hints that Mary is pregnant when the narrator observes her, again from first base, "about a hundred yards to my left, sandwiched between two nursemaids with baby carriages" (69). More obliquely, there are subtle indications that Mary is going to get an abortion, because she is sitting in foul territory and smoking a cigarette.

As the scene develops, Salinger offers more clues that support this reading. For instance, when the Chief goes to bring Mary to the field she never reenters the field of play but remains in foul territory-"She walked slowly behind the plate, with her hands in the pockets of her beaver coat, and finally sat down on a misplaced players' bench just beyond third base" (70). In this carefully worded scene, Salinger once again refuses to associate Mary with "home" and has her sit on a "misplaced players' bench just beyond third base" (70). Unlike the first baseball scene, Mary does not wave to the narrator from third, and when he goes to talk to her she tells him to leave her alone. Trying to make sense of her actions, the narrator tells us, "About midway along the third-base foul line, I turned around and started to walk backwards, looking at Mary Hudson" (70).

Here we should note the danger of walking backwards down the third-base foul line and the fact that, in baseball terms, it is one of the most dangerous places to be on the field. Thus, with the danger of the scene in mind, Salinger renders the rest of the scene carefully: "I couldn't have been more certain that Mary Hudson had permanently dropped out of the Comanche lineup. It was the kind of whole certainty, however independent of the sum of its facts, that can make walking backwards more than normally hazardous, and I bumped smack into a baby carriage" (70). We should note that Salinger bookends this complex scene with baby carriages and the narrator's looking at Mary. While at first she is "sandwiched between" them as she smokes, the second time she wants the narrator, a child, to leave her alone. Salinger might foreshadow this scene early on in the story when the narrator states, "If we had straight athletics on our minds, we went to Van Cortlandt, where the playing fields were regulation size and where the opposing team didn't include a baby carriage or an irate old lady with a cane" (57).

The passage appears to indicate that we should not have "straight athletics on our minds" as we read the baseball scenes that take place with Mary Hudson in Central Park. With this in mind, the narrator could be said to have a "some-girls-just-don't-know-when-to-go-home" look on his face as he watches Mary and bumps into the baby carriage with the "whole certainty" that "Mary

Hudson had permanently dropped out of the Comanche lineup" (70).

The other major indication Salinger gives that an unwanted pregnancy might be involved in the Chief and Mary's breakup comes through the death of the Laughing Man at the conclusion of the story. In the Chief's final telling of the Laughing Man serial to the Comanches, the events in the fictional world appear to blend with the real world and, in turn, childhood with adulthood. It would seem that, in the end, the Chief cannot save the Comanches from the fate of the Laughing Man any more than he can save his own child-which Salinger seems to indicate when the narrator first trips and falls and then states "I remember wishing the Chief had gloves" (71) before the final installment of 'The Laughing Man."**(E2)** With this in mind, the story transcends the teller, whether it is the Chief, the narrator, or even Salinger.

A true story cannot be altered in order to make the audience happy with the ending. If this were possible, the narrator (or Salinger) could alter his version of "The Laughing Man" to give it a happy ending-a point worth considering when reading "Bananafish" and "Teddy." For the Comanches, the death of the Laughing Man is as real as the death of one of their relatives. In the final scene of the story the narrator looks down at a piece of "red tissue paper" and he thinks it looks like "someone's poppypetal mask" (73), similar to the one the Laughing Man wore. The image coincides with that of a child seeing the harsh reality of the world unmasked. Here the dual frames of the "The Laughing Man" stories intersect: once the world of childhood innocence has been unmasked and the child becomes an adult, the magical world of one's childhood can only be reflected upon and recaptured in stories.

Tying "The Laughing Man" into the Cycle

In the final line of "Eskimos," Salinger tells us that as a child Ginnie Mannox had taken "three days to dispose of the Easter chick she had found dead on the sawdust in the bottom of her wastebasket" (58). Ginnie's childhood belief in the Easter story leads directly into "The Laughing Man," where Salinger illustrates both the magic of childhood and the loss of innocence. Just as the allusion to Easter provides a glimpse of the faith that Ginnie apparently loses in her adolescence, in "The Laughing Man" Salinger explores the loss of innocence from the point of view of both child and adult. Salinger also imports the spiritual overtones of the Easter allusion into "The Laughing Man." Ginnie's belief that the Easter chick might come back from the dead is a material belief based upon sight, but when she takes the chicken sandwich Salinger implies that she must internalize her faith and believe, "with difficulty" (50), in what she cannot see. With this in mind, we could replace the narrator of "The Laughing Man" with Ginnie and say that "a few years before," or "Once upon a time," she believed in the Laughing Man.

Accordingly, in "The Laughing Man," there's magic captured in the retelling of the story; it is a way that an adult can believe in childhood once again, and the arc of the story follows the path of every child into adolescent "knowledge." The "sound of one hand clapping" in "The Laughing Man" can be found in one of the most complex images of "glass" in *Nine Stories*. Salinger establishes the image through a complex web of allusions to the doctrine of original sin, *felix culpa*.

For instance, the narrator describes the bus that the Chief picks the Comanches up in as "condemned-looking" (56), and when Mary's picture first appears in the bus it is "above the rear-view mirror over the windshield" and she is "dressed in academic cap and gown" (62). The narrator's description of Mary recalls that of the Virgin Mary **(E3)** and is an image that recalls a prayer card. And the prayer on the back of the card with the image of the Virgin Mary, naturally, is the "Hail Mary," which contains the phrase, "blessed is the fruit of thy womb." Perhaps more importantly, Mary's photo being situated above both the rearview mirror and the windshield seems to denote that the image speaks to both the past and the future, or that it transcends the glass.

To take this reading a step further, as the narrator walks down the third baseline at the conclusion of the story, he tells us that he was "looking at Mary Hudson and holding on to my tangerine" when he bumps into the baby carriage. Here Salinger appears to connect Mary with *felix culpa* (the blessed fall) through the narrator's tossing of the fruit, his knowledge that Mary would no longer be playing in their games, and his stumble into the baby carriage. All of these details correspond with the Genesis account of the forbidden fruit: Adam and Eve's expulsion from Eden, the curse of death, and the pain of childbirth (Gen. 3). Salinger appears to foreshadow the narrator's and the Comanche's confrontation with original sin through Mary several times in the story. Not only does the narrator describe the Chief's bus as "condemned-looking," but when Mary does not show up, the Chief nonsensically demands "a little quiet in this damn bus" (68-69), and when Mary teases him on the baseball field, the narrator "picks up a stone and [throws] it at a tree" (65). This last detail might prove especially poignant in light of the tree of knowledge and the Christ-like way that the Laughing Man dies while "lashed to the tree with barbed wire" (72).

Salinger alludes to *felix culpa* throughout the cycle and it becomes the primary thesis informing Teddy's explanation of life and death in the final story. Central to *felix culpa* is the paradox that it was through the fall of man that a redeemer could come (a paradox that is central to deaths-both physical and spiritual-throughout *Nine Stories*). In "The Laughing Man," the death of the Laughing Man (presumably because of the death of Mary's child) is the event, the "fall," that brings this knowledge to the Comanches. Therefore, the image Salinger provides of "one hand clapping" comes through his meditation upon the story itself, a passage that bears repeating: "'The Laughing Man,' was just the right story for a Comanche.

It may even have had classic dimensions. It was a story that tended to sprawl all over the place, and yet it remained essentially portable. You could always take it home with you and reflect on it while sitting, say, in the outgoing water in the bathtub" (58). If "you" have read "The Laughing Man" and considered it through the eyes of a child and "reflect on it while sitting, say, in the outgoing water in the bathtub," then as the dirty water goes down the drain you will see through the "glass" of the water. The image that Salinger brings to mind upon reflecting on "The Laughing Man" is that of a baptism, which is, again, a symbolic act meant to recall the death, burial, and resurrection of Christ.

This image of baptism leads to the source of the work, Victor Hugo's novel, *L'Homme Qui Rit* (*The Man Who Laughs*). **(E4)** Critics have largely ignored the meaning behind the source other than the obvious connections between Salinger and Hugo's Laughing Men wearing masks over their faces to hide their grotesque features. Salinger's source for the story, however, seems in all likelihood to be the 1928 silent film adaptation, *The Man Who Laughs*. Throughout the film, the central character is referred to as "the Laughing Man," in addition to a number of parallels with John Gedsudski and the narrator's stories. One notable connection, in fact, is that the gypsies who buy and disfigure the Laughing Man are called Cormanchicos.

By setting "The Laughing Man" in 1928, Salinger draws attention to the silent film. Among other spiritual themes in the film, one of the primary conflicts explored is between physical and spiritual beauty. In *Nine Stories*, Salinger will again draw attention to "The Laughing Man" through a cryptic allusion in the story "De Daumier-Smith's Blue Period." The narrator of "Blue Period," who never reveals his true name, states that "his mother and father were divorced in the winter of 1928" (160). The detail proves important because Salinger parallels "The Laughing Man" with "Blue Period" on a number of levels and implies that the narrator was a member of the Comanche Club. The most revealing detail comes when the narrator, who is grieving the death of his mother for most of the story, writes a letter to a nun named Sister Irma. He tells her,

The happiest day of my life was many years ago when I was seventeen. I was on my way for lunch to meet my mother, who was going out on the street for the first time after a long illness, and I was feeling ecstatically happy when suddenly, as I was coming in to the Avenue Victor Hugo, which is a street in Paris, I bumped into a chap without any nose. I ask you to please consider that factor, in fact I beg you. It is quite pregnant with meaning. (160)

In this passage, Salinger appears to inform us that the narrator has bumped into "The Laughing Man" on his way to see his mother. The fact that Mary Hudson is depicted in "academic cap and gown," or as a nun, resonates with the fact that the narrator (or Jean) is writing the letter to a nun in "Blue Period." If we were to consider his meeting with the Laughing Man as "pregnant" with meaning "while sitting, say, in the outgoing water in the bathtub" (58), we might recall that the narrator of "Blue Period" has an epiphany that "everybody is a nun" (164). Even more, we should remember that a nun denies the material world and does not despair in the face of death because she follows Christ, who she believes has transcended death. Thus, according to Christian theology, the narrator has no reason to despair the death of his mother-or the death of the Laughing Man-if he understands the implications of the death of *Mother* Mary's child and the *fortunate fall*.

Endnotes:

E1: A number of major points from this essay come from an unpublished essay and conference presentation I did on "The Laughing Man" entitled, "'Some-Girls-Just-Don't-Know-When-To-Go-Home': Infield Chatter and Rite of Passage in J. D. Salinger's 'The Laughing Man.'"

E2: The narrator's wish that the Chief was wearing gloves here seems to correspond with the fact that Mary Hudson insists on playing with a catcher's mitt, and she cannot catch. This, of course, brings to mind Holden Caulfield's desire to protect children in *The Catcher in the Rye*: "I keep picturing all these little kids playing some game in this big field of rye and all. Thousands of little kids, and nobody's around "nobody big, I mean except me. And I'm standing on the edge of some crazy cliff. What I have to do, I have to catch everybody if they start to go over the cliff" (173). Yet Holden ultimately has to recognize that he cannot stop children from losing their innocence any more than he can stop someone from dying, as he states when he watches Phoebe on the carrousel, "All the kids kept trying to grab the gold ring, and so was old Phoebe, and I was sort of afraid she'd fall off the goddam horse, but I didn't say anything or do anything. The thing with kids is, if they want to grab for the golden ring, you have to let them do it, and not say anything. If they fall off, they fall off, but it's bad if you say anything to them" (211). Aside from the allusions to the Fall, Holden's speech raises some interesting questions about whether or not Gedsudski is a sympathetic or pathetic figure after he tells his final installment of "The Laughing Man." In the end, Holden recognizes that he cannot stop anyone from falling, which is a reading that seems to inform the conclusion of "The Laughing Man."

E3: By placing Mary in "cap and gown," Salinger invokes the image of the Madonna and seems to foreshadow Hudson's "immaculate conception," as well. Salinger also appears to choose the name Hudson (i.e. Henry Hudson) to symbolically convey the "corruption" of both the spiritual and physical worlds of the Chief and the Comanches. From this point of view, the narrator relates how Hudson invades the Edenic utopia of the Comanches on Manhattan Island. The fact that she wears a beaver coat offers another connection to Henry Hudson, who was a fur trader. Throughout his description of Mary Hudson, Salinger depicts her as an out-of-place intruder who is at odds with the natural world. In addition to wearing an animal skin (a fact which in itself contradicts the Laughing Man's befriending of the animals), the narrator tells us that when she played in the field, despite being of "unclassifiably great beauty," "it was a horrible sight" (65, 67).

E4: Another likely influence upon the story is F. Scott Fitzgerald's *The Great Gatsby*, which might provide the basic plot framework of "The Laughing Man." The self-made man John Gedsudski, from Staten Island, falls in love with a girl from an upper-class home in Long Island. Like Gatsby, Gedsudski's imaginative wish fulfillment ends tragically and invokes the paradox of the American dream. Another point worth remembering when making connections between "The Laughing Man" and *Gatsby* is that Nick Carroway states, "Gatsby turned out all right in the end," and adds, "it is what preyed on Gatsby, what foul dust floated in the wake of his dreams that temporarily closed out my interest in the abortive sorrows and short-winded elations of men" (8). These words could just as easily be placed in the mouth of the narrator of "The Laughing Man" concerning Gedsudski. Like Gatsby, or Jay Gatz, Gedsudski might be said to grant the Comanches with "an extraordinary gift for hope, a romantic readiness such as I have never found in any other person and which it is not likely I shall ever find again" (8).

Bibliography:

Bible. King James Version.

Blotner, Joseph L. and Gwynn, Frederick L. *The Fiction of J. D. Salinger*. Pittsburgh: Pittsburgh UP, 1958.

Fitzgerald, F. Scott. *The Great Gatsby*. New York: Scribner's, 1958.

The Man Who Laughs: Dir. Paul Leni. Perf. Conrad Veidt, Mary Philbin, Olga Baclanova, Josephine Crowell, George Siegmann, Brandon Hurst, Sam De Grasse, Stuart Holmes, Cesare Gravina, Edgar Norton. Kino, 2003.

Salinger, J. D. *Nine Stories*. Boston: Little Brown, 1991.

---. *The Catcher in the Rye*. New York: Bantam, 1967.

Teaching Salinger's Nine Stories

Discussion Questions and Possible Essay Topics:

1. Compare and contrast John Gedsudski's life with the story he tells about the Laughing Man.

2. How does Salinger use baseball in the story? Compare and contrast the two baseball scenes.

3. Explore Salinger's use of New York throughout the story-Hudson, Long Island, Manhattan, Central Park, Staten Island, etc.

4. Discuss the role of the storyteller in "The Laughing Man." Who controls the story? Is it the narrator, John Gedsudski, or Salinger?

5. With the previous question in mind, explore why the Laughing Man dies at the end of the story and how much control the storyteller has over the death of a character.

6. F. Scott Fitzgerald's *The Great Gatsby* had a tremendous influence on Salinger. Explore the parallels between *Gatsby* and "The Laughing Man."

7. Discuss the absence of the narrator's parents throughout the story. What does the story seem to imply about growing up in Manhattan?

8. Discuss the events of the story in light of the fact that it takes place in 1928, just before the Great Depression.

Down at the Dinghy

Overview

"Down at the Dinghy" begins with an obscure conversation in the kitchen between two maids, Sandra and Mrs. Snell, about, as we learn at the end of the story, Sandra's calling her boss, Mr. Tannenbaum, "a big-sloppy-kike" (86). Sandra's concern over the remark comes from the fact that Mr. Tannenbaum's four-year-old son, Lionel, heard what she said. As the two talk, Sandra claims that Lionel "goes pussyfooting' all around the house" eavesdropping on conversations and that she has to "weigh every word" she says around him. When Mr. Tannenbaum's wife, Boo Boo, or Beatrice Tannenbaum (Née Glass-the sister of Seymour and Walter Glass) comes into the kitchen, she looks for a pickle to lure Lionel out of the dinghy and back to the house. Mrs. Snell tells Boo Boo, "I hear Lionel's supposeta be runnin' away," and Boo Boo proceeds to tell her and Sandra about how Lionel's "been hitting the road regularly since he was two" (77, 78). According to Boo Boo, Lionel runs away whenever someone says something that upsets him, though she usually cannot make sense of the reasons he gives.

Boo Boo leaves the house and goes down to talk to Lionel at the dinghy. Initially Lionel will not allow Boo

Boo to come into the dinghy with him, and he tells her, "Nobody can come in" (83). Boo Boo tries to play along with Lionel, but when that does not work, she attempts to get him to tell her why he is running away after he promised he would not anymore. Lionel's response is to throw a pair of "underwater goggles" into the water. Boo Boo takes offense to Lionel's actions and tells him that the goggles used to belong to Lionel's "Uncle Webb," and "they once belonged to [his] Uncle Seymour" (84). Lionel does not care. Boo Boo then takes out a key chain that Lionel wants and says she should throw it into the water, and once again, Lionel says he does not care. But when Boo Boo throws the keys onto Lionel's lap, he proceeds to defiantly throw them into the water and then starts "crying mightily" (85). At this point Boo Boo steps down into the dinghy, and Lionel confesses that he is upset because "Sandra-told Mrs. Smell-that Daddy's a big-sloppy-kike" (86). Boo Boo, who "flinched" at Lionel's statement, responds by telling him, "That isn't too terrible," and adds: "That isn't the worst that could happen" (86). She then asks Lionel if he knows what a kike is? "It's one of those things that go up in the air," he says, "with string that you hold" (86). Boo Boo then tucks Lionel's shirt in and tells him they will go get some pickles, pick up "Daddy" and all go out for "a ride on the boat" together. The story ends with them racing back to the house and Lionel winning the race.

Analysis

Salinger uses the conversation at the beginning of "Down at the Dingy" to emphasize Sandra and Mrs. Snell's sense of materialism. While on the one hand Sandra labels the Tannenbaum family through ethnic stereotypes, Salinger identifies Mrs. Snell through the "Hattie Carnegie label" on the inside of the hat she has worn "not just all summer, but for the past three summers-through record heat waves, through change of life, over scores of ironing boards, over the helms of dozens of vacuum cleaners" (74). In addition to her hat, Mrs. Snell has a leather handbag that, though "extremely worn," has a "label inside it as impressive as the one inside [her] hat" (75). By associating Mrs. Snell and Sandra with labels that represent what they wear on the "inside," Salinger seems to confer a level of superficiality upon them. Salinger also might be alluding to Seymour's parable of the bananafish when he notes that Sandra has an enormous waistline. As Seymour warns Sybil, when the bananafish swim into the hole and "eat as many as seventy-eight bananas" they get "so fat they can't get out of the hole again. Can't fit through the door" (16). Sandra's weight embodies the type of gluttony that Seymour warns Sybil about, but Sandra's physical appearance only reflects her outward spite for the Tannenbaum family. As a way of drawing the reader's attention below surface appearances, Salinger contrasts Sandra's gluttony as a maid with Boo Boo's "hipless" and "styleless" appearance. Thus, the reader is forced to look beyond the social stigmas associated with them-such as the fact that the Tannenbaum's are a wealthy Jewish family and Sandra is a poor maid. Sandra supports the notion that she cannot swim out of the bananahole when, after she has called Mr. Tannenbaum a kike, she states that Lionel is "gonna have a nose just like the father" (76).

In contrast to Sandra's frivolous use of racial stereotypes and epithets, Lionel weighs "every word" (75). And as with Muriel and her mother, Mrs. Snell and Sandra are situated as unreliable narrators because their perspectives on the world are often limited to the material world. Salinger draws attention to this when Boo Boo calls to Sandra and she has to look, "alertly past Mrs. Snell's hat" (77). The irony in Sandra's concerned look comes from the fact that Lionel might have told Boo Boo what she has said. But when she looks "alertly," she is forced to look at the person beyond the "label." Further complicating the image of Sandra looking past the hat is that Hattie Carnegie was born Henrietta Kanengeiser, a Jew from Vienna, Austria.

Once Boo Boo begins talking to Sandra and Mrs. Snell about Lionel, she offers clues into the fact that he has been deeply affected by the racial slurs of other children, though he does not seem to connect them with race. Boo Boo tells them that one child said, 'You stink, kid," and another one "told him she had a worm in her thermos bottle" (79). The racial slurs do not make any sense when Lionel attempts to translate them to Boo Boo, any more than it makes sense that a "kike" is a "kite" in Lionel's eyes. Lionel's translations of the racial slurs suggests that even though he does not understand the words, he understands the meaning behind the words. Sandra, in turn, does not understand the meaning behind the words she chooses. Like most racial slurs, the word "kike" itself is an example of a word whose meaning was kidnapped by malicious intent since "kike" derives from the Yiddish word *kikel*, which means circle. Jews who immigrated through Ellis Island made their mark with a circle instead of an X to mark their names because they associated the X with the Christian cross. One of the fascinating implications of Salinger's use of language in "Down at the Dingy" is that it parallels his use of language throughout *Nine Stories*. While the language is often wrapped in obscure actions, the meaning behind the character's words conveys what is significant. Seymour's use of the bananafish parable is a primary example of this; understanding the meaning behind Seymour's words has more significance than the words themselves.

Accordingly, Salinger parallels Lionel's misinterpretation of a kite for a kike with his description of how Boo Boo first sees Lionel floating in the water off the edge of the pier down at the dinghy: "Boo Boo found it queerly difficult to keep Lionel in steady focus. The sun, though not especially hot, was nonetheless so brilliant that it made any fairly distant image-a boy, a boat-seem almost as wavering and refractional as a stick in the water" (80). The unfocused image foreshadows Lionel's definition of what a kike is at the conclusion of the story. As Boo Boo's looks out at Lionel on the water, he blends with the boat so that Boo Boo cannot tell the difference between the boy and the boat. The wavering movement of the boy and the boat in the water recalls looking at a kite in the sky. Even Salinger's description of Lionel sitting in the dinghy tied to the dock "at a perfect right angle away from the far end of the pier" mirrors the image of a kite in the sky.

Beyond these mimetic images, throughout the second half of the story Salinger explores the difference between what Boo Boo sees, the boy in the boat, and what Lionel perceives: his father as a "big sloppy" kite in the sky. What Boo Boo perceives from a distance with her eyes distorts her vision, and in this way, Boo Boo sees Lionel the way Sandra sees him. Salinger highlights this detail by portraying both Sandra and Boo Boo looking out the window to where the dinghy floats off the end of the pier. While Sandra looks "down" to where Lionel is sitting through "the lake-front window" (74), she does not appear to see him or to *see through the glass*. Similarly, Boo Boo looks out the window at Lionel, having "changed her position slightly, so that her back wasn't directly to the two women at the table" (78). As Boo Boo talks to Sandra and Mrs. Snell about Lionel, she reveals that she does not really understand why Lionel runs away: "It's all slightly over my head" (79). Yet, by the end of the story, Boo Boo will be able to translate what continues to upset Lionel (i.e. the labels people place on him).

After talking with Sandra and Mrs. Snell, Boo Boo stands at the top of the front lawn on the other side of the window and briefly watches Lionel before she goes down to him and attempts to understand why he is upset. Though she is beyond the glass of the window, she still does not see Lionel clearly, an indication that she will have to see the world from his perspective, down at the dinghy. Boo Boo's walk from the house and down the "slight downgrade of her front lawn" (79) to the pier also symbolically represents the bridging of the home with the boat-a bridge that needs to be re-established since Lionel has come to associate (or label) home and kites with a negative meaning because of Sandra. When Boo Boo walks the imaginary line down from the house to the boat, it is almost as if Salinger is trying to represent the house as a kite, and it will be Boo Boo's job to guide Lionel back and restore his faith in home.

Because Lionel associates Boo Boo with Sandra and the house, he will not allow her to come into the boat. He tells her, "Nobody can come in," (83) and that she "can talk to Sandra" (83). In her attempts to disarm him, Boo Boo asks him why he's running away, "After you promised me you were all through" (84). Lionel, "for answer" (84), takes a pair of underwater goggles and flips them into the water. Boo Boo scolds him for doing it and tells him that the goggles belonged to his Uncle Webb and once belonged to his Uncle Seymour, but Lionel is defiant: "I don't care" (84). To counter his defiance, Boo Boo takes out a key chain,

"Just like Daddy's," and tells Lionel that she "should throw this key chain in the lake" (85). When Lionel states "It's mine," she responds, "I don't care" (85). At this point, Salinger writes Lionel's "eyes reflected pure perception, as his mother had known they would" (85), and she tosses the key chain down into his lap. Once in his lap, Lionel "picked it off, looked at it in his hand, and flicked it-sidearm-into the lake" (85). Having flicked the keys into the lake, "He then immediately looked up at Boo Boo, his eyes filled not with defiance but tears. In another instant, his mouth was distorted into a horizontal figure 8, and he was crying mightily" (85).

The scene merits close examination due to the complexity of the details Salinger provides and the way they tie in with other parts of the story. Lionel's tossing the goggles into the water is an action that reveals the way Sandra's words have made him feel. Just as Sandra has disregarded his father, he disregards Boo Boo's feelings about the goggles. The kite and goggles are perfectly juxtaposed images in that one can only play with a kite when it is up in the air and goggles are only useful under the water. When Lionel throws the goggles *down* into the water, he essentially does the same thing to Boo Boo that Sandra has done to him. Though, as Boo Boo recognizes, Lionel has a "pure perception" of what his actions and words mean when he throws the keys into the water along with the goggles. The implied meaning is that both the goggles and the keys are representations of the material world and only have significance because of the people that Boo Boo and Lionel care about. When Lionel perceives this, he gives up the keys because he cares about his Daddy and ultimately how Boo Boo feels about his Uncles, as well. At this point in the story, Boo Boo goes on board the boat and sits in the "stern seat," where Lionel was sitting, and puts "the pilot on her lap" (85). While she tries to calm him down, Lionel blurts, "Sandra-told Mrs. Smell-that Daddy's a big-sloppy-kike" (86).

Since Boo Boo is now in Lionel's seat and Lionel is sitting on her lap, their roles are momentarily inverted in the story. Lionel's confession punctuates this inversion and makes Boo Boo flinch, "Just perceptibly" (86). When she regains her composure, she stands him in front of her and asks him, "Do you know what a kike is, baby?" (86). Here Salinger puts them on the same level for the first time in the story. Boo Boo could define or try to explain what a kike is to Lionel, but instead she allows him to define the word for her. This important scene anticipates Sergeant X's attempt to reconcile the despair of a Nazi official in "For Esmé, With Love and Squalor." Salinger was wrestling with the Holocaust in the wake of World War II and according to Kenneth Slawinski, "he began to take notes on reading materials he had brought with him: a chilling endorsement of ethnic cleansing contained in the Nazi treatise "New Basis of Racial Research" and an "article from *The New Yorker* entitled "The Children of Lidice" (173). Slawinski continues,

It was The New Yorker *article that captivated Salinger's attention, a shocking description of the savage slaughter of children during the war and the enslavement of those who had managed to survive because they looked German.* "We know," *Salinger recorded from the text,* "that more than six thousand Jewish, Polish, Norwegian, French, and Czech children were killed by gas at Chelmno and burned in the crematorium." (173)

With the Holocaust as a backdrop, Salinger's original title for "Down at the Dinghy," "The Killer in the Dinghy," is all the more compelling. The original title is echoed in Salinger's description of Lionel swinging "the dead tiller" of the dinghy as Boo Boo tries to talk to him. Not only does the image seem to imply that Sandra's words leave Lionel alone and rudderless, but it also brings the Dantean image of tilling up the dead of the Holocaust as well. **(E1)** In this way, we might consider how Salinger inverts the indoctrination of the Hitler Youth **(E2)** in the scene through the levelheaded way Boo Boo responds to Sandra's words. When Lionel tells Boo Boo that a kike is "one of those things that go up in the air . . . with string you hold," he puts the absurdity of the label into perspective and offers a "pure perception" of how racism takes something beautiful and defiles it. After she listens to Lionel re-define what a kike is, Boo Boo tucks his shirt in and tells him they will go "to the station and get Daddy, and then we'll bring Daddy home and make him take us for a ride in the boat" (86). She adds, "You'll have to help him carry the sails down. O.K.?" (86). In the same way that Sandra's words corrupt Lionel's view of an image as beautiful as a kite, Lionel's words allow Boo Boo to redefine a horrible racial slur and see it as something beautiful. From this point on, she does for Lionel what he has done for her, as she restores the meaning and re-establishes the order of Lionel's world. First of all, she says that they will pick up "Daddy;" second, she tells him they will all go out sailing on the lake; and third, the last line of the story, they race "back to the house" and Lionel wins (86). In both of the last images, Salinger re-establishes the images of the home and the kite that were corrupted in Lionel's mind. Not only does he run back home instead of running away, but the image of the kite is renewed in the image of the dinghy with its "main and jib sails" (79) sailing upon the lake.

Tying "Down at the Dinghy" into the Cycle

"Down at the Dinghy" is at the heart of *Nine Stories*. It is the one story in the collection in which a child and an adult arrive at an agreement on an equal level. Yet it is easy to overlook the story, especially in the wake of the fantastic and intricate storytelling of "The Laughing Man." The order of the child's world disrupted in "The Laughing Man" is re-established in the image of the mother and child running home and going to pick up "Daddy" to bring him home at the end of "Down at the Dinghy." Unlike Mary Hudson, Boo Boo Tannebaum Née Glass is a girl who knows "when-to-go-home," a detail Salinger reinforces by setting the story in Long Island, Mary Hudson's "home." Unlike the boys in the Comanche Club whose parents are hardly present and who idolize "The Laughing Man," Lionel's hero is his father. In this way, "Down at the Dinghy" is the exemplary story about family, parenting, and to some extent marriage, in *Nine Stories*.

By extension, the sound of one hand clapping in the story comes through the mirroring of the lake and the sky. The precise image that Salinger gives of the dinghy, "Tied and stripped of its main and jib sails" floating "at a perfect right angle away from the dock" (79), appears to create the image of a kite reflecting upon the water. Thus, if one were looking above at a kite in the air or down below at the dinghy upon the water, they would be mirror images. Along with this, when Boo Boo looks out upon the horizon and sounds "the call-a peculiar amalgamation of 'Taps' and 'Reveille'-three times" (82), Salinger focuses on the merging of the sky and the water. The Naval tradition that Boo Boo invokes through "Reveille" and "Taps" is one that essentially translates into a call to wake up and to rest. Because of "Taps" association with military funerals, Boo Boo's amalgamation of the two could be translated as a waking up of those who are dead or asleep. As Boo Boo salutes "the opposite shore," she is "profoundly moved" by "one of the virtues of naval tradition" (82) and forgets

Lionel is there. Ironically, though, Boo Boo is performing the "virtue" for Lionel, and it seems to call her to attention. Also noteworthy in the scene is that Salinger sets it in the late afternoon as day draws even with the night, and Boo Boo is facing east with the "late afternoon sun at her back" (83). Boo Boo's facing east obliquely alludes to the presence of the dead beyond the horizon and it is evident that she begins thinking about her dead brothers, Seymour and Walter, as she fixes the "sextant of her eye on the horizon" (85). The image of a sextant once again should draw the reader's attention to the meridian between the lake and the sky, as much as it appears to associate what Boo Boo sees with both Seymour and Walter.

In addition, Salinger allows us to "see more" through Lionel's act of tossing Seymour's "underwater goggles" into the lake. Lionel's actions are an "answer" to why he is running away after he promised Boo Boo he would not. Once he throws the keys into the water, Salinger hints at the fact that the key to the story is to see through Seymour's eyes—which might also correspond with the key that Seymour takes out of his robe. Once both the keys and the goggles are below the surface of the water, Boo Boo is able to go down into the dinghy, and from this point on, she and Lionel are able to understand each other. In fact, it might be said that, if viewed from the distance, mother and child become one in the scene. The scene recalls how Boo Boo sees Lionel and the boat merging together from the distance and the way both she and Sandra look down at the dinghy from the window. But the scene also brings to mind Sandra's statement about the family earlier in the story to Mrs. Snell: "none of 'em even go anywheres near the water now. She don't go in, he don't go in, the kid don't go in. Nobody goes in now. They don't even take that crazy boat out no more" (79). Reflected in this statement is the fact that Sandra's words corrupt Lionel's view of his home and his father so that his words become an echo of hers, "Nobody can come in" (87).

But once the goggles and the keys are underwater, both Boo Boo and Lionel seem to proverbially see through Seymour's eyes. At the end of the story, Boo Boo re-orders Sandra's statement as she tells Lionel that they will all go out sailing later in the day. The image of the family sailing, untethered, upon the water into the horizon and the sunset brings the three central planes of the story-home, sky and the lake-back into focus and reflects the balance between what is seen in the sky and under the water. This balance is ultimately a reflection between the material and spiritual worlds and might call our attention to the image of the cross that frames both a kite and a mast on a boat. As with other images in "Down at the Dinghy" and *Nine Stories*, the cross as defined by both Christians and Jews is often distorted (and Salinger's unique perspective comes as a result of being raised in both traditions). Because both kite and dinghy contain the image of the cross, the "killing" at the dinghy might be interpreted as a redemptive death, which brings Boo Boo's thoughts of Seymour and Walt into a completely different light.

Though the cross has been a historically divisive image, Salinger seems to draw the reader's attention to the meaning of the cross, beyond the label, throughout *Nine Stories*. According to the Bible, the death of Christ upon cross does not discriminate but is open to "whosoever believeth" (John 3.16). Even more, Salinger might have Christ's death on the cross in mind when he connects the earth with the sky: "And having made peace through the blood of his cross, by him to reconcile all things unto himself; by him, I say, whether they be things in earth, or things in heaven" (1 Cor. 1.20). Through his exploration of the meaning behind labels in "Down at the Dinghy," Salinger provides a way of interpreting his use of Christian symbolism throughout *Nine Stories*.

Endnotes:

E1: *The Divine Comedy* provides a subtext to "Down at the Dinghy." Boo Boo, whose real name is Beatrice, serves as a guide for Lionel throughout the story in the way that Beatrice leads Dante from hell and purgatory into paradise and the beatific vision.

E2: The Hitler Youth (The Hitler-Jugend or HJ) were central to Hitler's rise to power and the Nazi (National) party. Hitler was able to take control of the country through propaganda that taught children to value the National values over all others, even the values taught to them by their parents (especially if they conflicted with those of the Nazi party). Central to this propaganda was a hatred of Jews, gypsies and homosexuals. The Hitler Youth were taught that Jews were closest on the evolutionary ladder to apes and thus could be killed with the same disregard as an animal.

Bibliography:

Bible. King James Version.

Salinger, J. D. *Nine Stories*. Boston: Little Brown, 1991.

Slawenski, Kenneth. *J. D. Salinger: A Life*. New York: Random House, 2011.

Discussion Questions and Possible Essay Topics:

1. Explore the things Sandra says about Lionel with what he actually says and does in the story.

2. Compare and contrast Sandra and Mrs. Snell through their words, appearances and the cups of tea they are drinking.

3. Explore the social divisions Salinger presents in the story through the maids and the Tannenbaum family.

4. What role does race/ethnicity play in the story? Is the fact that Salinger hides the race/ethnicity of Sandra and Mrs. Snell significant?

5. Discuss Salinger's use of water, what Boo Boo calls "the bounding" (81), in the story.

6. Why does Boo Boo ask Lionel to define the word "kike" for her? Why does she choose not to tell Lionel what it means?

7. What is the role of Mr. Tannenbaum in the story?

8. Explore Salinger's use of Seymour's underwater goggles in the story. With this in mind, does Seymour's parable of the bananafish correspond with the themes of "Down at the Dinghy"?

For Esmé, With Love and Squalor

Overview

At the beginning of "For Esmé, with Love and Squalor" the narrator has been invited to a wedding that he and his wife decide they cannot attend because, among other reasons, his mother-in-law is coming to visit. He adds, however, that he has "jotted down a few revealing notes on the bride," since he is not "the type that doesn't even lift a finger to prevent a wedding from flatting" (87). "If my notes should cause the groom, whom I haven't met, an uneasy moment or two," he speculates, "so much the better. Nobody's aiming to please, here. More, really, to edify, to instruct" (87). The story begins, "In April of 1944," in Devon, England just before the D-Day landings. The narrator states that most of the soldiers who are with him in "a rather specialized pre-Invasion course" are "essentially letter writing types" (88), and there isn't "one good mixer in the bunch" (88). At the conclusion of the training he packs up all of his belongings, "including a canvas gas-mask container full of books [he'd] brought over from the other side" (88), walks into town in a thunderstorm, and eventually enters a church where he listens to a children's choir sing a hymn. As he listens to the choir, the narrator observes a young girl whose voice "led the way" and whose eyes "might very possibly have counted the house" (90).

Once he leaves the church, the narrator makes his way to a tearoom and sits down to reread letters from his wife and his mother-in-law. As he is reading, the young girl from the choir, Esmé, comes in with a young boy, her brother Charles, and a woman he presumes is their governess. Esmé comes over to talk to the narrator, having observed him sitting in a pew at the church, and they proceed to discuss her view on Americans among a number of other topics. The narrator observes that Esmé is a "small-talk detester," and she is wearing a watch "much too large for her slender wrist" (93). Esmé eventually reveals that the watch belonged to her father, who was "s-l-a-i-n in North Africa" (97). Esmé also tells the narrator that her mother died and asks, "Do you find me terribly cold?" (96). When Charles comes over to the table he tells the narrator a riddle, "What did one wall say to the other wall?" (99).

The riddle is repeated three times during the course of the narrator's interaction with Charles. In the midst of their conversation, the narrator tells Esmé that he considers himself "a professional short-story writer," and she asks him if he would "write a story exclusively for [her] sometime" (100). Esmé tells him she prefers "stories about squalor" and shortly after this she leaves the tearoom with Charles and her Aunt as the narrator confesses, "It was a strangely emotional moment for me" (102). The emotion of the moment is tempered, though, when they re-enter the tearoom because Esmé says that Charles wants to kiss him goodbye (102). Esmé reminds the narrator to "write the story" and to "Make it extremely squalid and moving" (103). Finally she tells him she hopes he returns "from the war with all [his] faculties intact" (103).

In the second part of the story, the "squalid, or moving part of the story," the narrator tells us, "I've disguised myself so cunningly that even the cleverest reader will fail to recognize me" (103). In this part of the story, the narrator refers to himself as Sergeant X and over a year has passed since he met Esmé in the tearoom in England. The narrator also reveals that Sergeant X has "not come through the war with all of his faculties intact" (104). X, for example, has to press "his hands hard against his temples" and hold on tight to keep his mind from dislodging "like insecure luggage on an overhead rack" (104). After his mind steadies, he picks up a book by Joseph Goebbels entitled *Die Zeit Ohne Beispiel*. The narrator explains the book belongs to the unmarried daughter of the family that lived in the house, that she "had been a low official in the Nazi Party" (105), and X had arrested her. X looks at the inscription inside the woman's book and reads what is written on the page in "small, hopelessly sincere handwriting": "Dear God, life is hell" (105). X attempts to refute the statement by writing a quote from the Fyodor Dostoyevsky's *The Brothers Karamazov*: "Fathers and teachers, I ponder 'What is hell?' I maintain that it is the suffering of being unable to love" (105). But when he looks at the page he sees that his words are "almost entirely illegible" (105). Frightened by the event, X opens up a letter from his brother and throws it away after his brother asks X to send "the kids a couple of bayonets or swastikas" (106).

At this point, Corporal Z (Clay) comes in the room and begins to talk to X. The narrator notes Z's various war commendations and contrasts his sanity with X's. Z observes that X has the shakes and tells him how his girlfriend Loretta "says nobody gets a nervous breakdown just from the war and all. She says you probably were unstable like, your whole goddam life" (109). In contrast, Z says Loretta diagnosed him as being "temporarily insane" (110) for shooting a cat when they were in combat. After this, Z invites X to go listen to Bob Hope on the radio but X declines. Z then leaves the room but not before he asks X if he will help him translate the German in his letters to Loretta because she thinks it makes him sound intelligent. Once Z leaves the room, X attempts to write a letter as a type of "therapy," but he cannot get the paper into the typewriter (112). Frustrated by his failure, X closes his eyes, and when he opens them, he sees a package wrapped in green paper that he discovers is from Esmé. Esmé's package contains a note that includes a postscript from Charles and her father's watch. After X reads the note, he holds it for a "long time" before he picks up the watch and notices the "crystal had been broken in transit" (114). The narrator tells us X does not have the courage to wind the watch and see if it still works but that "suddenly, almost ecstatically, he felt sleepy" (114). In the final line of the story, the narrator addresses Esmé directly and tells her that when a man is really sleepy "he always stands a chance of again becoming a man with all his fac-with all his f-a-c-u-l-t-i-e-s intact" (114).

Analysis

The narrator's preface to the story addresses marriage on two different levels. On the one hand, he communicates the nature of his own marriage when he states that though he wants to attend Esmé's wedding and has discussed the matter with his wife, "we've decided against it" (87). The important thing to note is that the narrator states that they both have decided against his attending the wedding after they discuss the trip. The glimpse he provides into his own marriage helps to put his notes "on the bride" into context. Marriage, after all, requires a great deal of self-sacrifice for one's spouse and family, a theme that provides the subtext of the story. Through this subtext, Salinger shows how authentic expressions of love come out of the squalor of life. Even as Esmé rhetorically asks the narrator, "isn't it a pity that we didn't meet under less extenuating circumstances" (103), Salinger might be suggesting that it is precisely because of the squalid circumstances that their meeting means so much to them both. If the narrator was not struggling with the impending conflict of D-Day, and if Esmé had not lost her parents in the war, her words and her gift would not have the value they do for the narrator. With this in mind, Salinger displays how a selfless love (or *agape*) comes only through enduring the squalor of life. Thus, the lesson the narrator provides for the groom is one that might cause him "an uneasy moment or two" (87). "So much the better," he tells us, "Nobody's aiming to please, here. More, really, to edify, to instruct" (87). The statement invites examination: what is it about the narrator's notes on Esmé that might cause the groom an uneasy moment or two? And how will the narrator's story keep the wedding from flatting? Both of these questions lead us back into the nature of love and squalor; the narrator appears to be acknowledging that most marriages based upon a superficial or purely physical love end up "flatting" when they experience squalor. Therefore, in relation to love, specifically with regards to marriage, the story translates the sacrificial love of *agape* through squalor.

  As the narrator begins his "notes" about how he met Esmé, the impending doom awaiting him and the other American enlisted men in the "specialized pre-Invasion training course" (88) establishes the ominous tone early in the story. The details the narrator provides in the first half of the story must be read with an understanding of what the soldiers are training for and where they are imminently headed. The narrator's statements that "there wasn't one good mixer in the bunch," and that "When we weren't writing letters or attending classes, each of us went pretty much his own way" (88), are indicative of the seriousness of the battle that the soldiers are being prepared to go into. Not only are the soldiers aware of the probability of their own death, but they are aware of possible deaths of their fellow soldiers. The intensity of the situation, naturally, leads them to activities that ease the tension of their training such as writing letters home and reading books. In fact, the narrator and his wife's decision for him not to make the trip overseas for Esmé's wedding could be connected, at least in part, to the trauma the narrator suffers during the war and the possibility that it might be too soon for him to return to Europe. The narrator draws attention to this when he states that the three week training course ended on a rainy Saturday and that "At seven that last night, our whole group was scheduled to entrain for London, where, as rumor had it, we were to be assigned to infantry and airborne divisions mustered for the D-Day landings" (88).

In contrast with the unfolding events, the narrator relates the gut-wrenching emotion of the situation through understatement, though death is foreshadowed in all of the details he provides. For instance, he writes, "By three in the afternoon, I'd packed all my belongings into my barrack bag, including a canvas gas-mask container full of books I'd brought over from the Other Side" (88). The books, in other words, are helping him to stay alive on the "Other Side" (88), which seems to represent the war's culture of death. Another compelling image the narrator provides comes when he describes himself "standing at an end window of our Quonset hut for a very long time" and watching the "slanting, dreary rain, my trigger finger itching imperceptibly, if at all. I could hear behind my back the uncomradely scratching of many fountain pens on many sheets of V-mail paper" (88). The objective correlative between the rain and the fountain pens anticipates the D-Day landing and *many* of the soldier's last words to their families. Through these soldier's letters, Salinger parallels Esmé's statement that her "father wrote beautifully" and that she is "saving a number of his letters for posterity" (99), namely Charles. As the narrator listens to the pens, his "itching" trigger finger corresponds with the "uncomradely" sound of the pens and what the words they are writing represent as he watches the rain falling on the *other side* of the window. Salinger appears to represent and honor these words not only in the letters of Esmé's father, but in her "note" to Sergeant X and in the narrator's "few revealing notes" "For Esmé" (87). The squalor of the "conflict" informs all of the letters and notes comprised within the story and establishes a correlation between how the words themselves become valuable because of the squalor. Corresponding with this squalor, as if he cannot stand to consider the scene anymore, the narrator leaves the window "abruptly," and prepares to head into town "after synchronizing [his] wristwatch with the clock in the latrine" (89). The scene not only anticipates the symbolism of Esmé's chronographic watch for the narrator, but the act of setting his watch with the clock in the latrine seems to coincide with how his "time" is now "synchronized" in accordance with the dirty and unpleasant conditions of squalor that are about to befall him.

Anticipating this squalid condition, the narrator walks into town and stops "in front of a church" (89) where he reads the bulletin board. He sees that at three-fifteen "there would be children's choir practice," looks at his wristwatch and before he enters the church reads "all of the names" (89). The glance at his watch should remind the reader of the squalor that his watch has been set to, and the reading of the children's names inverts the act of those who are reading the list of the names of the dead on the "Other Side." Once inside the church, the narrator listens to the children sing a hymn and hopes it has "a dozen or more verses" (90). The hymn, which the choir coach tells the children to sing absorbing the "meaning of the words" (89), cuts against the meaning behind all of the words the narrator has shared up to this point. As they sing, he describes how their "melodious and unsentimental" a capella voices make him feel, when he writes, "a somewhat more denominational man than myself might, without straining, have experienced levitation" (90). While the narrator listens to the children, he scans their faces and "one in particular" stands out, that of Esmé's, and he notes her "blazé eyes that, I thought, might very possibly have counted the house" (90).

The narrator also notices the manner in which Esmé's eyes seem uninterested even while they take account of the house (or the people in the audience). Just as the narrator accounts for the sound of the pens on the paper and the names of the children he reads while standing "in the rain" (89), Esmé eyes seem to count the house because of her parents' deaths. Salinger might imply here that the narrator is about to become "acquainted" with the squalor that affects Esmé's view of the "house" (91). The connection is made again when the narrator sees Esmé in the tearoom. While he notes her "house-counting eyes" (92) she states, "You were at choir practice....I saw you" (93). Even more, Esmé tells the narrator that she saw him sitting in the "house" immediately after he observes the object representative of her squalor, "a wristwatch, a military-looking one that looked rather like a navigator's chronograph" (93). The attention Salinger pays to the watches both the narrator and Esmé are wearing, in addition to the fact that she notices him in the church and comes over to him in the tearoom appears to connect him, however distantly, with her father. This connection is only strengthened when he confides to her that he likes to think of himself "as a professional short-story writer," and she responds, "My father wrote beautifully" (99). In the course of their conversation, these details only reinforce the significance of Esmé's loss, and her ability to endure the tragedy of her father and mother's deaths proves exemplary in the midst of the narrator's own squalor.

Along these lines, the conversation between Esmé and the narrator reaffirms their mutual need, helping to bridge the voids in their lives. Not only does the death of Esmé's parents continue to resonate in their relationship and in the person that it has made Esmé and, in turn, the narrator, but the narrator's "notes" about Esmé six years after they meet are meant to "edify" and "instruct" the groom and, in turn, the reader. But Salinger does not idealize Esmé. From the start of their conversation, Salinger draws attention to everything Esmé does not know about America and Americans. Accordingly, the narrator becomes representative of America (the New World) and Esmé of England (the Old World). As their conversation unfolds, Salinger subtly addresses the repercussions of failing to bridge the distance between the two worlds. When Charles asks his riddle, "What did one wall say to the other wall?" (98), the divides in the story are brought together in the answer, "meet you at the corner!" (99). The narrator and Esmé have to meet at the corner, the intersection between their respective worlds. When Esmé, for example, tells the narrator, "You seem quite intelligent for an American" (94), the narrator tells her "that was a pretty snobbish thing to say" (94).

Esmé attempts to defend her statement, but the narrator tells her that most of the soldiers she was talking about "were a long way from home, and that few of them had had many real advantages in life" (94). The narrator's statement reflects the perspective of a soldier who understands the enormous squalor of the war. While on the one hand there is no way to excuse people who, as Esmé observes, "act like animals" (94), on the other, war is a "method of existence that is ridiculous to say the least" (113). More importantly, in the greater context of WWII, when Esmé takes a position of snobbish superiority she only contributes to the worldview that began the war. Furthermore, the nature of the riddle is that it is essentially a truth that is always pursued and never finally arrived at. "He tells that same riddle to everyone he meets," Esmé explains, "and has a fit every single time" (99). For Charles, the riddle is made new every time and with every person (or every wall) he meets. When Charles asks the narrator the riddle a second time, the narrator tells him the answer and immediately regrets it because it upsets Charles. Yet the third time the riddle is told, the narrator tells it to Charles and allows him to provide the answer. In this way, the riddle changes every time it is told, and it reflects how the narrator figuratively "meets Charles at the corner."

The sequence of riddles that unfold between Charles and the narrator also parallels the narrator's interaction with Esmé. The first time she requests a story Esmé asks for it to be "about squalor" (100). The second time she tells him not to "forget to write that story for me," but adds, "It doesn't have to be exclusively for me" (103). Esmé tells the narrator to "Make it extremely squalid and moving," and then questions him, "Are you at all acquainted with squalor?" (103). The narrator's answer, "I was getting better acquainted with it" (103), foreshadows how the story he eventually writes for her will meet her at the corner in that-in response to her wedding invitation-he writes it with both *love* and *squalor*.

The narrator's "acquaintance with squalor" comes over a year later, "several weeks after V-E Day" (103), and he tells the reader that in "the squalid, or moving, part of the story" he has "disguised [himself] so cunningly that even the cleverest reader will fail to recognize [him]" (103). Since the narrator is clearly identified as Staff Sergeant X in the squalid part of the story, it would appear that in the time since he has left Esmé he has been changed so dramatically that he is not the same person. In fact, it seems that the narrator of the previous section has died and is now represented by Sergeant X. The narrator writes, "he was a young man who had not come through the war with all his faculties intact" (104). The squalor of his physical condition is represented by his inability to read, his 'chain-smoking for weeks,' his bleeding gums "at the slightest pressure," and thinking "he felt his mind dislodge itself and teeter" (104). Sergeant X's mental condition, furthermore, is associated with hell, as he opens up *Die Zeit Ohne Beispiel* (by the minister of Nazi propaganda Joseph Goebbels) "for the third time since he had returned from the hospital that day" and reads the inscription of the Nazi official, "Dear God, life is hell" (105). Tempted to *meet her at the corner* the third time he reads her inscription, Salinger writes,

> X stared at the page for several minutes, trying, against heavy odds, not to be taken in. Then, with far more zeal than he had done anything in weeks, he picked up a pencil stub and wrote down under the inscription in English, "Fathers and teachers, I ponder 'What is hell?' I maintain that it is the suffering of being unable to love." (105)

The Nazi official, an "unmarried daughter," epitomizes the condition of squalor. Her prayer signifies the natural conclusion of the secular world-represented here by the Nazi party-which Salinger illustrates by writing that "nothing led up to or away from it" (105). Sergeant X's response, taken from Fyodor Dostoyevsky's *The Brothers Karamazov*, offers a rebuttal to what appears "to have the stature of an uncontestable, even classic indictment" (105). But when he looks at what he writes, he sees "with a fright that ran though his whole body-that what he had written was almost entirely illegible" (105). Thus, the inability to write encompasses Sergeant X's squalor, a point Salinger reinforces when he cannot even type a letter as a form of "therapy" (112).

At the conclusion of the story, nearly overcome by the squalor of his condition, he opens Esmé's package and reads her "note." Esmé's note, of course, brings to mind "the extremely pleasant afternoon we spent in each other's company on April 30, 1944 between 3:45 and 4:15, in case it slipped your mind" (113). Esmé's attention to the precise time of their meeting recalls her father's watch, which she has enclosed to Sergeant X and tells him he can keep in his "possession for the duration of the conflict" (113). By sending Sergeant X the watch, Esmé symbolically shares her own squalor with him. But the gesture allows her to transcend the squalor of death by reaching out to Sergeant X, and in turn her father, from the *other side*. As he holds the watch that has, like himself, "been broken in transit" (114), the narrator addresses Esmé directly: "You take a really sleepy man, Esmé, and he always stands a chance of again becoming a man with all his fac-with all of his f-a-c-u-l-t-i-e-s intact" (114). His hyphenation of faculties is meant to correspond with Esmé's spelling out, for Charles benefit, that her father was "s-l-a-i-n" in the war. The last statement, addressed *to* or *for* Esmé, reveals the narrator has regained the ability to write again and, therefore, has overcome the squalor, or hell, of being "unable to love" (105). At last, the narrator meets Esmé at the corner between love and squalor by offering his own "notes" back to her as both her story and a wedding gift. The narrator's story exemplifies how it is only through squalor, as it is represented in its various forms in the story-including, lest we forget, the squalor of marriage-that true love is displayed. "You love God, don't you?" Nicholson proposes to Teddy later in *Nine Stories*. Teddy responds, "Yes, sure, I love Him. But I don't love Him sentimentally. He never said anybody had to love Him sentimentally" (187). Teddy continues, "If I were God, I certainly wouldn't want people to love me sentimentally. It's too unreliable" (187).

Tying "For Esmé" into the Cycle

In "For Esmé," Salinger refigures the koan riddle-"what is the sound of one hand clapping?"-in the riddle Charles proposes to the narrator, "What did one wall say to the other wall" (98). The answer, "Meet you at the corner!" (99), is a comic answer, a punch line to the koan. But it also coincides with the sense of balance that Salinger seems to be pursuing throughout *Nine Stories*. In "For Esmé," "one hand clapping" is portrayed through the "meeting at the corner" of a number of juxtaposed characters and themes. Central to this juxtaposition is, of course, the meeting between love and squalor, which is a conduit to understanding other themes that are central to the collection including the relationships between child and adult, husband and wife, war and peace, and life and death. The conjugation of the Old (East) and New (West) Worlds represents another way that Salinger illustrates a 'meeting at the corner' within "For Esmé." In accordance with this sense of juxtaposition, Salinger represents the Old World through a child (Esmé) and the New World through an adult (the narrator). We should also consider the implications Salinger makes between the two worlds as a crossing over from life to death-as the narrator states early on in the story when he crosses over to the "Other

Side" and slips his gas mask "through a porthole of the *Mauretania*" (88).

Increasingly in *Nine Stories*, Salinger represents the meridian between life and death through bodies of water. In "Down at the Dinghy," for example, Boo Boo Tannenbaum tells Lionel that they will all take a "ride in the boat" (86) at the conclusion of the story. We might connect the image of the family in the dinghy with Boo Boo's playing her "peculiar amalgamation of 'Taps' and 'Reveille'-three times" (82) and then saluting the "opposite shoreline" on the east side of the lake. Thus, Salinger moves them into the symbolic space, crossing the water, where there is a "peculiar amalgamation" of life and death or the material and spiritual worlds. Similarly, the narrator has to cross over to the "Other Side" in "For Esmé," and he has to die before he can truly live. From a material point of view, the narrator teaches Esmé about the "Other Side," America (the New World/the West), but from a spiritual point of view, Esmé teaches the narrator about the "Other Side," the United Kingdom (the Old World/the East). Therefore, when the material and spiritual come together, Salinger represents true love as a product of experiencing and understanding squalor.

Once this connection is made, it provides a means of interpreting Salinger's portrayal of squalor in *Nine Stories*. In "For Esmé," perhaps the most profound example of squalor comes through the inscription of the Nazi official within the flyleaf of Goebbels book of propaganda, "Dear

God, life is hell" (105). Salinger draws our attention to the specific details of the Nazi official's life: she is thirty-eight, unmarried, and still living with her family at home. The details of her life are an inversion of Esmé's, and everything that she has learned as a Nazi has led her to a condition of squalor. In contrast with the Nazi official, Esmé reflects her sense of upbringing by enduring the squalor. She even embraces it to some degree-as she tells the narrator, "I prefer stories about squalor" (100). The home of the Nazi official also recalls Boo Boo's question to Lionel in "Down at the Dinghy," "Do you know what a kike is, baby?" The Nazi official, who has learned what a "kike is" from, most notably, Goebbels, has come to the natural conclusion of this worldview: "life is hell."

This is what makes Boo Boo's response so compelling; she could just as easily be posing the question to Sandra and, in the end, herself. Lionel's response defies the definition of what a kike is because it is as absurd as Hitler and Goebbel's definition of Jews, homosexuals and gypsies. Boo Boo's question could be substituted with any number of words that would elicit just as many absurd responses: "do you know what a Nazi, a Christian, a redneck, a spick, or a honky is?" Accordingly, if Boo Boo chooses to label Sandra or even explain what a "kike is," in effect, she only continues the same cycle of squalor that Goebbels perpetrated (which she seems to indicate by biting "the rim" of Lionel's ear; 86). The far more distressing and convicting statement Salinger appears to make throughout *Nine Stories* is that the human condition has an evil within it that is prone to complicity with Goebbels and that this complicity comes through the same feeling of moral superiority the Nazi's claimed to have.

Salinger uses the hateful squalor of Nazi propaganda as a means to transcend it with love. The statement, "Dear God, life is hell," is one made apart from both God and love. Salinger's response seemingly teaches us that if one knows God the hell of life can be redeemed by love, which comes in the form of the quote X uses to counter the Nazi official's inscription: "Fathers and Teachers, I ponder 'What is hell?' I maintain that it is the suffering of being unable to love." Salinger takes the quote from a section of Fyodor Dostoyevsky's *The Brothers Karamazov* entitled "The Life of the Elder Zosima." Dostoyevsky writes "The Life of Elder Zosima" in nine sections that could be said to serve as a subtext to *Nine Stories*.

Among the sections are ones entitled, "A Reminiscence of the Youth and Early Manhood of the Elder Zosima While Yet in the Secular World. A Duel," and "Something Concerning Masters and Servants and Whether it is Possible for Masters and Servants to become in Spirit Mutually Brothers." Another section poses as its title the question, "Is it Possible to be a Judge of One's Fellow Men? Of Faith Unto the End." The first line of this section reads: "Bear in mind particularly that you can be no man's judge" (369). This last statement provides one of the clues to understanding the division between the material and spiritual in *Nine Stories*. Those characters who are on the road to enlightenment in the cycle are able to, or are given the lesson that will allow them to, love beyond the material world and see beyond judgment.

We should also note that when Dostoyevsky writes through Father Zosima that hell is "The suffering of no longer being able to love," he defines love through Christ: "Once, in infinite existence, immeasurable either by time or by space, a certain spiritual being was given, upon visiting the earth, the ability to say to itself: 'I am, and I love'" (371). Dostoyevsky illustrates God's love through Christ, whose love was defined by his gift-his death for mankind. In other words, Christ's love is tied directly to his suffering on the cross and that suffering is enveloped in his descent into hell after his death (Rev. 1.18). With this in mind, Dostoyevsky's epigraph to *The Brothers Karamazov*, taken from the Gospel of John, offers context to the squalor in "For Esmé": "Verily, verily, I say unto you, Except a corn of wheat fall into the ground and die, it abideth alone: but if it die, it bringeth forth much fruit" (12.24).

The fruit Esmé brings forth through the death of her parents restores the narrator/Sergeant X's ability to write. In turn, the narrator's experience with the squalor of death also brings forth the fruit of the epithalamium he writes for Esmé's wedding. In doing so, he seems to be asking the groom to "not just mouth" his marriage vows to Esmé but to "absorb the meaning of them" (89). Assuming that Esmé and her husband will be married in the church, as British nobility are, Salinger also might be alluding to the "uneasy moment or two" that the groom could have when the minister tells him that he is commanded to love Esmé "even as Christ also loved the church, and gave himself for it" (Eph. 5.25). And if he does absorb the meaning of these words, so much the better. He will be edified and instructed in the true meaning of *agape* in the midst of life's squalor, which may prevent his marriage from flatting.

Bibliography:

Bible. King James Version.

Dostoyevsky, Fyodor. *The Brothers Karamazov*. New York: Penguin, 1993.

Salinger, J. D. *Nine Stories*. Boston: Little Brown, 1991.

Discussion Questions and Possible Essay Topics:

1. Examine the narrator's introductory remarks to the story in light of how the story unfolds and ends.

2. What is the significance of the act of writing in the story? What are the various ways that Salinger portrays writing throughout the course of the story?

3. Discuss Esmé's statements about squalor and why the narrator writes her a story about love and squalor.

4. Explore the significance of Charles' riddle to the narrator. Why might the riddle be repeated three times in the story?

5. Compare and contrast how America and Europe are portrayed in the story.

6. Explore the significance of why Esmé sends her father's watch to Sergeant X. Is the "conflict" (113) over for the narrator/Sergeant X at the conclusion of the story?

7. Explore Salinger's allusion to Fyodor Dostoyevsky's *The Brothers Karamazov* and the nine sections from the discourses of the Elder Zosima as they might be applied to both "For Esmé" and throughout *Nine Stories*.

8. Discuss the juxtaposition of Esmé and the low official in the Nazi party and how they both impact the narrator/X's life.

Pretty Mouth and Green My Eyes

Overview

"Pretty Mouth and Green My Eyes" opens with a ringing phone and "the gray-haired man," Lee, asking Joanie, the woman he is in bed with, if she minds if he answers it. As the reader eventually discovers, the call is from Joanie's husband Arthur, and he is trying to figure out where she is. Joanie asks him, "God, I don't know. I mean what do you think?" But Lee does not think it makes "a helluva lot of difference one way or the other" (115). When Lee answers the phone, Arthur worries that he is waking Lee up and asks if he saw Joanie leave the party that they attended earlier in the evening. Lee lies and tells Arthur that he "didn't see a bloody thing all evening" (117). Both men speculate that Joanie could be with the Ellenboagens, who are from Connecticut, and Arthur states that he has had enough of his five-year marriage to Joanie. He tells Lee that Joanie "went to work on some bastard in the kitchen" and confides she has had a number of affairs, some of which he suspects she's had in their own home.

Arthur mocks Joanie as an "undeveloped, undiscovered actress, novelist, psychoanalyst, and all-around goddam unappreciated celebrity-genius in New York" (120). Though Lee attempts to defend Joanie, Arthur retorts she "hasn't got any goddam brains! She's an animal!" (120). "We're all animals," Lee responds, "Basically, we're all animals" (120). A little later, Lee changes the conversation and asks Arthur how his court case went. Arthur explains that he was about to begin his "summation" when "this crazy chambermaid with a bunch of bedsheets as evidence" (121) came in and he lost the case. Arthur then tells Lee that he "may go back in the Army" (122). Arthur's declaration causes Lee to give a "forbearing" look to Joanie, but she misses it because she has spilled an ashtray. Arthur continues to lament the fact that he did not leave Joanie and says he could not do it because he "felt sorry for her" (123). "That's out of my jurisdiction," Lee counters (123). Arthur says that Joanie is a "grown child," that he is too "weak for her" and tells Lee he is a "smart bastard" for never getting married (123-24). "She doesn't even love me," Arthur laments as he gets nostalgic about his courtship with Joanie, even going so far as to quote from a poem he once wrote for her: "Rose my color is and white, Pretty mouth and green my eyes" (125). He says the poem used to remind him of her even though she does not have green eyes.

Lee attempts to calm Arthur down and assures him that Joanie will "probably be there in about two minutes" (126). At last, Arthur asks Lee if he can come over and Lee tells him yes, but also that he thinks Arthur should just wait for Joanie. When he hangs the phone up, Joanie asks "God! What'd you say?" and Lee questions her, "You could hear me. Couldn't you?" She then tells him he was "wonderful" and that she feels "like a dog" (127). Just before Arthur calls back, Joanie tells Lee he is "on fire" (127), but it turns out to be "just an ash" (128). To Lee's bewilderment, Arthur reports that Joanie has returned home, and they are going to work things out. He considers the idea of moving out to Connecticut and resolves to go into work the next day to try and set things right with their boss, Junior, about the case he lost. Lee eventually excuses himself from the conversation because he has "a helluva headache all of a sudden" and hangs up the phone. He reaches for Joanie's cigarette out of the ashtray but drops it in his lap. When Joanie attempts to "help him retrieve it before anything was burned," he tells her to "sit still, for Chrissake," and the story concludes with Joanie pulling her hand back (129).

Analysis

As with other phone calls in *Nine Stories*, the two phone calls that take place in "Pretty Mouth" are accompanied by a sense of doom. Salinger describes Arthur's voice as "stone dead," yet "almost obscenely quickened for the occasion" (116). Here Salinger sets the tone of the story through an allusion to judgment day in 1 Peter 4.5: "Who shall give account to him that is ready to judge the quick and the dead." The question might be said to echo throughout the story as the two lawyers plead their cases before an unseen Judge. Along these lines, "Pretty Mouth" is a story in which Salinger invites the reader to actively engage with the story. As we read, we are allowed to become a Judge over the cases Lee and Arthur present for Joanie, and ultimately themselves. Yet by the story's conclusion, Salinger brings any sense of judgment full circle on the reader through the existential meditations he raises about morality. The question Salinger proposes is one of Pascalian absolutes. If there is no Judge (God) and people are only animals, what moral ground can we judge Lee upon? But by the conclusion of the story, Salinger reverses the question and considers what the consequence will be if there were a God to "judge the quick and the dead."

At the outset of the story, Lee appears to be in control of the situation, answering the phone call from Arthur casually and telling Joanie he does "not see that it made a helluva lot of difference one way or the other" (115). By the end of the story, Lee's tone changes completely, and he has a "helluva headache all of a sudden" (129). The shift compliments the parallel actions of the bedroom and courtroom Salinger establishes in the story. At one point, Lee changes the subject and asks Arthur how his case went earlier in the day. Arthur's "summation" essentially foreshadows Lee's conviction at the conclusion of the story: "before I'm all set to start my summation, the attorney for the plaintiff, Lissberg, trots in this crazy chambermaid with a bunch of bedsheets as evidence-bedbug stains all over them. Christ!" (121). Arthur tells Lee that he loses the case because of the "lousy bedbug mess" (129), which juxtaposes the action in the bedroom and on the telephone.

While Lee initially has the upper hand and seems to be entering a not-guilty plea, by the conclusion of the story he appears on the verge of confessing his guilt, "for Chrissake" (129). Kenneth Hamilton points out in his essay, "Hell in New York: J. D. Salinger's 'Pretty Mouth and Green My Eyes,'" Lee's swearing "is simply a low form of prayer. One cannot pray genuinely in hell, but one knows to whom prayer should be made. And as it is part of the misery of hell that one cannot pray, another part of the misery is the knowledge that others have access to divine love and forgiveness" (398). The same might be said of Arthur, who tells Lee that "for Chrissake" he would be a "goddam fool" if he did not try to straighten things out with Junior. According to Hamilton, Arthur concludes "his message about his new-found hope by saying that he was going to see Junior himself. This lets us see the extent of Arthur's hope and of Lee's despair. For Christ the Son of God is, in contemporary speech, quite accurately described by the name *Junior*" (399).

Salinger also draws attention to the moral overtones of the story through the exchange between Arthur and Lee after Arthur calls Joanie "an animal" (120). Lee defends Joanie, "Basically, we're all animals" (120), but Arthur rejects this notion, "Like hell we are. I'm no goddam animal. I may be a fouled-up twentieth-century son of a bitch, but I'm no animal" (120). Lee uses his view of himself and Joanie as "animals" to justify their actions. When he says that it does not make "a helluva lot of difference" if he talks to Arthur on the phone or not, he inherently denies the existence of any judge of his actions. As John Wenke observes, "Once [Lee] reduces the ontological status of the human, he surrenders moral imperatives" (54). Notably though, Salinger implies Arthur's call will sound an alarm for Lee to *wake up* throughout the story.

Another way Salinger might allude to the need for Lee to wake up is through his gray hair. Salinger constantly refers to Lee as the "gray-haired man" whose hair looks "a trifle 'distinguished-looking'" though "in disarrangement" (116). In spite of his gray hair, Lee offers no wise advice to Arthur, and he has to resort to lying and deceiving him so that he does not know he is sleeping with Joanie. This fundamentally tests Lee's moral sensibilities because if he truly believes his statement about being an animal and that it does not make a "helluva lot of difference" if he talks to Arthur or not, he will tell him that Joan is in his bed. Moreover, through Lee's gray hair, Salinger might ironically allude to the verse in the book of Proverbs that states, "The hoary head is a crown of glory, if it be found in the way of righteousness" (16.31). Salinger pays close attention to this detail when he observes the way Lee's hair, when in the light, "was particularly, if rather vividly, flattering to his gray, mostly white hair" (115-16). **(E1)**

Tying "Pretty Mouth" into the Cycle

In "Pretty Mouth" Salinger inverts the conditions of love and squalor. While in "For Esmé" the condition of squalor comes through tragedy that in turn leads to love, in "Pretty Mouth," the condition of squalor comes through the characters' inability to understand love. In other words, in "Pretty Mouth" there are no examples of authentic love; there is only squalor. The narrator's advice to the groom in "For Esmé" concludes with an admonition: "Nobody's aiming to please, here. More, really, to edify, to instruct" (87). These words echo in "Pretty Mouth" through Arthur's description of how he loves Joanie. As he attempts to define his "love" for Joanie, Arthur is noncommittal and unsure of himself. He tells Lee, "I don't love her any more, either. I don't know. I do and I don't. It varies. It fluctuates. Christ!" (125). Arthur admits to Lee that his love for Joanie is based upon an illusion symbolized by a poem he once wrote for her: "Rose my color is and white, Pretty mouth and green my eyes" (125).

Arthur also sentimentalizes the poem and says it "used to remind me of her" even though "She doesn't have green eyes-she has eyes like goddam sea shells for Chrissake-but it reminded me anyway" (125). The poem that reminds Arthur of his "love" for Joan contrasts with the story the narrator writes for Esmé. While Arthur bases his "love" for Joan upon a romantic illusion of who she is, the narrator of "For Esmé" illustrates how Esmé helped him to escape hell through an authentic expression of love. In comparison with the love and squalor Salinger associates with Esmé's "house-counting eyes," Arthur fictionalizes the color of Joan's eyes and the home he wants to create with her. "Anyway, so she's home," he lies to Lee at the conclusion of the story, "What I think maybe we'll do, if everything goes along all right, we'll get ourselves a little place in Connecticut maybe . . . . I mean she's crazy about plants and all that stuff" (128). Here Salinger reinforces the theme of home and the need for edification and instruction in marriage. Arthur's idealized vision of life with Joan in Connecticut, for instance, is countered by Eloise's *ennui* in "Uncle Wiggily." Like Eloise, Arthur romanticizes his past and it prevents him from seeing the present clearly.

The absence of children in the story (the only story in the collection without the presence of children) suggests another important aspect of "Pretty Mouth." Salinger constantly associates Arthur and Joanie with children. Lee calls Arthur a "boy" (126), tells him he talks like "an absolute child" (123), and they both refer to Joanie as a "kid" (129), while Arthur calls her a "grown child" (123). The behavior of the adults like children in "Pretty Mouth" undercuts the idealization of children in *Nine Stories*, and indeed the whole of Salinger's work. The balance Salinger explores between child and adult throughout *Nine Stories* seems completely lost in "Pretty Mouth," which results in a world defined by squalor.

The irony comes in the story being set within a time of peace, yet the characters are all defined by the inability to love authentically. In this way, the story recalls Franklin's absurd war, the war with the Eskimos. In fact, Arthur tells Lee he "may go back in the Army" (122), seemingly preferring the squalor of the Army to life with Joanie. In contrast to "For Esmé," Salinger portrays the internal wars of the characters in "Pretty Mouth" with the same squalor as those who experience war. Perhaps more dramatically, the characters in "Pretty Mouth" appear to lack sincere empathy and do not *meet at the corner*, a detail that Salinger might be drawing our attention to when Lee looks "where the wall met the ceiling" (116). The superior positioning of the ceiling to the wall effectively illustrates the superior positioning of the characters in "Pretty Mouth." Rather than *meeting* one another, the characters all seem to be in the inferior or superior position to one another, and it prevents genuine connection.

The superior position of the ceiling to the wall (which also might be viewed as the merging between the horizontal and vertical) also can be connected with the sound of one hand clapping in the story, as Lee becomes aware of a superior judge over his actions. "We're all animals," Lee tells Arthur early on in the story, "Basically, we're all animals" (120). But Lee's justification for his actions comes from a belief that his actions are instinctive like those of an animal. **(E2)** Joanie tells Lee, "God, I feel like a dog!" (127). Salinger underlines Joan's feigned contrition by inverting God with "dog," as if to imply that Joanie feels like a god-an echo of Lee's belief that "we're all animals" (120).

From both Lee and Joan's point of view, it would seem, that because they are "animals" they are the dogs/gods of their actions. For instance, feeling like a dog, Joanie tries to play God by saving him from hell. "I think you're on fire," she tells Lee before concluding, "No, it was just an ash" (127-28). Joanie then repeats, "God, I feel like an absolute dog" (128). Joanie's hand trying to brush the fire/ash off of Lee corresponds with her spilling the ashtray and "rapidly, with her fingers, brushing the spilled ashes into a little pick-up pile" (122). Here Salinger appears to connect Joan's hand with death through the ashes; furthermore, as she sweeps up the ashes, Salinger writes, "her eyes looked up at him a second too late" (123). Salinger suggests that Joan's eyes "missed seeing" (122) how her actions affect those around her.

Throughout the story, her eyes, along with the ashtray, are the best representations of seeing through the glass. For example, the first representation of her eyes comes while the phone is ringing for the first time at the beginning of the story and she turns toward Lee "one eye-on the side of the light-closed tight, her open eye very, however disingenuously, large, and so blue as to appear almost violet" (115). Shortly after this, her first words are revelatory: "God, I don't know" (115). The "violet" color of her eye seemingly foreshadow the burning Lee feels at the conclusion of the story when he finally appears to feel guilt over having her in his bed.

The story's climax occurs after Arthur calls the second time and lies to Lee, telling him Joan came home. Lee is thrown by what appears to be Arthur's closing argument. Salinger indicates Lee's sense of conviction through the ringing phone and Lee's secular prayer, "Christ!" (128). As he talks to Arthur, Lee becomes blinded by "a helluva headache," and for the first time he is not looking at the world through his own eyes (129). "His eyes, behind the bridge of his hand, were closed" (129), Salinger writes. Lee's conviction culminates when he picks "a burning cigarette-the girl's-out of the ashtray and started to bring it to his mouth, but it slipped out of his fingers" (129).

Salinger suggests that when Lee smokes Joan's cigarette, he is complicit in partaking of the deceit that comes from her "pretty mouth" (129). When he drops the cigarette, he is "on *fire*" (127); though, when Joan tries to "retrieve it before anything was burned," he tells her to "sit still, for Chrissake" (129). Lee apparently recognizes Joan cannot save him from burning and rebukes her like a child. In the last line of the story, Salinger writes that Joan "pulled back her hand" (129). As Joan pulls her hand back, it's as if Lee feels the proverbial hand of God convicting him when the cigarette from the ashtray burns the "bedbug mess" (129).

So many passages in *Nine Stories* are concerned with proper and improper instruction, and Lee's instruction to Joan to "sit still" here is noteworthy because, all at once, his actions do "make a helluva lot of difference one way or the other" (115). His instruction to Joan-though rather meaningless here-should recall the narrator's in "For Esmé," who does not aim to "please" but to "edify, to instruct" (87). "Pretty Mouth" offers a different kind of instruction to its readers-a warning against illusions of love based on the color of a lover's eyes or the prettiness of their mouth. Here and elsewhere, *Nine Stories* itself teaches the reader by taking a look at the material and moral squalor of life in search of the presence of authentic love. The reader may have to experience Lee's burning dilemma in order to see and value the redemptive love among the ruins-the love which Salinger implies is available to all those who will "sit still, for Chrissake" and pull back their hands (129).

Endnotes:

E1: Flaubert's *Madame Bovary* is another significant allusion Salinger makes in the story. Salinger seems to parallel the adulterous relationship between Lee and Joanie with Madam Bovary and the young law student

Léon. The allusion to *Madame Bovary* is significant not only because of Salinger's attention to Flaubert's principle of *le mot juste* (*the right word*) throughout *Nine Stories*, but because of its satire upon bourgeoisie culture, which seems to approximate the post-war affluence and decadence in New York.

E2: On the heels of "For Esmé" and X's encounter with Nazi Germany and, presumably, concentration camps, Lee's statement resonates with the propaganda of Goebbels, who compared Jews to animals and justified their extermination based upon this belief. Salinger might also be making a subtle allusion to the Nuremberg Trials in the story when Arthur states, "Lissberg, trots in this crazy chambermaid with a bunch of bedsheets as evidence" (121). Lissberg is a Bavarian community located outside of Nuremberg where Salinger's division helped to liberate Jews from concentration camps.

Bibliography:

Bible. King James Version.

Hamilton, Kenneth. "Hell in New York: J. D. Salinger's 'Pretty Mouth and Green My Eyes.'" *Dalhousie Review* 47 (1967): 394-399.

Salinger, J. D. *Nine Stories*. Boston: Little, Brown. 1991.

Slawenski, Kenneth. *J. D. Salinger: A Life*. New York: Random House, 2011.

Wenke, John. *J. D. Salinger: A Study of the Short Fiction*. Ed. Gordon Weaver. 26 vols. Boston: Twayne, 1991.

Suggested Reading:

Hagopian, John. "'Pretty Mouth and Green My Eyes': Salinger's Paolo and Francesca in New York." *Modern Fiction Studies* 12.3 (1966): 349-354.

Discussion Questions and Possible Essay Topics:<

1. Discuss how the characters and events in the story parallel a courtroom trial. (Try appointing a judge and divide the classroom into two parts that will attempt to make the case for either Arthur or Lee).

2. Explore Salinger's use of cigarettes throughout the story. What do they tell us about the characters?

3. Why does Salinger refer to Lee as the "gray-haired man"?

4. Discuss the significance of the poem Arthur sends to Joanie when they are dating.

5. Explore Salinger's attention to eye imagery and vision throughout the story.

6. What is the significance of the fact that most of the story takes place on the phone?

7. Discuss the implications of Arthur and Lee's differing points of view on whether or not Joanie is "a grown child" (123) and that "We're all animals" (120).

8. Explore Salinger's allusion to *Madame Bovary*.

De Daumier-Smith's Blue Period

Overview

"De Daumier-Smith's Blue Period" begins with the narrator dedicating the story to his "late ribald stepfather" (130). He explains that his stepfather, Robert Agadganian, Jr. (Bobby), married his mother in 1928 after his parents had divorced and that they moved from New York to Paris, France, after the 1929 stock market crash. The narrator returns to New York with his stepfather nine years later following the death of his mother. Grieving his mother, the narrator despises being back in America and living in New York. To escape his grief and his loneliness, he immerses himself in his art and paints-in a fit of adolescent solipsism-seventeen self-portraits.

Attempting to escape his life with his stepfather in New York, the narrator applies for a job teaching art in Montreal under the pseudonym Jean de Daumier-Smith.

He lies about being a relative of the artist Honoré Daumier and about knowing Pablo Picasso. He lies about a number of other details as well, and even tells the curators of the school, M. and Mme. Yoshoto, that his wife died of stomach cancer. When he gets the job, the narrator tells Bobby and Mrs. X, an attractive younger woman Bobby is dating. While Bobby partially objects and wants to know more about the job, Mrs. X encourages the narrator to go and that the opportunity "sounds *very* exciting" (138). The narrator imagines Mrs. X is flirting with him and fantasizes that her "eyes sparkle with depravity" as she waits for him to slip his "Montreal address" to her "under the table" (138).

When M. Yoshoto picks up "Jean" from the train station, Yoshoto says nothing to him, and Jean states that his expression "was inscrutable" (138). Jean feels the need to validate his lies to M. Yoshoto on the way back from the station, but M. Yoshoto continues to say nothing. When they arrive at the school, Les Amis Des Vieux Maitres (The School of The Friends of Old Masters), Jean describes Mme. Yoshoto as "every bit as inscrutable as M. Yoshoto, if not more so" (140). The couple show Jean to their son's recently vacated room and apologize that there are no chairs to sit in. That night, Jean hears one of the Yoshoto's moaning "in his or her sleep" (141). The sound, he says, seems to come from "either a tragic, subnormal infant or a small malformed animal" (141). He sleeps for less than two hours before M. Yoshoto wakes him up for work.

Hardly able to swallow Mme. Yoshoto's cooking, Jean eats his breakfast with the Yoshotos in silence. After breakfast Jean spends a depressing morning translating "corrections from French into English" (143), excuses himself at lunchtime, and finds a lunch bar where he bolts "four 'Coney Island Red-Hots' and three muddy cups of coffee" (144). When he gets back to Les Amis, M. Yoshoto gives him three envelopes and asks him to "correct a few lessons" (145). Correcting the work of the first two artists-Bambi Kramer and R. Howard Ridgefield-leaves Jean in a state of despair, contemplating some form of protest to M. Yoshoto. However, the portfolio of the third artist, Sister Irma, redeems the faults of the previous two. Jean describes at length the answers Sister Irma gives on her questionnaire and one of her paintings, "a highly detailed depiction of Christ's being carried to the sepulcher in Joseph of Arimathea's garden" (149).

Elated over the contents of Sister Irma's envelope, Jean hides it in his shirt so that he can work on his response to her in his room. That night he writes a long letter to Sister Irma and works on her painting. He mails the package to her in the middle of the night and comes back to the sound of moaning from the Yoshoto's room. He imagines himself comforting Mme. Yoshoto and sharing the joy Sister Irma has given him with the Yoshotos. His joy begins to "seep through" the following day when M. Yoshoto brings him two more envelopes with the work of artists less talented than Bambi Kramer and R. Howard Ridgefield, and he wonders how he will make it to "the Monday when Sister Irma's next envelope was due" (156). Over the next few days Jean works on the other artists' envelopes, goes to the movies, and attempts sketching Sister Irma's painting from memory. Shortly after this, Jean gets word that Sister Irma will no longer be studying at the school.

Distraught by the news, Jean expels his other four students from the school, skips dinner and writes a letter to Sister Irma asking her why she quit, offers his services "gratis" (161), and says he would like to come visit her. He then dresses up in a dinner suit and plans to go an expensive restaurant, taking the letter with him for the "tragic occasion" (161). Unable to find his way to the restaurant, Jean eats more "Coney Island Red-Hots" and makes his way back to the school. But on his way back he looks into the window of "the orthopedic appliances shop" below the school, sees a girl dressing up a wooden dummy and has what he terms a "transcendent" experience (163). The experience causes him to go back to his room and give "Sister Irma her freedom," in addition to reinstating his four expelled students (164). The story concludes shortly after this with the school being closed down and the narrator joining Bobby in Rhode Island.

Analysis

The narrator's dedication of the story to his late "ribald stepfather" Bobby foreshadows his transformation over the course of the story. The dedication also illustrates how the narrator/Jean comes to deal with the passing of his stepfather since he dedicates the story to him after his death. As the title indicates via its allusion to Picasso's Blue Period **(E1)**, the story explores death on a number of levels. Indeed, all of the narrator's actions in the story should be viewed in light of the grief he experiences over the death of his mother. The narrator's disdain for his life in New York with Bobby three months after his mother's death, for example, exemplifies the way that her death affects his outlook on the world.

Throughout the story, Salinger associates Jean's conflict with death with his inability to find a seat. Early in the narrative he says, "it seemed to me that all the seats from all the buses in New York had been unscrewed and taken out and set up in the street, where a monstrous game of Musical Chairs was in full swing" (132). "I think I might have been willing to join the game," Jean continues, "if I had been granted a special dispensation from the Church of Manhattan guaranteeing that all the other players would remain respectfully standing till I was seated" (132). When Jean realizes that no one sympathizes with his pain, he takes a "more direct approach" and prays "for the city to be cleared of people, for the gift of being alone-a-l-o-n-e: which is the one New York prayer that rarely gets lost or delayed in channels, and in no time at all everything I touched turned to solid loneliness" (132).

Jean's alienation from those around him comes first from his anger and his solipsism, which leads to his prayer to be alone. Jean's relating his dilemma to the Church of Manhattan and making his New York prayer foreshadows his vision later in the story that he "would always at best be a visitor in a garden of enamel urinals and bedpans, with a sightless, wooden dummy-deity" (157) answering his solipsistic prayers. As a representation of modern man, he desires that others serve him, and when they do not he rejects them. Jean's pilgrimage throughout the story will require him to see beyond his narrow view of the world as he seeks to overcome his grief. Perhaps as a way of informing this journey, Jean notes on his "voyage to America" his "uncanny physical resemblance to El Greco" (132). El Greco's ability to reinterpret traditional religious subject matter in his art coincides not just with Jean's pilgrimage in "Blue Period" but Salinger's approach to religion in *Nine Stories* as a whole.

As he does in much of *Nine Stories*, Salinger pivots "Blue Period" on a pilgrim's progress from the secular to the sacred. This pattern corresponds as much with the artists that Salinger alludes to as it does with Jean's journey. For instance, other than El Greco, Salinger alludes to Honoré Daumier, Picasso, Walt Disney, Rembrandt, Titian, Sargent and Antonello da Messina. The cumulative effect of these many allusions to artists is to bring Jean's confrontation with himself as an artist beyond mere paint on a canvas. Seeing himself as El Greco allows Jean to romanticize his personal appearance. But Jean also represents himself through cartoon caricatures associated to his namesake, Honoré Daumier. Yet when his students Bambi Kramer and R. Howard Ridgefield use caricature and satire in their work, he rejects it without irony.

In doing so, Jean unconsciously rejects himself. While contemplating his protest he thinks he might tell M. Yoshoto, "My mother's dead, and I have to live with her charming husband, and nobody in New York speaks French, *and there aren't any chairs in your son's room*" (147). Jean's elements of protest to Kramer and Ridgefield are reflective of the way his grief has led to his complaint with the world. Furthermore, after Jean makes his internal confession, he states that he is "long self-trained in taking despair sitting down," and rather than protest to M. Yoshoto about the quality of the artists, he "managed very easily to keep [his] seat" (147). Salinger draws our attention to the scene through the detail of Jean's keeping his seat because even though he has found a seat by leaving New York, he is confronted with caricatures of himself, which leaves him in a state of despair.

Jean's despair, however, leads to joy when he opens Sister Irma's envelope. In contrast to Jean and the other artists, Sister Irma writes and paints without ego. She includes a "snapshot of her convent" (148) instead of a personal photo and does not sign her paintings-a detail that contrasts with Bambi Kramer's and Ridgefield's signing or initialing their work. Sister Irma's painting of Christ's burial manages to be just as self-effacing in its subject matter. Jean offers a detailed description of the painting, paying particular attention to a woman he identifies as Mary Magdalene, who "wore no part of her grief" (149) and also "a woman in the left foreground, facing the viewer . . . .frantically signaling to someone-her child, perhaps, or possibly the viewer-to drop everything and hurry over" (149).

Jean seems to identify with the "woman" and with Mary Magdalene because they reflect his internal strife. The woman might be said to represent both his mother and Sister Irma; the two will become mirrors of each other in the story. Jean explains early on that both he and Bobby are in love with his late mother and tells the Yoshotos that his wife, not his mother, has died. Furthermore, Jean imagines himself going to visit Sister Irma at her convent before she has "taken her final vows and was still free to go out into the world with the Peter Abelard-type man of her choice" (158). But Jean's identification with the woman he thinks is Mary Magdalene also comes through the "serious" flaw (150) in the painting, Mary's face. The flaw in Mary's face corresponds with Jean's flaw, his self-obsession. In this way, Jean's desire to correct the flaw in Sister Irma's art illustrates one of the central lessons of his pilgrimage, seeing beyond the material world. The "flaw" Jean desires to correct in Sister Irma's art reveals his own flaw—a flaw Salinger will connect with his need for grace or mercy.

Central to Jean's understanding of and identification with Mary appears to be his feeling that his lies will be revealed, M. Yoshoto will "unmask" him, and he will be "stoned from all directions" (145). Thus, when Jean identifies with Mary Magdalene, Salinger seems to allude to her unmasking when Christ told the scribes and Pharisees who wanted to stone her, "He that is without sin among you, let him first cast a stone at her" (John 8.7). **(E2)**

But when Jean first identifies Mary, he thinks he can fix her flaw without recognizing that correcting the external flaw on the canvas cannot atone for the internal flaw, something Mary Magdalene knows and Sister Irma represents by the fact that when Christ dies the woman in the painting wears "no part of her grief" (149). Another detail worth pointing out concerns Jean's stoning of others; Salinger represents his pilgrimage through his need to identify with everyone and not just those he idealizes.

In addition, unlike Mary, Jean wears every part of his grief; rather than trying to correct the external "flaw" of the painting, he must learn to accept the invitation of the woman waving to "the viewer" from the painting and "hurry over" (149). But instead of 'hurrying over,' Jean states, "I kept my seat. I didn't care to risk having Sister Irma taken from me" (150). Though his "seat" has turned from despair into joy, Jean's suggests his solipsism by thinking he can possess Sister Irma. Later, however, Salinger foreshadows his epiphany when he hears the moaning from the Yoshoto's room and imagines how he might comfort them: "I would reach down into Mme. Yoshoto's throat, take up her heart in my hand and warm it as I would a bird. Then, when all was put right, I would show Sister Irma's work to the Yoshotos, and they would share my joy" (155). But Jean does not share his "joy," and, fittingly, it begins to fade away the next morning when he has to look at the work of two artists "who had less talent for drawing than either Bambi or R. Howard Ridgefield" (156).

Salinger suggests that the object of Jean's joy diminishes since he does not internalize the meaning of the work. Jean must learn, like the "major figure" in Sister Irma's work, to call the viewer into the painting. Indeed, Sister Irma's painting makes Jean begin to consider this as he implies by alluding to both Antonello da Messina and St. Francis of Assisi in his letter to her. **(E3)** Accordingly, Jean's epiphany coincides with the death, burial and resurrection of Christ. It begins on "Wednesday evening" when he tries "to sketch from memory Sister Irma's picture of Christ's burial" (157). This reproduction of Sister Irma's work leads to his "macabre" Thursday evening, represented by a blank diary page. Jean explains that the page is blank because when he looks into the "window of the orthopedic appliances shop . . . . something altogether hideous happened": "The thought was forced upon me that no matter how coolly or sensibly or gracefully I might one day learn to live my life, I would always at best be a visitor in a garden of enamel urinals and bedpans, with a sightless, wooden dummy-deity standing by in a marked-down rupture truss" (157). Jean's vision brings him into a confrontation with the emptiness of his unthinking conception of God as a "sightless, wooden dummy-deity" and his existence apart from Him. This recognition leaves him despondent, "a total blank," lying "awake for hours, shivering" (157-58).

The culmination of Jean's symbolic death comes on Friday when he receives word that Sister Irma will no longer be his student. His first reaction is to expel his other students from the school. Later he tries to get Sister Irma to return to the school and offers his "services gratis" (161). He also tries to persuade Sister Irma to follow his own life as a visitor in the service of a "wooden dummy-deity": "The bare truth is as follows: If you do not learn a few more rudiments of the profession, you will only be a very, very interesting artist the rest of your life instead of a great one. This is terrible, in my opinion. Do you realize how grave the situation is?" (160). The tragedy of the situation, though, only applies to Jean, who confesses to Sister Irma, "The worst that being an artist could do to you would be that it would make you slightly unhappy constantly" (160).

He then adds that the unhappiness "is not a tragic situation in [his] opinion" because on the happiest day of his life he was on the way "to meet [his] mother, who was going out on the street for the first time after a long illness, and [he] was feeling ecstatically happy when suddenly, as [he] was coming in to the Avenue Victor Hugo, which is a street in Paris, [he] bumped into a chap without any nose" (160). Jean's story about his unhappiness as a representation of the physical world's squalor recalls his earlier words "that happiness is a solid and joy a liquid" (155). In other words, his happiness on "the happiest day" of his life comes because of his mother's sickness (which is yet another example of love meeting squalor at the corner.)

But Jean sees the man without a nose as a representation of being "slightly unhappy" constantly; instead, he needs to take off his own mask and see beyond the physical world.

Therefore, when Jean has his "transcendent" experience, he returns to the site of his "macabre" Thursday evening standing in front of the window to the orthopedic appliances shop. When he looks into the window he is "startled to see a live person in the shopcase" who is "changing the truss on the wooden dummy" (163). The woman on the other side of the glass seems to be representative of Sister Irma, but she could just as easily be his mother. When the girl sees him, she is startled and falls down. Jean tries to reach out to her but hits "the tips of [his] fingers on the glass" (163). He then has his "Experience":

> *Suddenly . . . . the sun came up and sped toward the bridge of my nose at the rate of ninety-three million miles a second. Blinded and very frightened-I had to put my hand on the glass to keep my balance . . . . When I got my sight back, the girl had gone from the window, leaving behind her a shimmering field of exquisite, twice-blessed enamel flowers.* (164)

In contrast with the first time he looks inside the window and sees a "wooden-dummy deity," he appears to recognize that the girl on the other side of the glass, like

Sister Irma, is trying to serve "her Lord" (148) and that he has only caused her to fall by noticing her. Even more, Jean cannot help the girl from falling anymore than he could stop his mother from dying; in fact, his attempts have caused her to fall. In this way, Jean must recognize his complicity in the girl's fall and in "losing" Sister Irma.

From a spiritual perspective, Jean must recognize *felix culpa* and how the woman in the painting invites him to come over, to fall, in order to see Christ. From this point of view, the people in Sister Irma's paintings are real live people and not simply orthopedic appliances. The "bridge" of Jean's nose connects to the man without a nose and allows him to see beyond the material world and through Mary Magdalene's eyes wearing "no part of grief" or unhappiness. This leads him directly to declaring in his brief diary entry, "I am giving Sister Irma her freedom to follow her own destiny. Everybody is a nun" (164).

By giving Sister Irma her freedom, Jean also gives his mother her freedom and is freed from his own grief. As a representation of this freedom, he reinstates the students he had earlier expelled and states that the "letters seemed to write themselves" because, "before sitting down to write, I'd brought a chair up from downstairs" (164). Since it is the first time Salinger notes Jean sitting down in the story (outside of his references to keeping his seat in the midst of both his despair and his joy), the detail of moving his seat to the upper room is noteworthy.

Here we might recall that the apostles famously gather in the upper room after Christ has been raised from the dead in the book of Acts; likewise, Salinger seems to imply that Jean has found the Mercy Seat at the conclusion of the story. His ability to see everyone as a nun-as Sister Irma, and by association his mother-reveals the sense of grace that he has found. One possible way to interpret Jean's epiphany comes through the book of Romans when St. Paul conveys the Mercy Seat as Christ's "propitiation through faith in his blood, to declare his righteousness for the remission of sins that are past" (3.25).

In addition, Salinger draws our attention to Jean's finding the Mercy Seat through his Pauline type conversion of being blinded by the light and also by the fact that he takes the name Jean, which means God is gracious. Finally, the narrator's joining Bobby in Rhode Island at the conclusion of the story and his dedication of the story to him speaks to how his relationship with the world has shifted. Over ten years after he returns from his pilgrimage to Montreal, the dedication to Bobby illustrates how his "Experience" in Canada is not a joy that he loses over time; rather, it gives him an enduring happiness: an ability to see beyond himself and to treat others with the grace of Sister Irma.

Tying "Blue Period" into the Cycle

Following the squalid love triangle in "Pretty Mouth," "Blue Period" explores a love triangle from a different point of view. Jean appears to parallel Joan in the sense that he is a boy who has little regard for those around him and is a type of "grown child" for most of the story. Also, Jean seems obsessed with identifying Mary Magdalene whose major sin, like Joan's, is adultery, and he tells his lies with "conviction" (159), like the lawyers, Lee and Arthur. "Blue Period" provides a means of interpreting all of the characters in *Nine Stories*, not just those in "Pretty Mouth." As easy as Salinger makes it to throw stones at a number of characters through a strong identification with his protagonists, Jean's epiphany provides a means of humanizing all of the characters in the collection when he proclaims "everybody is a nun." Jean's statement transcends the polarizing hierarchy of "phony" characters and actually seems closer to Holden's vision of "missing everybody" at the conclusion of *The Catcher in the Rye*.

Salinger also communicates this sense of transcendence through the way that boundaries are broken down over the course of "Blue Period." While the story begins with Jean rejecting his American roots after nine years in France, by the conclusion of the story he embraces chasing "the American Girl in Shorts" (165)-an altogether different way of seeing a "nun" but just as important in the greater ("pretty mouth and green my eyes") scheme of things. But there are further examples of how Salinger crosses boundaries in "Blue Period." For instance, Jean states that he "considered Canada as part of America" (139), and he tells M. Yoshoto he is a student of Buddhism, though he discovers the Yoshotos are Presbyterians who are from Japan. In the end, all of these boundaries are erased by Jean's epiphany, and Salinger brings us to the knowledge that Jean's pilgrimage is everyone's pilgrimage. Indeed, he appears to exhort the reader through Jean as much as the "major figure" of Sister Irma's painting, who is "frantically signaling to someone-her child, perhaps, or her husband, or possibly the viewer-to drop everything and hurry over" (149).

The erasure of boundaries also provides the first of a series of parallels between "Blue Period" and "The Laughing Man." For instance, as John Gedsudski tells his installments to the Comanches, he relates how the Laughing Man goes "back and forth across the Paris-Chinese border" (61). While the narrators of both stories remain essentially unnamed, it is unlikely that they are the same person since the narrator of "Blue Period" states that his parents were divorced "during the winter of 1928, when I was eight," and the narrator of "The Laughing Man" tells us he was nine. Still, the direct allusion to "The Laughing Man" might imply that the narrator of "Blue Period" was a member of "The Comanche Club." This would provide insight into one of the central passages of the story, when Jean bumps into the man without a nose on the Avenue Victor Hugo on "the happiest day of [his] life" (160; see "The Laughing Man" chapter).

Of this event Jean states, "I ask you to please consider that factor, in fact I beg you. It is quite pregnant with meaning" (160). One way to interpret this detail, other than the way already proposed above, is that Jean comes face to face with his boyhood hero, the Laughing Man, on his way to see his mother. As the narrator of "The Laughing Man" tells us, "Actually, I was not the only legitimate living descendant of the Laughing Man. There were twenty-five Comanches in the Club, or twenty-five legitimate living descendents of the Laughing Man" (62).

Seeing this "descendent" in the flesh might be akin to a spiritual experience for Jean, and it prefigures his "Experience" when he crosses the boundaries between the material and spiritual worlds. The idea of meeting the Laughing Man in the flesh also makes the fictional story transcend the material world so that the two become one—which follows the pattern established when Jean seems to enter Sister Irma's painting in "Blue Period." In "Blue Period," though, the nun considers herself an adopted daughter of Christ, and Jean has to come to this realization as well. Along these lines, Christ must become more than just a character in a story for him to be able to believe. Salinger seems to reinforce this connection in "The Laughing Man" through the narrator's reflection: "I happen to regard the Laughing Man as some kind of super-distinguished ancestor of mine . . . . with the ascribed virtues held under water or blood" (61).

The one hand clapping in "Blue Period" comes when Jean attempts to reach through the glass of the window and hits "the tips of his fingers on the glass" (163). In the scene Salinger posits the manner in which Jean needs to look beyond the material to see everybody as "a nun." At last, Sister Irma's art teaches Jean more than he can ever teach her. Jean recognizes Sister Irma's work is composed with a conviction that transcends the material world, even if he does not yet share this conviction. As he writes to her of St. Francis of Assisi, "He said as follows: 'Brother Fire, God made you beautiful and strong and useful; I pray you be courteous to me.' You paint slightly the way he spoke" (153). Sister Irma's painting is crafted with such conviction in fact that it burns itself into Jean until the material world becomes a reproduction of her painting. When this occurs, Jean is blinded by the convergence and has to "put his hand on the glass to keep [his] balance" (164).

When he regains his sight, Jean sees that the "girl had gone from the window, leaving behind her a shimmering field of exquisite, twice-blessed, enamel flowers" (164). The flowers provide an allusion to the *Fioretti di San Francesco d'Assisi* (*The Little Flowers of St. Francis of Assisi*), and the flowers (miracles) connect St. Francis's words to Sister Irma's painting. Salinger reinforces this connection through Jean's description of the "quite transcendent" event: "I'd like, if possible, to avoid seeming to pass it off as a case, or even a borderline case, of genuine mysticism. (To do otherwise, I feel, would be tantamount to implying or stating that the difference in spiritual *sorties* between St. Francis and the average, highstrung, Sunday leper-kisser is *only* a vertical one)" (163). The difference, as Sister Irma teaches Jean, is also horizontal. As St. Francis once explained to Brother Leo, perfect happiness consists of enduring "evils and insults with joy and patience, reflecting that we must accept and bear the sufferings of the Blessed Christ patiently for love of Him" (Brown 60).

Endnotes:

E1: Picasso's Blue Period (1901-1904) represents the time during which Picasso's canvases were infused with various shades of blue that represented his grief over the death of his friend Carlos Casagemas.

E2: Though the myth that Mary Magdalene was a prostitute and the adulteress portrayed in John 8.7 has been largely discredited by scholars, it continues to be a part of Christian folklore and one of the favorite biblical illustrations of both writers and speakers.

E3: Jean's allusion to "reproductions of the paintings by Antonello da Messina" seems to be a reference to his series of works entitled, *Ecce Homo* ("Behold the Man"). The paintings portray Christ before his crucifixion and are based upon Pilate's words in John 19.5: "Then came Jesus forth, wearing the crown of thorns, and the purple robe. And Pilate saith unto them, Behold the man!" However, Messina depicted Christ's crucifixion in other works and his paintings echo a number of religious themes. Because *Ecce Homo* portrays Christ (God incarnate) as man, the theme intersects with Jean's journey towards belief in Christ as a real man and not just a subject for artists. When Jean tells Sister Irma that her paintings remind him, "in many pleasant ways" (153), of the way St. Francis of Assisi spoke, he suggests that her work has made him feel a kinship with the world that God has made through his suffering: "Brother Fire, God made you beautiful and strong and useful; I pray you be courteous to me" (153). Though he has not internalized it at this point, Jean intuits that the suffering of St. Francis (and Christ in Sister Irma's painting) is not solipsistic because it is in service to others and God.

Bibliography:

Bible. King James Version.

Brown, Raphel. *The Little Flowers of St. Francis*. Garden City: Doubleday, 1958.

Salinger, J. D. *Nine Stories*. Boston: Little Brown, 1991.

---. *The Catcher in the Rye*. New York: Bantam, 1967.

Discussion Questions and Possible Essay Topics:

1. Explore Salinger's allusions to various painters throughout the story. What do they reveal about the story?

2. Discuss how the death of the narrator's mother affects him throughout the story.

3. Why does the narrator take on the pseudonym, Jean de Daumier-Smith? Compare this pseudonym with the narrator/Sergeant X's in "For Esmé."

4. Explore the relationship between Europe, America, and Canada in the story. What does Salinger seem to imply through the narrator's journey throughout the story?

5. Why does Jean state, "Everybody is a nun," at the conclusion of the story?

6. Compare and contrast Sister Irma's painting with Jean's experience at the window of the orthopedic appliances shop.

7. What is the significance of the narrator's dedication of the story to Robert Agadganian, Jr.?

8. Discuss the paintings of R. Howard Ridgefield and Bambi Kramer and Jean's reaction to them in comparison with Sister Irma's work.

Teddy

Overview

"Teddy" begins in the McArdle cabin on board an ocean liner as they are crossing from Europe to America. Teddy's father asks him to get off the Gladstone bag that he paid "twenty-two pounds for" (168). Teddy continues to stand on the Gladstone in order to look out the porthole of the ship. Salinger suggests that both Mr. and Mrs. McArdle are sunburned and lying almost nude under the sheets of their beds out of the discomfort from both their sunburns and how hot it is within the cabin-"October, for God's sake," Mr. McArdle states, "If this is October weather, gimme August" (166). While Mr. McArdle repeatedly asks Teddy to get down off the bag, his mother tells him to stay on it, to "Jump up and down," and to "Crush Daddy's bag" (168).

Mrs. McArdle's statement sets off an exchange between the McArdle's in which he suggests kicking her "head open" and she imagines him dying of a heart attack (168-69). As the scene plays out, Teddy offers the information that they "passed the Queen Mary at three-thirty-two this morning" (169), and his father tells him, again, to get down off the bag and to get a haircut. Teddy mentions a conversation he had with a teacher (Nicholson) about "that last tape" he made (170).

A little later someone throws orange peels out of a porthole near their cabin, and while Teddy observes the peels floating on the surface of the water, meditating aloud that the peels will soon be floating only "inside my mind" (172), Mrs. McArdle asks where his sister Booper went. Teddy tells her he gave her the Leica camera and Mr. McArdle turns his attention from the Gladstone to the Leica: "I want that camera, Teddy. You hear me?" (172). Teddy then gets down from the Gladstone, cleans up the ashes from Mr. McArdle's cigarettes, kisses his mother and considers that once he leaves the room he "may be an orange peel," before he sets off to find Booper.

When Teddy leaves the cabin, he picks up the "ship's daily paper" and walks past "an enormous mural of Saint George and the Dragon" before he ascends the stairs to the Main Deck (174). On the Main Deck he goes to "the Purser's desk" and asks the Ensign behind the desk what time a word game is being played later in the day. He has a brief exchange with her and then goes up to "the Promenade Deck" (175) where he finds Booper. Booper has arranged all of the shuffleboard discs into "two tangent stacks" (176) and shows them to Teddy while she rebukes a small boy named Myron for standing in the light.

Booper mocks Myron for his ignorance about backgammon, among other things, and calls him "the stupidest person in this ocean" (176), a point Teddy rebukes. Teddy locates the camera and briefly puts it around his neck before giving it back to Booper and asking her to take it back to the cabin because he needs to write in his diary. Booper tells him that she hates "everybody in the ocean" as he walks away (178). Teddy walks down from the Sports Deck to the Sun Deck and sits in the chairs marked for the McArdles and proceeds to read his previous diary entry.

The diary entry consists mainly of a meditation on poetry and words he needs to look up in the dictionary. After reading, Teddy writes his diary entry for October 28, 1952 and alludes to the day he will die, "today or February 14, 1958" (182). While Teddy writes, a man who turns out to be Nicholson watches him from the distance; Salinger notes that the man leaves and then comes back onto the deck and eventually sits down next to Teddy. Nicholson talks about the weather and asks Teddy about his trip to Europe. Teddy tells him that he was interviewed in Edinburgh, Scotland and Oxford, England and asks Nicholson if he is a poet because "Poets are always taking the weather so personally" and "sticking their emotions in things that have no emotions" (185). Nicholson responds that he is not a poet but asks rhetorically if emotions are not "what poets are primarily concerned with?" (185). Teddy responds by quoting two haikus that are "not full of a lot of emotional stuff" (185-86).

This conversation leads directly to their discussion of Teddy's lack of emotions, his belief in reincarnation, and God. Teddy relates that he does not see what emotions are "good for" and that if he were God he "certainly wouldn't want people to love me sentimentally. It's too unreliable" (186-87). Teddy explains how in a past life he was "a person making a very nice spiritual advancement" and that he fell in love with a woman and had to "get incarnated in an American body" because he lost his focus on God (188). He then explains that he was six when he saw "that everything was God" (189). Teddy associates this pantheistic idea with a need to get rid of the logic represented by the "apple" Adam and Eve ate in the Garden of Eden. He says that once "you vomit it up" you "see things as they really are" (191). He compares this to dying and says death represents an awakening into the presence of God.

When Nicholson asks about prophecies Teddy made to various teachers and philosophers concerning their deaths, Teddy tells him, "in their hearts they really didn't want to know" when they are going to die because, "even though they teach Religion and Philosophy and all, they're still pretty afraid to die" (193). Teddy refutes this fear of death by forecasting his own death for Nicholson, explaining how he might die when he goes to his swimming lesson because Booper might push him into the pool, which might have been drained of its water. "What would be so tragic about it, though?," he asks (193). Shortly after this, Teddy gets up to leave, but Nicholson presses him to stay for a little longer and asks him for advice about how to educate children. Teddy tells him that he would educate children by getting them to "empty out everything their parents and everybody ever told them" so they could "vomit up every bit of the apple" Adam and Eve ate in the Garden of Eden (196).

Nicholson directs this form of teaching towards an ontological way of thinking, but Teddy explains that he would want the children to "begin with all the real ways of looking at things" and explains that he could not be a doctor because they "stay too right on the surface" (196). After this, he leaves quickly while Nicholson sits "motionless" with his cigarette smoking. Nicholson seems to meditate on Teddy's words for a little while before he appears to realize something Teddy said, and he gets up and begins, somewhat quickly, to descend the decks of the ship until he arrives at D Deck and the pool. When he is "halfway down the staircase," the story ends abruptly as he hears a girl's scream, "as though it were reverberating within four tiled walls" (198).

Analysis

In the opening exchange between Teddy and Mr. McArdle, Salinger pays close attention to their physical appearances. Mr. McArdle has a "sunburned, debilitated-looking body" and lies "supine" with his head "propped up just enough to rest uncomfortably, almost masochistically, against the very base of the headboard" (166). Through Mr. McArdle's positioning and physical description, Salinger portrays him almost as if he were lying dead in a coffin and in a type of hell. This sense is only furthered when he reaches out "a nude, inflamed-pink, right arm and flicked his ashes" and complains about the heat, "October, for God's sake ... If this is October weather, gimme August" (166). Mr. McArdle's statement about the heat in October establishes one of the early themes of the story, the consequences of the Fall from "that apple Adam ate in the Garden of Eden" (191).

In contrast to Mr. McArdle's physical description, Teddy is standing up and looking out the porthole of his parent's cabin. His ruddy physical appearance, dirty oversized shorts, "ankle-sneakers, no socks," a T shirt with a "hole the size of a dime in the right shoulder," and a head needing a haircut, all suggest a casual disregard for physical appearances. Salinger also notes that the single formal aspect of his outfit, a "handsome, black alligator belt" is 'incongruous" with the rest of his outfit (167). In contrast with the burnt skin of Mr. and Mrs. McArdle (and Booper), Teddy's skin is "unsuntanned" (179).

Salinger furthers the material and immaterial divide between Teddy and those around him when Mr. McArdle insists he get off the Gladstone bag he is standing on in order to look out the porthole. In spite of the fact that Teddy's "face was considerably more outside than inside the cabin," Salinger notes, "he was well within hearing of his father's voice-his father's voice, that is, most singularly" (167).

Throughout the scene Salinger intones that Teddy is caught between the material and spiritual worlds. He hears "his father's voice" in the material world and his Father's voice (God's) in the spiritual world. Of course, Teddy already knows he might die on this "exquisite day" (166), and he appears to be listening to his other Father's voice while his face is out the porthole. Salinger also might indicate the confluence of the material and spiritual through Teddy's "slightly crossed" eyes (168).

Teddy's "crossed" vision and his physical appearance are, as Mr. McArdle states, to make him look "precocious, for God's sake" (169). In other words, Teddy's appearance and physical features imply his ability to see God through the surfaces of the material world.

Once again, the Gladstone bag illustrates Salinger's use of these surface details to contrast Teddy's vision of the world with his father's. While Mr. McArdle wants Teddy to get off the bag because he might damage it, even going so far as to say how much he paid for it, Teddy stands on the bag so that he can "see out of his parents' open porthole" better (167). Salinger's use of the "Gladstone" as the prop Teddy stands on becomes a pun that can be read on a number of levels. On a superficial level, Teddy's standing on the bag does not make his father glad. But, as

Teddy will tell Nicholson later, he is not interested in staying "right on the surface" (196).

Therefore, from a spiritual perspective, the glad stone Teddy stands upon could be interpreted as the stone of God. In the Bible, Christ is repeatedly referred to as the foundation stone of the Church, and when Lazarus is raised from the dead it states, "they took away the stone from the place where the dead was laid" (John 11.41)-a foreshadowing of the stone being rolled away from Christ's tomb. Yet another reference comes in the book of Revelation, "He that hath an ear, let him hear what the Spirit saith unto the churches; To him that overcometh will I give to eat of the hidden manna, and will give him a white stone, and in the stone a new name written, which no man knoweth saving he that receive it" (2.17).

This reference in particular seems to coincide with Teddy's hearing the voice of the spirit of God over the voice of his father and being given a "new name written" that defies the material limitations of logic ("no man knoweth"). A little later Mrs. McArdle tells Teddy to "Crush Daddy's bag," to which Mr. McArdle responds, "That's a Jesus-brilliant thing to say" (168). The exchange between the two might suggest the need for Mr. McArdle to get rid of his baggage in order to see beyond the material world (i.e. "Jesus"). But with the "Gladstone," Salinger also creates a rift between Mr. and Mrs. McArdle that seems to parallel St. Peter's words, to "them which be disobedient, the stone which the builders disallowed, the same is made the head of the corner, and a stone of stumbling and a rock of offence" (1 Peter 2.7).

Yet the irony of the exchange between Teddy and Mr. McArdle is that the Gladstone will be trivial in light of Teddy's death and will proverbially, "Crush Daddy's bag" (168). But Teddy seems to be attempting to offer his parents advice about how to deal with the possibility of his impending death. When a whole "can of orange peels" are thrown "out the window" (171), Teddy tells them, "Some of them are starting to sink," and that "In a few minutes, the only place they'll still be floating will be inside my mind" (171). The sinking of the orange peels doubles with Teddy's death at the conclusion of the story and the fact that soon he will only exist in the minds of his parents.

Similarly, Teddy's standing on the Gladstone parallels the image of the peels floating on the surface of the water. Just as the peels are a representation of the outside layer of the orange, Teddy knows that he has to empty himself out by vomiting up the apple of logic (191). While Mr. and Mrs. McArdle profanely joke about the other dying on a superficial level, they do not consider it from an existential point of view. Thus, as Teddy leaves he alludes to the orange peel as a type of parable for his parents: "After I go out this door, I may only exist in the minds of all my acquaintances. ... I may be an orange peel" (174).

Salinger doubles this sense of surface representation through the Leica camera Teddy gives to Booper. While

Mr. McArdle once again dwells on the value of the camera, Teddy assures him the camera is safe because he "showed her how to hold it" and "took the film out, naturally" (172). The fact that Teddy shows her how to hold it but takes the film out becomes an extension of his looking through the "porthole." The camera lens, like the porthole, only creates an illusion of a moment when it is captured on film, but Teddy takes the film out so that the moment can be captured "naturally" through the lens. Teddy's action of cleaning Mr. McArdle's ashes off the glass table top and centering the ashtray like a camera lens (173) also symbolically represents an attempt to help him see beyond the surface planes of the material world. Finally, the scene also might indicate the reason Booper pushes Teddy into the pool-she most likely gets scolded for having the camera by Mr. McArdle and blames Teddy.

As Teddy leaves the cabin and goes down the hallway, he passes "an enormous mural of Saint George and the Dragon" (174), an intricate allusion that Salinger clearly wants us to acknowledge. Saint George and the Dragon is a medieval legend of Eastern origin that tells of how Saint George "subdues the beast" (Robertson 51). After subduing it, George led it to the people of "Silcha, in Libya" to convert them to Christianity and "slays the creature" (51). Duncan Robertson, however, in his book *The Medieval Saints' Lives*, contends that the Saint George myth is "absorbed" (52) from St. Theodore, and "George becomes associated with St. Theodore" over time and "in the course of various crusade-interventions" (52). Robertson also adds, "Theodore's legend had included a dragon-encounter as of the earliest Greek texts" (52).

In Christopher Walter's *The Warrior Saints in Byzantine Art and Tradition*, St. Theodore of Tiron is referenced as the "greatest of the martyrs" (44), and Walter writes later that in several historical plates, "Theodore and George" are pictured "on horseback [and] direct their spears at two serpents entwined around a tree" (56). Salinger seems to connect Teddy (or Theodore), whose name means gift of God, to the slaying of the dragon through the alligator belt that he wears; thus, it is fitting that in some versions and illustrations of the legend the dragon is depicted as an alligator. Salinger might be alluding to the Old Testament prophet Isaiah here: "Awake, awake, put on strength, O arm of the Lord; awake as in the ancient days, in the generations of old. Art thou not it that hath ... wounded the dragon?" (51.9).

For example, the second time Salinger mentions the alligator belt comes when Teddy tightens it after explaining to Nicholson that "he wouldn't wake up till he died himself" (194). In this way, Teddy could be seen as slaying the dragon of death in the story. From a biblical point of view, the dragon represents Lucifer, the dragon who tempted Adam and Eve to eat the apple in the first place. Therefore, the second Adam, Christ, has to slay the dragon of death on the cross. As St. Paul writes in his first letter to the Corinthians, "O death, where is thy sting? O grave, where is thy victory?" (15.55). In this regard, as with the Saints before him, Teddy's role in the story is to slay the dragon of death and help others to understand that death is an illusion (or a porthole) so others might see through the illusion of death and follow God.

Teddy eventually ascends the various decks of the ship until he finds Booper, "high up on the Sports Deck" (175), and a young boy named Myron standing next to her. Booper has made two "tangent stacks" of red and black shuffleboard discs that she is proud of, and she tells Teddy to "Look!" (176). She then scolds Myron for "making it all shadowy" so that Teddy "can't see" (176). After Teddy admires the symmetry of the stacks, Booper mocks Myron because he has "never even heard of backgammon" (176). The scene turns almost comical when Booper, who has mistaken the shuffleboard court for a gigantic backgammon table, states, "All I need now is two giants ... They could play backgammon till they got all tired and then they could climb up on that smokestack and throw these at everybody and kill them" (177).

Salinger implies that Booper confuses shuffleboard with backgammon as easily as she does life with death. For instance, she tells Teddy that Myron's father "was killed in Korea" and "if his mother dies, he'll be an orphan" (176). Yet, when she imagines the giants killing everyone, she tells Myron, "They could kill your parents" and "if that didn't kill them, you know what you could do? You could put some poison on some marshmallows and make them eat it" (177).

Booper's words seem cruel at first, but they should be read with the understanding that she does not really *know* what she is saying. In this way, Salinger indicates that the reader has to get rid of their logic (from the Tree of Knowledge), or what they have been taught about the meaning of words, in order to see beyond the surface meaning of Booper's words. As Teddy will later explain to Nicholson about how he would instruct children, "I'd get them to empty out everything their parents and everybody ever told them. I mean even if their parents just told them an elephant's big, I'd make them empty that out. An elephant's only big when it's next to something else-a dog or a lady, for example" (195).

"I might show them an elephant, if I had one handy, but I'd let them just walk up to the elephant not knowing anything more about it than the elephant knew about them," Teddy continues, "The same thing with grass, and other things. I wouldn't even tell them grass is green. Colors are only names. I mean if you tell them the grass is green, it makes them start expecting the grass to look a certain way-your way-instead of some other way that may be just as good, and maybe much better . . . I don't know" (195-96). At last, Teddy concludes, "I'd just make them vomit up every bit of the apple their parents and everybody made them take a bite out of" (196). Naturally, Teddy's vision of how to instruct children coincides with a prelapsarian view of the world and seems to clue the reader into how Booper's teaching, most likely from the violent inflections of her parents' speech, informs her view of the world.

Moreover, Salinger appears to build the scene with Booper and Myron around a question that Teddy asks to Ensign Mathewson about the "time that game starts today?" (175). Teddy explains, "You know. That word game they had yesterday and the day before, where you're supposed to supply the missing words. It's mostly that you have to put everything into context" (175). The game Teddy seems to refer to, Exquisite Corpse, is a surrealist word game in which every person adds a word to a sequence by following a rule-such as one can only see the previous word before adding one of their own-and, notably, derives from a game called "Consequences." With Exquisite Corpse in mind, Booper's words take on a different meaning entirely for Teddy (and for the reader), and they also appear to inform his instructions to Nicholson about how to teach children. As Booper tells Myron, "Move your carcass," then shuts her eyes and waits "with a cross-bearing grimace" (176), Salinger parallels her words with Teddy's meditating in order to empty his body (carcass) out and in that way get closer to the burden Christ bore upon the cross. In contrast to Booper, Myron does not *know* (which makes him "the stupidest person" Booper has "ever met"), and thus Myron is closer to

Teddy's educational model because he has less of the apple to empty out of himself.

Salinger's game of Exquisite Corpse continues later through Teddy's conversation with Nicholson-after Teddy has descended below the Sports Deck onto the Sun Deck. Nicholson observes aloud, "God, what a divine day," and then adds, "I've been known to take a perfectly normal rainy day as a personal insult. So this is absolute manna to me" (183). Teddy responds by asking if Nicholson is a poet because poets are "always sticking their emotions in things that have no emotions" (185).

After making this statement, Teddy looks "abstractedly toward, or over, the twin smokestacks up on the Sports Deck" (185). Teddy's look prefigures his sister as a giant, who is bored with her game of backgammon, killing him. Teddy's looking up from the Sun Deck (which, in the context of Exquisite Corpse, could also be read as, Son Deck) also seems to coincide with the way he will be looking up to her from the bottom of the pool at the end of the story. Teddy attempts to tell Nicholson that his death will not be tragic because of the fact that he will only be waking up to be with God. Thus, because Teddy has seen that "everything was God," his fall into the pool should be viewed as if Booper "was pouring God into God" (189).

Through the game of Exquisite Corpse, Salinger also alludes to Teddy's "spiritual advancement" by way of reincarnation. A way of interpreting this is that Teddy's journey from corpse to corpse has been a way of emptying himself of the logic inscribed on words so that he can become "exquisite." This, of course, adds a new dimension to the first words he intimates in the story, which are known only because his father repeats them: "I'll exquisite day you, buddy" (166). Unlike Nicholson's putting his emotions into the weather, Teddy's "exquisite day" coincides with waking up to God. Accordingly, the two ancient haiku's he quotes are "not full of a lot of emotional stuff" and both appear to relate to his proverbial "exquisite corpse":

Nothing in the voice of the cicada intimates how soon it will die

Along this road goes no one, this autumn eve. (185)

Like the cicada, Teddy does not speak of his death in emotional terms because he does not "have names and emotions for everything that happens" the way others do (194). Finally, on the eve of autumn, Teddy will empty himself out and become "no one," and by being "no one," from his point of view, others should not feel emotional when he dies.

Tying "Teddy" in the Cycle

Throughout "Teddy," Daumier-Smith's epiphany that "everybody is a nun" is echoed in the way Teddy sees others around him. Teddy writes in his diary, "it is very tasteless of Professor Walton to criticize my parents. He wants people to be a certain way" (181). Teddy also refuses to judge Booper when he speculates with Nicholson that she might push him into an empty pool and that he could "die instantaneously" (193). "My sister's only six, and she hasn't been a human being for very many lives, and she doesn't like me very much," Teddy states but wonders, "What would be so tragic about it, though" (193). Because he does not view life from a material point of view, Teddy associates the event with Booper's path of "spiritual advancement" (188).

It is fitting that Booper is six years old, and Teddy tells Nicholson that he was six when he saw "that everything was God," and that Booper, "was only a very tiny child then, and she was drinking her milk, and all of a sudden I saw that she was God and the milk was God" (189). Therefore, when Booper pushes Teddy into the pool she will be forced to consider the boundaries of life and death the way that Teddy has and this might, in Teddy's estimation, eventually lead her to the realization that she 'pushed God into God' (189). Still, it could be argued that Teddy also wants people to be a certain way.

For example, when Nicholson questions how he would teach children, Teddy's response is not based upon indoctrination, but on an emptying out of logical thought so that the individual can "begin with all the real ways of looking at things" (196). Though Teddy shares this with Nicholson and the people who ask him questions, he does not impose his beliefs upon others. Teddy appears to understand that each individual's path to God is a personal quest and that part of the inner-life cannot be understood from a material point of view. Daumier-Smith's (Jean's) "spiritual advancement," therefore, comes out of an understanding that allows him to see beyond the tragedy of his mother's death, a connection Salinger develops quite intimately between the two stories.

In Jean's first experience in front of the "window of the orthopedic appliances shop" (157), for example, he describes himself, without God, as "a visitor in a garden of enamel urinals and bedpans, with a sightless wooden dummy-deity standing in a marked-down rupture truss" (157). Jean's vision causes him to "lay awake for hours, shivering" and then imagining himself with Sister Irma as a "Peter Abelard-type man" (158). In the first vision, Jean sees only the material world and his terror at the prospect of it is only calmed through a fantasy of fulfilling his fleshly desires.

Teddy addresses these desires when he tells Nicholson that what stopped him from making a "spiritual advancement" was when he "met a lady, and [he] sort of stopped meditating" (188). As a result of meeting the lady, Teddy "had to get incarnated in an American body" (188). He then tells Nicholson, "it's very hard to meditate and live a spiritual life in America. People think you're a freak if you try to" (189). Teddy's statement about the difficulty of leading a spiritual life in America applies not only to Salinger's use of East and West in "Blue Period," but all of *Nine Stories*. Consider, for instance, Jean's reference to volumes "36, 44, 45 of the *Harvard Classics*" (154).

The allusion provides the best textual evidence for the connection between Eastern and Western religious thought in the cycle in that they contain sacred writings from Christian, Buddhist, Hindu and Mohammedan writers-they also contain "Hymns of the Christian Church" that could provide a possible link to the hymn being sung in "For Esmé."**(E1)** With regards to the relationship between East and West, from the perspective of Jean, it seems that the narrator's journey from America (because of the Great Depression) to Europe and back to America (because of his mother's death) portrays the West as a type of hell or purgatory. For both Teddy and Jean, who considers "Canada part of America" (139), the journey back to the West from the East might be viewed as a path to spiritual enlightenment through death. Indeed, the difficulty of the spiritual journey in the West seems to be the reason that Teddy maintains his focus upon God-which provides another example of the convergence of love and squalor-instead of getting distracted by a lady in the East where it seems to be easier to "live a spiritual life" (188). Fittingly, Teddy has crossed back to the East and appears to find the balance between East and West when he dies.

Even more, Jean's second, "Experience," at the window of the orthopedic appliances shop offers some illumination of the balance between East and West. When Jean sees "a light on" and a "live person in the shopcase" (163), he begins to see beyond the "wooden dummy-deity" (157) of the material world. **(E2)** As Teddy explains to Nicholson about his arm, "You know it's called an arm, but how do you know it is one? Do you have proof that it's an arm?" (190). Teddy states that he has to "get out of the finite dimensions" (190) in order to get rid of the logic and get closer to God. Concurrently, Jean describes his vision in terms of escaping the "finite dimensions," and when he gets "his sight back" he sees "a shimmering field of exquisite, twice-blessed enamel flowers" (164). The exquisite flowers that represent Jean's epiphany parallel what seems to be Teddy's "final Illumination" when he falls through the *porthole* of the pool on an "exquisite day" (166).

Furthermore, Salinger appears to relate this sense of enlightenment to identity. Like the narrator of "Blue Period," Teddy acts older than his age and almost seems like an adult. The chief distinction between them, though, might be in the fact that Teddy is more spiritually mature than the narrator of "Blue Period." While the narrator of "Blue Period" changes his name in order to mask himself

Teaching Salinger's Nine Stories

and escape his misery and despair, Teddy embraces his identity in spiritual terms. Teddy's identity is not wrapped up in the superficial titles of the material world, but in his sense of spiritual advancement. In this way, he values both who he is and everyone else around him because he sees everyone, in one way or another, on a path to becoming one with God: "most people don't want to see things the way they are. They don't even want to stop getting born and dying all the time. They just want new bodies all the time, instead of stopping and staying with God, where it's really nice" (191). Teddy's statement indicates that he, too, wants people to be a certain way. But his philosophy is not self-serving or based upon logic, and thus, from his point of view, it will lead others to God rather than a "wooden dummy-deity" (157).

At last, in terms of one hand clapping, "Teddy" brings together the various lenses of the material and spiritual worlds Salinger presents throughout the cycle. Each story can be read through the spiritual signification Teddy gives to life and death. From Seymour's own "lady" and "spiritual advancement," to the tragedy of the Laughing Man's death and Teddy's understanding that God "never said anybody had to love Him sentimentally" (187), the connections that can be made in "Teddy" are too numerous to mention here and will hopefully provide a framework from which thousands of student essays will be written. In terms of "Teddy" itself, Salinger multiplies the glass imagery, it would seem, as a way of alluding to the fact that for Teddy the division between the physical and spiritual worlds is increasingly hard to determine. As Teddy leans "his face" more "outside than inside" the porthole, for example, Salinger shows us that though he is "well within range of his father's voice" (167), he does not hear him. It is only when his father shouts that Teddy comes back inside the cabin and Salinger reveals his crossed eyes. Along these lines, Teddy seems crossed between two worlds, a point that Salinger only punctuates with the orange peels that Teddy observes are "starting to sink" (171) outside the porthole.

Salinger also relates the conflict of Teddy's thoughts through the fact that he does listen to his father's request for him to get the camera back from Booper. Teddy does not seem to be intentionally disregarding his father's words about the Gladstone. It is just that he, like Christ with his earthly parents, might be said to be about his "Father's business" (Luke 2.49). However, before obeying Mr. McArdle's request for the camera, Teddy clears off his father's cigarette ashes and places the ashtray on the center of the glass table. The action, which is the last service that Teddy will do for his father (outside of offering him a pillow to make him comfortable), seems representative of a type of photograph Teddy leaves for him. In other words, when Teddy falls through the glass (the empty pool) at the conclusion of the story, his father might see through the glass. Salinger also alludes to the erasure of surface planes when Teddy gives "his right ear a light clap with his hand"

and tells Nicholson, "I still have some water in my ear from yesterday" (186).

Ridding his body of the water appears to be symbolic of Teddy emptying himself of the physical world so that by the conclusion of the story he sees no distinction between the spiritual and physical worlds. From another point of view, when Teddy falls into the pool at the conclusion of the story, for him there is no difference between falling into a pool with or without water, as there is no distinction between one or two hands clapping.

Another illuminating detail comes from Teddy's journal entry in which he writes, "do not lose consciousness in the dining room if that waiter drops that big spoon again. Daddy was quite furious" (180). Salinger might be alluding to what Salvador Dali called the "slumber with a key." Dali used the "slumber with a key" technique to resolve the "problem of 'sleeping without sleeping,' which is the essence of the dialectics of the dream, since it is a repose which walks in equilibrium on the taut and invisible wire which separates sleeping from waking" (36). Dali used the "slumber with a key" technique to revive his "whole physical and psychic being" (37).

The technique essentially involves meditating with a heavy key balanced upon one's hands to wake them up when they lose consciousness, and Dali describes it in detail in his book *50 Secrets of Magic Craftsmanship*. Dali also practiced the technique with a spoon and attributes his "knowledge of the 'slumber with a key' to the fact that it was practiced by the Capuchin monks of Toledo" (36)-a sect that seeks to live a primitive life of poverty and follow the example of St. Francis of Assisi. Applied to "Teddy," the "slumber with a key" technique would reinforce Teddy's increased detachment from the world. Instead of waking up when the spoon drops, Teddy loses consciousness.

Of course, Teddy would argue that by losing consciousness in the logical world, he is actually waking up to the real world. Significantly, Salinger indicates Teddy's transcendence beyond the material world through his final descent far below the surface of the water to "D Deck," when he falls into the pool. As with the peels that have fallen into the ocean, Teddy seems to have rid himself of the logic of the world so that he has gotten rid of the apple and can now stay "with God, where it's really nice" (191). The reader, like Booper, Nicholson and those who knew Teddy, is left only to consider Teddy's words (his *exquisite corpse*) after he has died. Each individual's journey through the glass is his or her own, but it is only through the squalor of death, Salinger seems to imply, that we consider the sound of one hand clapping and God's love.

Endnotes:

E1: It is also possible that the hymn being sung is "Softly and Tenderly," which was written by Will L. Thompson in 1880. The lyrics resonate with a number of themes in "For Esmé" and *Nine Stories* including the lines, "See, on the portholes He's waiting and watching," and "Come home, come home, / You who are weary, come home."

E2: Salinger's use of the Exquisite Corpse game here might be an allusion to the Corpus Christi play cycle. In his analysis of the Corpus Christi plays as a cycle, V. A. Kolve writes that it added to the medieval drama something "unique to the Corpus Christi kind-the capacity of the cycle drama to celebrate in its fullest significance what the Middle Ages took to be the supreme gift of God, His body for man's sin" (50). Teddy's discussion of "that apple Adam ate in the Garden of Eden" (191) might have a direct bearing here. For example, in 1 Corinthians 15.45 St. Paul writes, "And so it is written, The first man Adam was made a living soul; the last Adam was made a quickening spirit." Throughout the passage Paul discusses the body that "is sown in corruption" and "raised in incorruption" (15.42); "The first man is of the earth, earthy: the second man is the Lord from heaven" (15.47). The Corpus Christi cycle drama ties in with Salinger's use of the allusions to the Middle Ages. Another notable point comes when Kolve cites that in preparation for the "birth of Christ in the cycle sequence" a fast was observed, and "We can trace the observance in English documents such as the *Penitential of Theodore* (emanating from Theodore of Tarsus, Archbishop of Canterbury; 161). Finally, we should observe how Salinger connects his use of the Vedantic theory of reincarnation with the Christian theology of how believers become part of the body of Christ: "For as the body is one, and hath many members, and all the members of that one body, being many, are one body: so also is Christ. For by one Spirit are we all baptized into one body, whether we be Jews or Gentiles, whether we be bond or free; and have been all made to drink into one Spirit" (1 Cor. 12.12-13).

Bibliography:

Bible. King James Version.

Dali, Salvador. *50 Secrets of Magic Craftsmanship*. Mineola, NY: Dover, 1992.

Kolve, V. A. *The Play Called Corpus Christi*. Stanford: Stanford U. P., 1966.

Robertson, Duncan. *The Medieval Saints' Lives Spiritual Renewal and Old French Literature*. Lexington: French Forum, 1995.

Salinger, J. D. *Nine Stories*. Boston: Little Brown.

Walter, Christopher. *The Warrior Saints in Byzantine Art and Tradition*. Burlington: Ashgate, 2003.

Discussion Questions and Possible Essay Topics:

1. Explore the opening scene and Teddy's interaction with his parents. What does Teddy say about his parents later on in the story?

2. What is the significance of the fact that the story takes place upon an ocean liner in the middle of the ocean?

3. Explore Salinger's allusion to Saint George and the Dragon in the greater context of the story.

4. Discuss Booper's explanation of the game that she wants to play. Does it shed any light on her view of death? Examine this scene in light of how Teddy says he would teach children.

5. What do Teddy's diary entries reveal about him? Examine the conflict in the story between knowing and what Teddy calls vomiting up the apple.

6. Explore Teddy's point of view on East and West and the reason that it is hard to "live a spiritual life in America."

7. Explore the conclusion of the story through the various ways Salinger foreshadows Teddy's apparent death. What do they reveal or imply about his death? Why does Salinger resist stating that Teddy is dead?

8. Compare and contrast the events and characters in "Teddy" with "Bananafish."

Part II

Nine Essays

The View from Shore:
Seymour Glass in The Waste Land

Joseph A. Thompson
University of Mississippi

That J. D. Salinger was influenced by T. S. Eliot is obvious to readers: Eliot haunts Salinger's prose through allusions in the long litanies of influential quotes, or as a name casually dropped into his characters' dialogue (cf. *Franny and Zooey*), or, most tellingly, through direct quotes of "The Waste Land"-as in "A Perfect Day for Bananafish," when Seymour himself tangentially muses in Eliot's language, "How that name comes up. Mixing memory and desire" (9). Yet, it is less obvious just how importantly Eliot specifically functions in Salinger's fiction. However, *The Waste Land* provides an analytic for the collection and organization of *Nine Stories*, beginning with "Bananafish." The story is not merely an interpretation of Eliot's poem, which informs the character of Seymour and the story itself. Rather, "Bananafish" exclusively relies on the figures of *The Waste Land* to address the same question posed by Eliot: if the condition of the Modern world is characterized as barren, self-involved, and dead, how does one restore human connection in a life-giving way? Salinger's interpretive response to this question in "The Waste Land" is through Seymour's death in "Bananafish." Consequently, the events of Salinger's story must be primarily understood through the dialectic that Eliot's poem provides.

"The Waste Land" preceded Salinger's first publication by eighteen years. The poem functions in multiple ways: it is a catalog of stylistic adaptations in the tradition of Western literature, a cutting examination of the aftershock of the First World War, and a deeply personal complaint based on those examinations. Yet, Eliot's poem provides more than just the "rhythmical grumblings" of a stodgy expatriate; *The Waste Land* deploys a mixture of language, metaphor, and myth to position traditionally meaningful figures against a cultural decline of an age "when men seem more than ever prone to confuse wisdom with knowledge, and knowledge with information and to try to solve problems of life in terms of engineering" ("Classic" 129-130). The poem suggests that the product of such an age is a culture of disorder and infertility, resulting in physical decay and spiritual death.

J. D. Salinger had first-hand experience of this culture during his deployment overseas to fight in World War II. His time in the war was destructive if his fiction is any indicator; *Nine Stories* itself contains a bleak account of the cost of fighting in that horrific war in "For Esmé." The First

World War produced a new kind of horror that became the subject for Modernism as a cultural response and *The Waste Land* was principal among those responses. However, at the advent and conclusion of the Second World War, the horror had not subsided or altered, proving the persistence of the waste created by these new modern wars. It comes as no surprise, then, that Salinger looked to "The Waste Land" to inform his post-war short fiction, which he developed into *Nine Stories*.

When "Bananafish" appeared in the *New Yorker* in 1948, Salinger's professional writing career was well established. He had had steady work up until then, publishing at least one short story every year since 1940. However, with "Bananafish," Salinger started garnering more attention. The story's mature plot mastered the tonal shifts between the mysterious and trite conversation of a young married woman and her mother, the charm and allegorical wisdom of Seymour Glass as he interacts with 3-year-old Sybil Carpenter, and Seymour's unprecedented and unexplained suicide in the presence of his sleeping wife. Perhaps it was the daring shock of violence that brought Salinger the attention that followed "Bananafish," yet it is more likely that the story's merits originate from and express Salinger's deliberate use of *The Waste Land* as the immediate context of Seymour's actions leading up to his suicide.

This essay intends to do two things: firstly, it will track the presence of "The Waste Land" through "A Perfect

Day for Bananafish" and investigate how the poem functions in this story to extend Eliot's meanings into new territory. Secondly, this essay will identify how this reading of "Bananafish" sets a trajectory for *Nine Stories* that answers the questions of how one can combat the oppressions of the waste land, what is at stake in that enterprise, and what is the outcome of such resistance. For instance, how does a war-tired sergeant regain spiritual sanity, or how does someone salvage innocence in the ugly face of racism? As *Nine Stories* builds toward the resonating pitch of Teddy McArdle's death in the final story of Salinger's collection, "The Waste Land" aids in the collection's development to determine new boundaries of cultural decline and the limits of effective responses.

"The Waste Land" in title, context, and content, concerns itself with infertility and the decline of vital forces in Western societies. The introductory phrase, "the dead land," (51) and the subsequent repetition of the word dead-11 times- demonstrates Eliot's subject in relation to the "Unreal City" of post-war London (53). While Eliot uses the images of agricultural infertility, his attention is trained on infertility as an anthropological issue. The voices of the women in "A Game of Chess" discussing the options of birth control (56-57) as well as the bleak tryst in "The Fire Sermon," in which sex is perfunctory at best and self-destructive at worst (60), indicate the detrimental threat of an increasingly childless world. The poem illustrates the lack of distinction between the living and the dead to suggest that a world without its future presently within it (i.e. without children) is one that is living out its own extinction.

Yet, *The Waste Land* also proposes several solutions rooted in mysticism, liturgy, custom, and the function of ritual. Eliot's admitted reliance on Jessie L. Weston's book, *From Ritual to Romance,* and Sir James Frazer's *The Golden Bough* shows how attentive he was to a natural inclination of man to what Weston and Frazer call vegetative rites that helped structure culture through their attention to fertility and life-giving functions. "The Waste Land," then, is an illustration of the pressures of a Modern era that veers violently away from organic maturation of culture stemming from life-giving ritual. It also gives a response that shows the rich and varied life of determinate cultures, which suggests a restorative power for this crisis. Hence, Eliot's configuration lets *The Waste Land,* as an artifact, be at the same time a diagnostic tool and a prescription for curing the fatal disease afflicting Western culture.

The congruence of *The Waste Land* and "Bananafish" becomes evident in the seemingly offhand comment of Seymour during his conversation with the 3-year-old Sybil. Seymour quotes the poem, "mixing memory and desire," and from this central moment the two works begin to speak to and for each other. Immediately, the connection emerges between the Sybil of "Bananafish" and the Cumaean Sybil in the epigraph of the poem, who explains to the young boys, ["I want to die"], (*The Waste Land* 49).

However, the roles of the Sybils are reversed – instead of the young boys asking the Sybil what she wants, it is the young girl, Sybil Carpenter, who interrogates the young man, Seymour, who does indeed want to die. As the dialogue between the two works continues outward in both directions from this central instance of overlap, it becomes clearer that they are inseparably linked.

The most compelling identification between the two occurs in the alignment of the central figures of each text, namely, Seymour and the Fisher King. Eliot confesses in his notes that he borrowed this figure from Weston, who identifies the Fisher King in Arthurian legend as the figure whose wound brings about the devastation of the land and he must be healed by the grail in order to restore his lands. This begins the identification between the two central figures, Seymour and The Fisher King. What the reader has gathered about Seymour from the telephone conversation in the previous section informs his relationship to The Fisher King, especially in terms of the "fatal wound."

Seymour's mental state is, at very least, not normative: Seymour's mother-in-law narrates that her husband has sought counsel with a psychologist about particular aberrations in Seymour's behavior: "The trees. That business with the window. Those horrible things he said to Granny about her plans for passing away. What he did with all those lovely pictures from Bermuda-*everything*" (3). Furthermore, the reader learns from word-of-mouth reports that Seymour was hospitalized during his stint in the Army, "Well. In the first place, [the psychologist] said it was a perfect *crime* the Army released him from the hospital-my word of honor" (ibid). Though Seymour's mother-in-law's response is unattractively melodramatic, nevertheless, Seymour does seem to have a condition as a result of the war, which links him in character to the Fisher King and his unfortunate wound.

The correlatives extend further. In the poem, the Fisher King first appears in "The Fire Sermon," in the setting in the wreckage of the Thames.

> *While I was fishing in the dull canal*
>
> *On a winter evening round behind the gashouse*
>
> *Musing upon the king my brother's wreck*
>
> *And on the king my father's death before him.* (58)

This bleak reverie is broken by the voice of children. "*Et O ces voix d'enfants, chantant dans la coupole!* (And O the voice of children, singing among the dome) (59). In "Bananafish," Seymour is on the shore of the Florida beach, but he is interrupted by the voice of three-year old Sybil and they, like the mythic figure of the poem, go fishing. The bananafish they seek are determinately metaphorical so that Seymour can express and diagnose the greedy, gluttonous consumption he sees after he returns home from the war. "Well, they swim into a hole where there's a lot of bananas. They're very ordinary-looking fish when they swim *in*. But once they get in, they behave like pigs. Why, I've known some bananafish to swim into a banana hole and eat as many as seventy-eight bananas...Naturally, after that they're so fat they can't get out of the hole again...Well, they get banana fever. It's a terrible disease" (*For Esmé* 11). Seymour's parable expresses his own complaint against the immorally obese of his age in a different way than Eliot, but the assessment is still the same. Indeed, the figurative bananafish matches Eliot's rat creeping "softly through the vegetation/dragging its slimy belly on the bank" (*The Waste Land* 58) while the Fisher King sits and fishes.

The Fisher King reappears at the end of *The Waste Land*, and through his voice Eliot provides the closest thing to restoring the waste land yet:

>*I sat upon the shore*
>
>*Fishing, with the arid plain behind me*
>
>*Shall I at least set my lands in order?* [. . .]
>
>*(Then in the fire that refines he hid)*
>
>*(When will I be like the swallow).* (67)

Eliot references Dante and a first century Latin poet at this point to pair with the voice of the Fisher King, who is beginning to expect the restoration of his land. In doing so, Eliot suggests that there is a requisite suffering before any peace or restoration may occur. In Dante, it is clear that the refining fire of Purgatory is destructive and painful yet it is paired with the irrefutable promise of heaven. Hence, to "be like the swallow," that is, to signal the coming of spring and summer (the fertile seasons), is to begin turning back toward a regenerative and life-giving culture through a necessary suffering. These few lines are critical in understanding the motives for Seymour's suicide at the end of "Bananafish."**(E1)**

It is unclear from the story what kind of moral judgment Salinger makes about Muriel Glass or Seymour, or if he is even bothering to make one at all. Yet, it is nevertheless clear that he presents Seymour's imaginative power and sensitivity as virtues juxtaposed to the non-serious but spiritually exhausting vices of his wife; the division of the story into three main events asks for a kind of syllogistic reckoning of the two characters in order to come to the conclusion of the suicide. While the suicide seems motivated by more external circumstances than Salinger gives in the story, *The Waste Land* establishes that Seymour, as the Fisher King, is setting in motion the restoration of his lands. Hence, the violence and possible cruelty of the act resembles and demonstrates the Purgatorial fires, which promise salvation only through the horror of cleansing fire. While an initial reading seems like an escape from the spiritual squalor of his wife's narcissistic character displayed in the first part of the book, "The Waste Land" provides the means to analyze the story in order to display the critical importance of this act in bringing order to a disordered society.

In fact, Salinger aligns Seymour's final act to the final section of Eliot's poem thoroughly and, in doing so, effects the complete predication on Seymour's suicide as one that is an act of sympathy, charity, and-contrary to his mother-in-law's expectation "that Seymour may com*plete*ly lost control of himself" (*For Esmé* 3)-self-control. It is the very sound of the gun that, though unheard, ends the story. Although the results of Seymour's suicide are lost in verbal silence, they resound in meaning, especially during comparison to Eliot's final resolving section, "What the Thunder Said." In the notes to the poem, Eliot states that the answer is provided in the *Upanishads* as the one word, "Da," which has plural meanings. **(E2)** The original spiritual text explains, "The storm cloud thunders: 'Da! Da! Da!'-Be self-controlled! Be charitable! Be compassionate!" (Prabhavananda and Manchester 112).

The thundering bang of Seymour's Ortgies automatic **(E3)** signals in one syllable three virtues that determine the morality of his suicide. Part of the horror of Seymour's suicide, added to the traumatic gore involved, is its immediate unaccountability. However, "The Waste Land" gives an account for the thunderous conclusion to

"Bananafish" and even challenges the reader to understand the suicide as righteous, in spite of its apparent insensitivity. Seymour's actions provide the requisite suffering to warrant the restoration that is promised to follow, just like the Fisher King. The suicide, though violently loud, causes and completes shockwaves that effect change throughout the rest of *Nine Stories*.

The Waste Land continues to function throughout the collection but specifically through the effects of "Bananafish." The images of the story–"Sex is Fun–or Hell," Seymour's death, the setting of water, the effective grace of children carry through either thematically or literally, informing the collection with the predications on "Bananafish" made possible by *The Waste Land*. The most effective uses are tonal. For instance, there is a tension in "Uncle Wiggily in Connecticut" between the fact that Eloise has a child and the childless neighborhood where she lives: "Eloise, yawning, shook her head. 'There are no little boys in the neighborhood. No children at all. They call me Fertile Fanny behind my-' (*For Esmé* 19). This childless environment brings about the crisis Eloise faces when her daughter, Ramona, clings too dearly to her imaginary playmate. There is a further tonal similarity between the great crowd of souls flowing over London Bridge in "The Burial of the Dead" and the crowd seen from above in "Just Before the War with the Eskimos": "[Franklin] looked down at the street, scratching his spine with his thumb. 'Look at 'em,' he said. 'God-damn fools. . . . They're all goin' over to the god-damn draft board,' he said. 'We're gonna fight the Eskimos next'" (35). Franklin perceives the crowd's foolish adoption of war's solvent power as worth condemning and it calls to mind the endless crowds of the dead in London, flowing over the bridge in "The Burial of the Dead." Again, the two books dialogue through Salinger's attempt to facsimile what Eliot calls the substance of the poem **(E4)** in "Pretty Mouth and Green My Eyes."

Salinger recognizes Eliot's meaning and rewrites the scene in "Pretty Mouth and Green My Eyes" in order to revive the urgency of the message. The story displays pathetic male posturing, insulting deception, and the sterile and joyless character of sexual affairs; in doing so, Salinger brings us to the heart of Eliot's poem, the substance seen by Tiresias. The loveless partners in the poem match in tone and effect Salinger's painful and morally bereft characters: Lee, Arthur, and Joanie. What Tiresias sees and what the reader subsequently discovers is the notion described in the first pages of *Nine Stories*, that "Sex is Hell" when it becomes an attitude of satisfying selfish desires instead of serving a social function of human communication. Salinger and Eliot pointedly use this image to describe the threat of perfunctory, anti-social sex and its part in bringing about the waste land. **(E5)**

Yet, there are some more literal references to the central images of *The Waste Land*-for instance, as "The Laughing Man" reaches its pitch in the developing romance between the Chief and Mary Hudson, the accompanying fiction of The Laughing Man begins its final chapter in the cruel month of April (48). That April is cruel is demonstrated in the Chief's brooding conclusion of his make-believe, a conclusion which traumatizes several if not all of his young Comanche ball-players. Moreover, the setting for the rising action in "For Esmé-With Love and Squalor" is in April, as well (65), exhibiting yet another moment of cruelty in which an unsuspecting, sensitive, author turned regimental soldier suffers incapacitating war trauma. Salinger's free usage of the opening line of *The Waste Land* deliberately repeats what he suspects of his contemporary culture, namely, that it tends to be exceedingly cruel. **(E6)**

But it is not simply that Salinger employs *The Waste Land* throughout *Nine Stories*. Rather, like in "Bananafish," the poem is an informative allusion that operates through all nine stories and it works effectively to unite the collection. This is only through its function in "Bananafish," where it justifies and explains Seymour's suicide as a sacrificial restoration and the beginning of an escape from the wreckage of "the dead land" and the "Unreal City." Salinger indicates this as each story hinges on a self-reflective action of the characters, which restores them to a more ordered existence. Eloise in "Uncle Wiggily" is brought back to a desire to be "a nice girl;" Ginnie dissolves her bitter dispute with Selena over money by consciously accepting the gift of half a sandwich in

"Eskimos;" Boo Boo Tannenbaum salvages her son's wounded innocence in "Down at the Dinghy;" the protagonist of "De Daumier Smith's Blue Period" has a quiet revelation that brings him to drop his pretenses and lovingly accept the faults of others, which are his faults, too-an act which registers with the last lines of "The Burial of the Dead," "mon sembable, mon fri ɑ re!" (My likeness, my brother!) (*The Waste Land* 53); the mentally and spiritually damaged Sergeant X in "For Esmé" attempts to communicate his troubles to the outside world and through this discovers a token of love that draws him out of his spiritual and physical squalor and restores his "f-a-c-u-l-t-i-e-s."

All these instances originate from Seymour's suicide, which, as sacrifice, operates to "put [his] lands in order" like the Fisher King of *The Waste Land*. Seymour is principal to *Nine Stories* and his actions resonate throughout the rest of the collection until they come to their resolution in the reflective and startlingly cogent precociousness of Teddy, whose death reflects Seymour's own. Teddy's prescience of his own death alters the way in which Seymour's own premeditation must be read. In fact, the two figures meet their deaths so unflappably that they exhibit precisely what Eliot approximates as "the peace which passeth understanding" in the closing words of *The Waste Land*, "Shantih shantih shantih." Hence, the concluding reiteration of Seymour's restorative sacrifice in "Teddy" extends its reach outside the story and ought to have resonating, "reverberating" (*For Esmé* 149) effects in the reader as they finish the book. The restoration that Salinger performs throughout the book is not limited to the characters in it but to the reader who encounters *Nine Stories*.

It does not take a great stretch of imagination to link Eliot and Salinger as accomplices in literature. In fact, this type of dialogue is more and more the norm throughout the twentieth century. Salinger never shied from giving credit in his fiction to those who influenced him and "Bananafish" is no different as it all but discloses that *The Waste Land* is its primary conversant. And while Salinger is borrowing liberally from the poem, he is nevertheless discovering new territories and retracing the boundaries of where the waste of western culture can be found. After all, the story ends on a cruise line that is *leaving* the dead land of Eliot's poem, England, and heading for the shores of America, where Seymour sat at the beginning of the collection surveying the wreckage around him. Salinger expresses the urgency to resist any continuation of the cultural waste land and suggests that in a different land, the view from the shore is that restoration is possible and is achieved through great sacrifice, which collects, repurposes, and reinvents life out of "a heap of broken images," which both Eliot and Salinger have effectively "shored up" to keep their world from ruin.

Endnotes:

E1: Yet, it is in this helpful metaphor that a difference arises, as well. In the Arthurian myths that detail the Fisher King's situation, the wound, and therefore the land, is only healed by obtaining the Holy Grail. Hence, the Fisher King is an impotent agent who must idly wait before he goes about restoring his land. Seymour, however, does not have to wait but exhibits a more capable agency in his determinate action at the end of the story. This difference between the two central figures of each work indicates Salinger's extension and application of *The Waste Land* and in this way he refreshes the poem and its subject as a valid and pressing cultural question. Seymour goes beyond the Fisher King as the sole arbiter of change, even though he follows the pattern of that change in the act of his suicide.

E2: The *Upanishad* relates a time when gods, men, and asuras lived and learned with Prajapati, the great teacher.

"Then the gods said: 'Teach us, sir!' In reply Prajapati uttered one syllable: 'Da.' Then he said: 'Have you understood?' They answered, 'Yes, we have understood. You said to us, "Damayata-be self-controlled."' 'Yes,' agreed Prajapati, 'you have understood.' Then the men said: 'Teach us, sir!' In reply Prajapati uttered one syllable: 'Da.' Then he said: 'Have you

understood?' They answered, 'Yes, we have understood. You said to us, "Datta-be charitable."' 'Yes,' agreed Prajapati, 'you have understood.' Then the asuras said: 'Teach us, sir!' In reply Prajapati uttered one syllable: 'Da.' Then he said: 'Have you understood?' They answered, 'Yes, we have understood. You said to us, "Dayadhwam-be compassionate."' 'Yes,' agreed Prajapati, 'you have understood.'" (Prabhavananda and Manchester 112)

Salinger's penchant for Eastern mystic texts makes it easy to see how this text in particular, especially given as a solution to Eliot's "Waste Land," would resonate within his work.

E3: Seymour's weapon of choice, the Ortgies 765 caliber, has an embossed "D" on its handle, providing yet another example of Salinger's talent for seamlessly weaving together the symbolic and the realistic-the instrument of Seymour's sacrifice is itself marked by the heavy sound of the thunder.

E4: When Tiresias appears in *The Waste Land* he is, "the most important personage in the poem...the two sexes meet in Tiresias" (70) and he functions as the most perceptive character, who "perceived the scene, and foretold the rest" (60). What Tiresias sees is a pathetic display of passionless sex, in which there is no human communication-both parties are involved in selfish pursuits, the "young man carbuncular . . . makes a welcome [of her] indifference" and she, "bored and tired" wants only to get through it (ibid). Tiresias, "who [has] sat by Thebes below the wall/And walked among the lowest of the dead" (ibid) is compelled to comment on what he has observed and the outcome is that sexual attitudes that do not hinge on human communion provide fates graver than death itself.

E5: To confirm this assessment one need only to look at the voices at the end of "A Game of Chess" mentioned earlier, who discuss quite frankly and unaffectedly the banalities of birth-control:

... and think of poor Albert,

He's been in the army four years, he wants a good time,

And if you don't give it him, there's others will, I said.

... I can't help it, she said, pulling a long face,

It's them pills I took, to bring it off, she said

(She's had five already, and nearly died of young George.)

The chemist said it would be all right, but I've never been the same.

You are *a proper fool, I said.*

Well if Albert won't leave you alone, there it is, I said,

What you get married for if you don't want children? (*The Waste Land* 56-57).

E6: However, these stories do not depict mere cruelness just as Seymour's suicide is not merely cruelness to his wife. Since Seymour is the paradigm for the rest of the stories in the collection, the deaths in these two stories- i.e., the Laughing Man's death and the death of Esmé's parents-work through the semblance of cruelty to accomplish particular restorations. In the latter case, it is Esmé's dead father's watch that is able to restore Sergeant X to his faculties and rescue him from his wasted self, brought about by the squalor of World War II.

It is less clear in the case of "The Laughing Man." While the Chief's narrative functions in a way to perpetuate a kind of childishness, its harsh conclusion shocks the boys back into a less forgiving world of compromise. The first thing that the narrator sees when he gets off the bus, in fact, is a bit of waste paper that reminds him of the red poppy petal mask of the Laughing Man. The restoration in this case is illuminative to the young Comanches, even if it is insensitive.

Works Cited:

Eliot, Thomas S. *The Waste Land*. San Diego [u.a.: Harcourt Brace, 1988. 49-74.

---. and Frank Kermode. "What is a Classic?" *Selected Prose of T. S. Eliot* New York: Harcourt Brace Jovanovich, 1975. 115-31.

Prabhavananda, Swami, and Frederick Manchester. *The Upanishads: Breath of the Eternal : the Principal Texts*. New York: Mentor, 1975.

Salinger, Jerome D. For Esmé-with Love and Squalor *and Other Stories*. London: Penguin, 1994.

---. *Franny and Zooey*. Boston: Little, Brown and Company, 1961.

Uncle Wiggily's Haunted House

Olivia Carr Edenfield
Georgia Southern University

The motif of domestic space in American short fiction has been primarily and practically associated with women simply because they were normally relegated to the home to nest and nurture. Throughout history and present in literature is the social and political conclusion that women usually contend best with feelings of dislocation and flux if they have a secure and defined space. The home, typically a woman's place, became a bastion against the unknown and potentially dangerous wilderness. Kerstin W. Shands defines this idea of home as "a sheltered solitude in which we, shuddering as we withdraw from the cold into snug warmth, are pleasantly aware of stark contrasts" (113). Against the unknown wilderness, home became a sanctuary.

The short story has provided a record of the varying landscapes of the American home, its focus a way to suggest a character's potential for negotiating within the expected framework of social codes and behaviors. From

Washington Irving to Tobias Wolff, American writers of short fiction have concluded that the ability to move through crisis to reach a sense of healing has in part hinged on the level of comfort within one's domestic sphere. For Eloise Wengler, in J. D. Salinger's "Uncle Wiggily in Connecticut," home feels anything but comfortable, and she is at odds with everything and everyone around her. Each reference she makes to her house reveals her discontentment.

She cannot find a comfortable pillow; she hates the rug in her living room, the room in her house where the majority of the action takes place. She avoids her kitchen, typically the center of domestic life and representative of a place of nourishment and warmth. Instead, she has surrendered that space to her housekeeper, Grace, whom she both dominates and is embarrassed by, aware that her maid is a better caretaker of her daughter than she. Her house serves as a metaphor for her entrapment. Isolated, Eloise lives in the past, unwilling or unable to let go of her former self, a girl who had good qualities that she now desires. Discontented, she rejects both her husband and her daughter as she resists being the wife and mother she ought to be.

As with many of Salinger's protagonists, Eloise is dealing with death, living with loss, but not very successfully. She clings to the memory of Walter Glass, her former boyfriend killed in a freakishly random accident when a stove that he was packing for an army officer exploded in his face. She believes that she is still in love with him, and though half a dozen years have passed, she is still haunted by his memory. Paul Levine asserts that she "can find no object, she thinks, worthy of her love. Thus she loves nothing-neither husband, home, nor child-but the memory of Walt" (110). Eloise's problem is exacerbated by the fact that she has no one to talk to, no one with whom to share the real depth of her grief. She has not found anyone since Walt who can make her laugh, and her need for some levity is clear. John Wenke also comments on her sense of entrapment, stating that "she imprisons herself and tortures others" (39).

Eloise is insensitive to the people around her, yes, but not necessarily because she wants to be cruel; rather, intensely depressed, she is living in a well of loneliness with the ghost of Walt as present in her life as her daughter, Ramona's, imaginary friends, Jimmy Jimmereeno and Mickey Mickeranno, are to Ramona. Emotionally lazy, she blames others for her unhappiness. She does not try to reach out to those around her; instead, she shuts herself off, unwilling to make an authentic connection with her husband or child.

Eloise's house is in a suburb in Connecticut, miles away from the activity and stimulation of New York, where her previous life took place. She appears to be trapped in a neighborhood without anyone to whom she can connect, in a marriage that does not fulfill her, with the expectation that she should mother a child she is too depressed really even to see, much less love. This confinement in her home and in the prescribed roles that she fails at playing are, for her, conceptualized as restrictive and stifling. In present discourse, Shands has discovered a trend in American fiction that being "settled is negatively associated with . . . absolutes and closures, with linear time and limitation" (9). Whether Eloise has actively chosen such isolation or not, her insularity has left her without anyone to whom she can confide. She broods instead on memories of Walt, living in cyclical time in her remembrances of their short romance. He has become emblematic of the girl she used to be, a "nice" girl who stands in sharp contrast to the bitter woman she has become.

Except for those college memories that seem more real to Eloise than her current existence, the only action that takes place outside of the house occurs in the opening scene. Eloise has gone out to the driveway to meet her former roommate, Mary Jane, who had gotten lost on her way to visit. Mary Jane missed a turn though she has visited her friend twice before. The fact that she loses her way suggests that a good bit of time has passed since the two have seen each other, a point Mary Jane makes later on in the narrative. She had planned to come for lunch, a meal now ruined due to her late arrival, everything "burned-sweetbreads, everything" (18). By the time she shows up, it is mid-afternoon, and Eloise stands with her collar turned up, "her back to the wind," waiting (18). This outward posture mirrors the storm she is weathering internally. Out of sync with her current life, she has hunkered down within herself, present, whether in real time or in memory, only to those people who remind her of her former life before she, too, got lost.

The only detail Salinger gives of the landscape surrounding Eloise's house is "soiled snow" (19), a fitting description for the extension of her domestic sphere. She is seemingly trapped in a marriage that bores her, focused inwardly, selfishly unaware of her daughter and willfully contemptible towards her husband, living in a house where she is not comfortable in a landscape that mirrors her cold heart. Doreen Massey has pointed out that space "is not a 'flat' surface . . . because the social relations which create it are themselves dynamic by their very nature" (265). Eloise has changed as her life has become increasingly less satisfying. She has not matured into the role of mother or wife; instead, the narrator refers to her as a girl (19). Even the title itself connects her to a character from a children's story, and her life in Connecticut is more fantasy than fact. As Shands states, "Throughout the centuries, feminists have implied that women's lot has overwhelmingly been one of confinement, a word . . . that carries associations to both birth and death, to beginnings and endings, to imprisonment and restriction as well as to oppressive boundaries and limited horizons" (59). Eloise's house is no safe warren against the world. Instead, it is a haunted house peopled by a ghost and her daughter's imaginary playmates.

Therefore, it is not surprising that, though she plays hostess, Eloise is not the one who has arranged Mary Jane's visit; instead, it is Mary Jane who has gone out of her way to see her former roommate. The two are seemingly connected by bonds of the past, not by anything they currently have in common. Neither finished college, both having left without completing their second year. Likewise, both married men whom they did not really know. Mary Jane's husband "spent two of the three months Mary Jane had been married to him in jail for stabbing an M.P." (19) while Eloise's husband, at least from her point of view, is "too damn unintelligent" for her to confide in (30). Divorced, Mary Jane has a career in the city while Eloise has gotten married, had a child, and moved to the suburbs. The former college roommates can talk about superficial things, gossiping about girls they knew from school, but Mary Jane has not been a friend to whom Eloise could confide.

Left alone in the living room while Eloise mixes their second cocktail, Mary Jane is uncomfortable and "wanders," having "little or no wherewithal for being left alone in a room" (21). She moves towards a window: "She drew aside the curtain and leaned her wrist on one of the crosspieces between panes, but, feeling grit, she removed it, rubbed it clean with her other hand, and stood up more erectly" (21). The dirty widows in the Wengler house focus the action internally rather than externally and further reinforce the lack of perception-the inability to see outside of herself-that plagues Eloise. Conversely, Mary Jane is more in tune with the conditions outside of the house, the slush turning to ice that will complicate her getting on down the road to her boss's house where she is expected. She moves past the bookshelves without noticing the titles and instead picks up a mirror to study her teeth. This disinterestedness in the internal landscape of her friend's home reflects her inability to comprehend Eloise's depression.

Ironically, the young Ramona comes much closer than Mary Jane does in connecting to Eloise's pain. Levine sees Ramona's make-believe world "mirroring not only her own loneliness but her mother's marital predicament" (110). Like her mother, Ramona has no friends in the neighborhood. Each is cut off in their upper-middle class suburban house, and, desperate for connection, Eloise conjures Walt's ghost while, in turn, her daughter brings to life first Jimmy and then Mickey. These imaginary males provide an escape for the females who suffer from loneliness and isolation. Mother and daughter are trapped, in contrast to the images they concoct.

Eloise's memories of Walt are kinetic. She remembers the two of them in motion: running for a bus; riding on the train, yet snuggled like rabbits under her coat, his hand on her stomach. That he should find comfort there is a positive sign of their connection at the time, as her womb, a potential warren for their children, would have been beautiful to him: "Anyway, all of a sudden he said my stomach was so beautiful he wished some officer would come up and order him to stick his other hand through the window. He said he wanted to do what was fair" (29). **(E1)** Walt is more to Eloise than just a boy who made her laugh. He made her happy, and this sense of fairness made her feel safe and loved.

Likewise, Eloise remembers running for a bus and falling down, injuring herself and being soothed by Walt, who rubbed her ankle, comforting her: "He said, 'Poor Uncle Wiggily.' He meant my ankle. Poor old Uncle Wiggily, he called it. . . . God, he was nice" (28). This story from her past both sets up the conflict in the present action and foreshadows her later fall into grief over Walt's death. She remains uncomforted due to her unwillingness to share her pain with anyone. In the Uncle Wiggily stories by Howard Garis that Walt alludes to, the title character, a sweet elderly rabbit, is rheumatic and myopic. When Walt first calls Eloise "[p]oor Uncle Wiggily," the reference is unfortunately portentous, suggestive of the woman she will later become: she lives in a fantasy world, emotionally crippled, without a clear vision of what to do to make her life any better.

She cannot see how to move ahead in or away from her marriage to Lew, nor will she bring into focus the possibilities for love available in a relationship with her daughter. Her life is in stasis, and her unhappiness has hardened her and made her cold; her home has become the igloo referenced in the novel her husband admired, where the characters starve-much in the way that Eloise is deprived of and in turn withholds the nourishing sense of connection that they all need. Where Walt was nice, she has turned bitter, overcritical, self-deprecating, living in the past rather than embracing the life she has before her. As Wenke says, "Eloise has consigned herself to an emotional penal colony: she imprisons herself and tortures others" (39). She is trapped while her memories of Walt occur in motion, offering her temporary movement away from her misery.

In Connecticut, where Eloise lives with a man she defines as unimaginative and limited, she has disconnected from her daughter, who she says looks so much like her husband and mother-in-law, with whom there is obvious conflict, that Ramona has become a living reminder of what was not to be. "When his mother comes over," she tells Mary Jane, "the three of them look like triplets" (23). Eloise may fear that she has reproduced Lew, and she spends most of her time with her child correcting her behavior, in part, perhaps, to condition her away from her father. In fact, Ramona is much like her mother, having inherited her loneliness, evidenced by the imaginary friends who fill her days just as the ghost of Walt Glass fills her mother's. Neither mother nor daughter has anyone in the neighborhood with whom they connect. Isolated, each lives in an imaginative world.

Mimicking her mother, Ramona has conjured a figure capable of action, a boy who wears boots and carries a sword, which, as Wenke rightfully states, "provides an image of power and romance" (39). This imaginary friend is always with Ramona; he is her "beau," as her mother tells Mary Jane: "Goes where she goes. Does what she does" (24). Since Ramona can seem to do nothing that escapes her mother's criticism, having a boot-clad boyfriend armed with a weapon would be a comfort. Though she will not kiss her mother's friend, in spite of Mary Jane's very friendly overtures and compliments, she holds Jimmy Jimmereeno's hand, a further connection to her power source that mirrors the bond Eloise still has for Walt; however, the true dominance in her relation to Jimmy over her mother's memory of Walt is that she claims she can see her beau. She tells Mary Jane that he is there, with her, in the living room. Mary Jane at first cannot tease out what Ramona means: "I don't get it," she says to Eloise, who ironically responds, "Don't look at *me*" (25).

Eloise cannot see that she is responsible for her child's make-believe friend. Because Ramona lives outside of her mother's affections, she seeks it, in the same way that her mother does, from her own imagination. It is Mary Jane, for all of her inability to understand her friend's unhappiness, who actually sees Ramona, who speaks "cordially" to Jimmy, leaning forward politely in her efforts to engage Ramona (25). Alas, however, Jimmy cannot speak to Mary Jane any more than Ramona will connect with her. Unfortunately, as Bernice Goldstein and Sanford Goldstein point out, the "child Ramona with her childlike spontaneous imaginative power is on the verge of having these qualities eradicated by her mother" (83). Eloise's treatment of her daughter has already made the child suspicious and closed off, and the condescending way in which she treats Ramona's make-believe world will eventually wear away the child's attempts to build a structure of support, even if the system is imaginary rather than real. Of coursethis make-believe world that Eloise mocks is patterned after her own behavior, and Eloise's ill treatment of her daughter is compounded by the way she speaks to her, talking down to her, falling into commands rather than engaging in conversation.

David L. Stevenson sees in Salinger a pattern of characters who "exist outside the charmed circle of the well-adjusted," aware "of the uncrossable gulf between their need for love and the futility of trying to achieve it on any foreseeable terms" (39). Likewise, William Wiegand sees the Wenglers as part of the characters who suffer from banana fever, a "diagnosis" that "applies to all the Salinger invalids. . . . What is unbearable is that experience is fleeting" (125, 126). He holds Eloise accountable for not picking up the pieces and moving on, calling her a "bitch" who is compensated enough by being able to act on that fact (128) and suggests that since she makes life hell for her husband, she should be satisfied that he is equally miserable. He concludes that Eloise "knows the consequences of her bitchiness" (129), seen in her reaction to her daughter's taking her playmates to bed, making room for one and then the other. In the end, Wiegand's analysis seems unfair and fails to take into account the awareness that comes to Eloise in the final scene. Ramona's apparent ability to replace Jimmy with Mickey proves an ironic catalyst that will move Eloise to examine herself and her relationship to her child.

Eloise has accepted Jimmy and insists that Ramona give Mary Jane all the facts. Ramona describes her friend, his green eyes and black hair; interestingly, he has no parents, a detail apparently no more significant on the surface that the fact that he has freckles. When Mary Jane presses her for information, the child looks back with eyes "behind thick, counter-myopia lenses," that "did not reflect even the smallest part of Mary Jane's enthusiasm" (25). This is not a happy child, and her eyesight symbolizes both her mother's and her own inherited inability to see beyond their immediate pain and isolation. While Mary Jane is interested in Ramona, stating three times that she is "dying to see her" (23), her mother speaks to her child with her eyes shut.

In spite of the worsening weather, Ramona had been left alone to play outside. When she does come in on her own from the cold, she eavesdrops, listening in from the hall on the women's conversation. Once she is discovered, Eloise immediately sends her out to the kitchen to have her wet shoes removed. The maid, Grace, takes care of Ramona since Eloise lacks what the housekeeper's name suggests, grace as a mother, grace towards the child she should love and protect rather than criticize and ignore. When Mary Jane asks about Ramona's eyes, if they have gotten worse, Eloise hardly knows the answer: "God! I hope not. . . . She won't tell anybody" (24). That the little girl is "lousy with secrets" is another trait she has inherited from her mother, a fact that Wenke also notes (40). Undemonstrative, she solemnly stands before Eloise, accepting her criticisms: "Stop that" (24). "Stand still." "Cut that out. But immediately."

No matter how "provocatively" (25) her mother's friend smiles at her, no matter that she flatters her pretty dress, Ramona simply wants to escape, to go outside and play and to recover Jimmy's sword that he has left outside. Asking only for a burned match in the ashtray, and corrected by her mother for her manner of asking, the child leaves, telling her friend, "C'mon, Jimmy," calling him by his name, a courtesy her mother never grants her (27). As Ruth Prigozy points out, from the story's opening, Eloise is characterized by her speech as hypercritical of everyone: "Linguistic patterns are again both subtle and obvious. Eloise never addresses Ramona by name, and she is consistently critical and irritable. . . . Eloise censures and corrects; she is unresponsive, indeed blind, to her daughter's obvious loneliness and misery" (50). Eloise does not see her child, but turns selfishly inward, focusing only on herself.

Eloise has nothing new in her life worth talking about. Though she and Mary Jane seem not to have seen each other in a while, there is nothing to report. She talks about the past instead, old friends from college, details about their clothes, seemingly random and unimportant, but everything tied to a specific time that is all that matters anymore to Eloise. Each memory down to the "darling blue cardigan" (29) is there because of its relationship to Walt. Mary Jane belongs to that time when Eloise was connected to Walt, when, she believes, she was still a nice person, and their conversation is about the people they remember from school. The depth of Eloise's sadness is revealed in her response to the news that their former professor is dead: "Whiting got cancer last summer and died and all. She only weighed sixty-two pounds. When she died. Isn't that terrible?" "No," Eloise answers.

Unsurprisingly, Mary Jane misses the point. Eloise is not "hard as nails" (22), as her seemingly cruel remark suggests. Rather, she is too sensitive for her own well being. Her current life is so unsatisfying, her depression so intense, that death for her would not be such a terrible thing. Just as Whiting lost weight, shrinking down to a child's size, Eloise, too, is disappearing. She is most content in her memories, ghostlike, more connected to the dead than to the living. To compensate for her unhappiness, she makes jokes, gossips, and drinks too much. And she picks at her daughter as a way to distance herself, not willing or able to invest in her current life in any meaningful way. Fulfillment may come to Eloise only in death, and her many references to dying have been remarked upon. **(E2)** When Mary Jane says that she needs to leave, that her boss is expecting her, Eloise is insensitive, ignoring her friend's concern that the roads are getting dangerously icy, that her car is low on anti-freeze: "Let it freeze," she tells her friend. "Go phone. Say you're dead. . . . Call up and say you were killed" (27).

Death, apparently, is desirable, an excuse that she can use to avoid obligations. Though she is at first unaware of Ramona's presence in the hallway where she listens in on her mother's conversation, the child has overheard; that death is not so terrible makes an impression on the young girl that only becomes apparent later in the narrative.

Like her daughter, Eloise is a secret keeper. Though she finally does share with her friend the details involving Walt's death, apparently revealing the story for the first time to anyone, Mary Jane never really understands the degree of Eloise's suffering. Though she does the best she can to be sympathetic, her perception is limited. Nevertheless, she gives good advice. She urges Eloise to engage in the life that she has rather than rejecting it for a past life that is impossible to reconstruct. When Eloise talks about Walt's ability to make her laugh, Mary Jane asks, "Doesn't Lew have a sense of humor?" (28)

She also encourages Eloise to share her pain with her husband, but Eloise immediately rejects this: "Oh, you can tell them stuff. But never honestly. I mean never *honestly*. . . . they'll listen very *maturely* and all that. They'll even look intelligent as hell. But don't let it fool you. Believe me. You'll go through *hell* if you ever give 'em any credit for intelligence. Take my word" (30-31). She lies by omission to her own husband, yet she expects her friend to take her at her word; she is being dishonest with everyone around her, including herself. Eloise has romanticized her affair with Walt to such a degree that she is unable to reconcile herself to her current situation, which will always pale in comparison. The routines of daily life, full of mundane responsibilities, rarely measure up to an idealized fantasy world. Since Walt is no longer living, he can never disappoint. Full of the limitations of flesh and blood-and, ironically, of the possibilities-husband and daughter suffer by comparison.

Eloise, therefore, shares nothing with Lew, who knows little of Walt beyond his being somebody she "went around with," some "wisecracking G.I." (32). She tells Mary Ann that the last thing she would do would be to tell her husband that Walt had been killed. "He'd be a ghoul" (32), she tells her friend. She rejects Mary Jane's advice to open up and is stuck with a man with whom she insists she has nothing in common. While she is smart and funny, she sees her husband as a stupid oaf, suggested by his taste in books. She tells Mary Jane that, while she married Lew because she thought he read Jane Austen, she later learned that he had never read even one of her novels, that he lied about her books meaning "a great deal to him" (31).

In contrast, his favorite author is L. Manning Vines, though he isn't "honest enough" to come out with the real reason why he likes his work, "because it was about four guys that starved to death in an igloo or something. He has to say it was beautifully written" (32). Ironically, she condemns Lew for his dishonesty when she, herself, is living a lie every day. Eloise has married a man she is determined not to know, who, she has decided, will judge her unfairly if she confides in him. To compensate, she lives in her imagination, disconnected from the world around her. She rejects her family without ever giving husband or daughter a chance. For a woman who claims to admire fairness, she shows little of her own.

When Eloise does attempt to share her pain, opening up to her friend about her feelings for Walt and her present unhappiness, Mary Jane, unfortunately, does not understand the depths of her depression. **(E3)** Realizing this, Eloise leads their conversation back towards general gossip. Later, when she tells Mary Jane about Walt's accident, she begins to cry, her hand wrapped around an empty glass. In that moment, Mary Jane gives her the best advice she can: "Don't cry. . . . I mean it isn't worth it or anything" (33). Immediately, the front door opens, and Ramona returns from outside. Into the middle of her misery walks the best hope Eloise has for overcoming her melancholy, love from an imaginative child capable of forgiveness who could offer the gift of healing grace. Instead, Eloise rejects this opportunity and sends Mary Jane out to the kitchen to see about Ramona's supper rather than seeing to her daughter's nourishment. Perhaps that room is too painful a reminder of how she came to lose Walt, who was killed by a stove that blew up in his face: "[T]ell whosis to give her her dinner early. . . . I don't feel like going out to that damn kitchen right this minute" (33). She avoids that space and, likewise, avoids the housekeeper, Grace, whose name she cannot bring herself to speak, just as she avoids the restorative grace inherent in her child.

To heal, Eloise needs the redemptive power of love. She must reach out to her child, and the first step towards that is recognizing the injury she has done to her daughter by her emotional distance. Rather, she keeps away from Grace, sidestepping any such connection with the one caretaker in the house. It is Grace who takes off Ramona's wet galoshes, who takes her upstairs to eat her supper in isolation, who puts her to bed. Eloise selfishly pretends that Ramona has a fever, inventing an excuse to get rid of her daughter so she can drink and tell stories from her past.

Eloise wakes in the dark to a ringing phone. Though she is supposed to meet her husband's train, she is drunk, so she lies to him to keep from driving to the station. This exchange is a metaphor for their current relationship. Lew is stuck outside of the house that is haunted by his wife's ghost. Eloise fibs and is obviously unconcerned with her husband's welfare, joking with him that he should "form a platoon and march home. . . . You can be the big shot" (35). The reference to the army denotes her memory of Walt, with whom she rode happily on a train, and this association intensifies her sadness: "I'm not funny. . . . Really, I'm not," she tells Lew. "It's just my face" **(E4)** (35). Such self-deprecation is evidence of her own self-loathing. She knows she is a bitter woman whose unhappiness makes her over-critical.

Her insensitivity continues in the scene that follows. She walks unsteadily away from the phone and back into her living room. She sits in the dark in her haunted house, shivering from the last shot of Scotch. Into this hopeless scene, Grace appears, metaphorically indicative of Eloise's need. Grace turns on the dining room light, which illuminates her, a symbol of all of the redemptive possibilities that her name and her responsibilities in that house suggest. This encounter with Grace sparks the epiphany that follows. Earlier in the afternoon, Eloise had confided in Mary Jane that she had done everything to get Grace to follow her to the suburbs. She is presently incapable of taking care of her house or her child on her own. She needs Grace. Yet Grace stands disconnected, rejected by Eloise, who will not even allow her employee's husband to spend the night to save him the potentially dangerous drive back into the city. Eloise is selfish, perhaps jealous of the thought of two people who love each other in bed together under her roof. "I'm afraid he can't spend the night here, Grace. . . . I say I'm afraid he can't spend the night here. I'm not running a hotel" (36). Her choice of words is revealing; Eloise is afraid, fearful of the person she has become.

Her fear, turned to anger, is played out when she climbs the stairs to her daughter's room and flings the child's rubber boot, left in hallway, over the banister, throwing with as much force as possible. It "struck the foyer floor with a violent thump" (36). Rather than following the shoe over the railing, a real possibility after all of her many references to death, she moves towards her daughter's room. Elevated now by having moved to the second floor of her house, away from the living room where the day's events have been more connected to the past than the present state of living, she stands framed in her daughter's bedroom door. She has moved from the darkness of the hallway, turning on the light in Ramona's room. For seemingly the first time all day, she actually looks at her child, seeing her in full light. "Wake up. Wake up," she tells her (36). She moves quickly towards Ramona, pulling her out of sleep to interrogate her, and Salinger writes, "Her eyes opened wide, but she narrowed them almost at once" (37); without her glasses, folded neatly on her bedside table, Ramona is unable to clearly see her mother, who frightens her. In the exchange that follows, Eloise learns that the space in the bed next to Ramona has been reserved for her daughter's new imaginary friend, Mickey Mickeranno. Ramona will not obey her mother, who commands her, shrieking at her to "get in the center of that bed" (37).

Ramona does not want to hurt Mickey, who has replaced Jimmy, who died after willfully disobeying Eloise's warning to stay out of the street. Asserting her own will, the child has been able to do what the mother would or could not. She has moved on from the death of her imaginary friend, filling his void with a new beau whom she is careful not to hurt. By comparison, Eloise has not progressed, and she has not been mindful, as her daughter has been, of the male who shares her bed. Incensed, she screams at her daughter to move over, and Salinger details how "Ramona, extremely frightened, just looked up at Eloise," who eventually drags her by the ankles. The child, Salinger continues, "let herself be moved without actually submitting to it" (37).

Just as her mother has looked at her, she, too, in spite of her bad vision, sees her mother and does not fully give in to her anger. Knowing how she must appear to her child, Eloise commands her, "Close your eyes. . . . You heard me, *close* them" (37). This perception of herself, actually seeing herself through her daughter's eyes, temporarily overwhelms her. When she takes her child by the ankles, the action mirrors Walt taking her own ankle years before, right after she fell. She stands now, about to fall again by failing to connect to her child. She turns off the light, momentarily suggesting that she is back to the same unawareness that she was in before she ascended the stairs.

However, in the half-light of the doorway, neither in nor out, but in between, Eloise stands "for a long time" (38). She is in a state of becoming and again, in quick action, she rushes into her child's room. Like the night years ago, she injures herself, crashing into the foot of the bed, "but too full of purpose to feel pain" (38). Though she is wounded, she is full of will, and she makes her way over to her daughter's glasses, letting go, crying as her tears wet the lenses. "Poor Uncle Wiggily," she says over and over, stroking this extension of her child. She holds her daughter's glasses against her cheek, suggesting that she finally sees exactly how her daughter perceives her. What she should have loved, she has ignored in place of her memories, her pain, her selfish bitterness. She has made a mess of things, and she carries this though by carelessly returning the glasses lenses down. She loses her balance as she attempts to tuck in Ramona's blankets. The child, too, is crying, has been crying. Now her mother attempts to comfort her by kissing her on the mouth while wiping the hair from her eyes, caressing her daughter who, from lack of habit, does not like to be hugged. **(E5)**

Eloise surely recognizes that she needs to reach out to her child and to do so must become the person she assures herself she used to be, whom she is still capable of being. Descending the stairs, leaving this elevated moment of awareness, she wakes up Mary Jane as a way to continue and assert what she wants to recapture in herself: "I was a nice girl" (38), she pleads. If this is true, and of course it must be or she would not be struggling so now, she can find her way back there again. But whether or not she can renew herself depends on her receptivity to Grace, an inability earlier evidenced and symbolically suggested by her bad treatment of her house-keeper. Yet it was Grace who turned on the light in the dining room, an action which brought her back to herself, and this chain of events led her up the stairs to an example played out by her daughter of the exact grace that she needs: the ability to move on from the memory of Walt in the way that her daughter has moved on from Jimmy.

When Eloise strokes her daughter's spectacles at the end of the story, she is reminded of Walt's Uncle Wiggily and at the same time realizes how her own melancholia, her own concentrated inwardness, has rubbed off on her child. Living in a haunted house, Ramona has mimicked her mother, creating her own ghosts with whom to pass the time. In her moment of epiphany, aware of her child's ability to move on from the death of one friend into concern for another, she understands what she must do. That she wants to return to a previous state of innocence is clear. As Arthur Heiserman and James E. Miller, Jr., have written, "love is the dominant trait of all Salinger's heroes, and when it is thwarted the hero either shoots himself . . . or goes berserk or melancholic. . . . But when, on the other hand, a person finds a way to love the world, then that person is saved from madness and suicide. . . . Salinger thus diagnoses the neurosis and fatigue of the world in one simple way: if we cannot love, we cannot live" (200). Eloise has been dangerously close to suicide, suggested by all of her earlier references to death. Her strongest attachment is to a young man no longer living. Part of her attraction to him is that he has attained that peaceful world of the dead, though he goes on living in her memory.

To live, to really live the life that she has before her, she must surrender Walt to the past and embrace her child in present time. As Wiegand summarizes, her "sense of loss ought to be overcome . . . remembering too much is a bad thing" (10). Whether or not she can sustain this desire to love remains outside of the story's frame, but as Levine rightfully asserts, the "only thing that remains for Eloise is to reaffirm the possession of innocence in the past" (110). This innocence can come through her acceptance of the grace available to her as she forgives her past mistakes and embraces her child. In doing so, her tears, connecting her to the tears she cried in college before her fall from grace, will start a cleansing so that she can better see her way through to love her child and rid their house of ghosts.

Endnotes:

E1: Bernice Goldstein and Sanford Goldstein make much of Walt's wanting to do what is fair. "Being fair from a Zen point of view is not to separate joy from pain; it means that 'beauty' or 'pain' or 'death' or 'sorrow' is not a separate category in which things, moments, persons are given names, are described by adjectives. Walt is well on the road to awareness" (83). Though Goldstein and Goldstein never go on to nail down specifically how this "fairness" fits into the text, perhaps it can be explained here. Walt has one hand that is warm and connected to Eloise's stomach; to balance that warmth, he looks for someone to command his other hand to the cold outside of the train. Wenke sees Walt's "odd remarks" as a "way of speaking about love, the words suggesting rather than denoting the nature of the feeling." He was, as Wenke says, "Eloise's lost idyll" (39).

E2: As Wenke points out, Eloise "seems close to desperation." He correctly asserts that her "language, at times, betrays a fixation with death" (40). Even her mention of Akim Tamiroff, who, perhaps not consequently, had won a nomination for best actor in the 1943 movie adaptation of Ernest Hemingway's *For Whom the Bell Tolls*, can be read with death in mind.

E3: Levine is particularly hard on Mary Jane and the conversations the two have: "Eloise's language is constantly impoverished by the mundane, by movies and clothes. Not only is the means of communication lacking but also the object of it. The irony lies in the discrepancy between Eloise's need to get outside of herself and the means and object left open to her: the insensitive, stupid girl friend, Mary Jane" (110). This criticism is too severe. Mary Jane is not stupid, but preoccupied with where she knows she should be, on the road towards her boss's house, fulfilling her responsibilities. These feelings are set against the obligations she feels towards her friend, mirroring the entrapment that Eloise feels. Mary Jane, for the most part, is simply uninformed. Eloise is not forthcoming, but by and large hides the details of her suffering behind deceptively simple conversation.

E4: Frederick L. Gwynn and Joseph L. Blotner conclude that "the motifs of Eloise's overt inhumanity and her secret innocent love" are brought together later in the narrative by "her sudden identification of herself with Ramona. To appreciate this climax," they assert, "the reader must utilize a fact about Eloise almost concealed by Salinger-her unprepossessing face" (23). For Gwynn and Blotner, the mother sees her own unattractiveness reflected in her "myopic daughter," and that creates "an active bond, albeit brief and drunken" (23).

E5: Goldstein and Goldstein are not convinced that Eloise reaches any epiphany: "Eloise's symbolic gesture at the end of the story, a gesture that finds her replacing her daughter's glasses lens down . . . reveals the lack of vision of the adult whose perpetual conflict is her marriage to her husband and the death of the spontaneous Walt" (83). While they conclude that Eloise is incapable of redemption, David D. Galloway sees this scene as Eloise's "alcoholic vision of the sophisticated squalor of her life and a moment of visionary love with her escapist daughter." Through "the innocent love of a child Eloise achieves a moment of salvation." He concludes, however, that her awareness is "temporary and unstable" (40). Gwynn and Blotner are equally convinced that Eloise's "salvation-by-child" is "abrupt" and "temporary" (23). Dominic Smith, on the other hand, sees the final scene as an "extreme" epiphany "with an extreme reliance on the present, dramatic moment. We don't pull out of the action and filter the epiphany through a changed state of consciousness . . . ; rather, we let the moment speak for itself" (646).

Works Cited:

Galloway, David D. "The Love Ethic." *J. D. Salinger*. Ed. Harold Bloom. New York: Chelsea House, 1987. 29-52.

Goldstein, Bernice and Sanford Goldstein. "Zen and *Nine Stories*." *J. D. Salinger*. Ed. Harold Bloom. New York: Chelsea House, 1987. 81-94.

Gwynn, Frederick L. and Joseph L. Blotner. *The Fiction of J. D. Salinger*. Pittsburg: University of Pittsburg Press, 1958.

Heiserman, Arthur and James E. Miller, Jr. "Some Crazy Cliff." *Salinger: A Critical and Personal Portrait*. Ed. Henry Anatole Grunwald. New York: Harper & Row, 1962. 196-217.

Levine, Paul. "J. D. Salinger: The Development of the Misfit Hero." *J. D. Salinger and the Critics*. Eds. William F. Belcher and James W. Lee. Belmont: Wadsworth, 1962. 107-15.

Massey, Doreen. *Space, Place, and Gender*. Minneapolis: University of Minnesota Press, 1994.

Prigozy, Ruth. "Nine Stories: J. D. Salinger's Linked Mysteries." *Modern American Short Story Sequences: Composite Fictions and Fictive Communities*. Ed. J. Gerald Kennedy. New York: Cambridge University Press, 1995. 119-20.

Salinger, J. D. "Uncle Wiggily in Connecticut." *Nine Stories*. Boston: Little, Brown, 1948. 18-38.

Shands, Kerstin W. *Embracing Space: Spatial Metaphors in Feminist Discourse*. Westport: Greenwood Press, 1999.

Smith, Dominic. "Salinger's *Nine Stories*: Fifty Years Later." *The Antioch Review*. 61.4 (2003): 639-49.

Stevenson, David L. "The Mirror of Crisis." *Salinger: A Critical and Personal Portrait*. Ed. Henry Anatole Grunwald. New York: Harper and Row, 1962. 36-41.

Wenke, John. *J. D. Salinger: A Study of the Short Fiction*. Boston: Twayne, 1991. 123-36.

Wiegand, William. "Seventy-Eight Bananas." *Salinger: A Critical and Personal Portrait*. Ed. Henry Anatole Grunwald. New York: Harper and Row, 1962. 115-36.

From York to Lexington:
A Pilgrimage through Allusions in "Just Before the War with the Eskimos"

Sarah Marshall
Nyack College

The symbolic nature of J. D. Salinger's short stories, and specifically his collection *Nine Stories* (1953), has already been well established. In his article "Religious Symbols in Salinger's Shorter Fiction," James Finn Cotter identifies three important symbols-glass, ashtrays, and the Fat Lady (a symbol for Christ), **(E1)** particularly in connection with their religious significance. However, while symbols, like allusions, point to unseen realities, they are quite different in nature. Symbols are vehicles through which ideas may flow, whereas allusions are specific points of connection between the world of the reader and the author's fictional world that carry with them meanings and associations imbedded in history and culture. These meanings and associations can, in turn, provide a subtext for the main plot, which deepens the themes explored and illuminates enigmatic passages.

In "Just Before the War with the Eskimos" there are allusions to historical events, literature, films, the Bible, and geographic locations. While the allusions might at first seem to be unrelated, there is a common thread that connects them together: war. In light of these allusions to war, Salinger seems to suggest that the main character, Ginnie Mannox, is on a spiritual pilgrimage. This journey physically begins and ends on two different avenues, York and Lexington, both of which have names connected with war. The word "avenue" itself originally derives from a 17th century French military term meaning "way of approach" ("Avenue"). For Ginnie, war is symbolically a way of approach to enlightenment, stripping away social niceties to uncover spiritual realities. Worth noting in Ginnie's "way of approach" is the way it reflects Salinger's own experiences. Kenneth Slawenski, in his 2010 biography of Salinger, argues that the maturation and deepening of the themes that occurred in Salinger's fiction as he grew older is due at least in part to his time spent in active duty on the Western Front during WWII; as Slawenski posits, "through his writings, he sought answers to the questions that his service experiences had exposed, questions of life and death, of God, of what we are to each other" (139).

These questions are at work in "Eskimos" and are most vividly seen through the allusions imbedded in the story. However, in order to appreciate the importance of the allusions, it is necessary to first understand the quality of

Ginnie's character. She tends to be slightly snobbish, and to make quick, superficial judgments; she openly considers "Selena the biggest drip at Miss Basehoar's-a school ostensibly abounding with fair sized drips" (57). Not only does Ginnie have an attitude of superiority towards others, it seems that her family also participates in and encourages this mindset. In a parenthetical comment, Salinger notes that "at dinner one night, for the edification of the entire Mannox family, Ginnie had conjured up a vision of dinner over at the Graffs'; it involved a perfect servant coming around to everyone's left with, instead of a glass of tomato juice, a can of tennis balls" (57). Ginnie does not share this "vision" in order to edify, which means "to instruct and improve especially in moral and religious knowledge" ("Edify"); instead, Ginnie simply shares this image in order to entertain, so that she and her family can indulge in a few laughs at the Graff's expense. The scene contains echoes of the snobbery of old money, chuckling at the pride of the *nouveau riche*; the central background information that is conveyed about Selena, apparently the *only* substantial fact that Ginnie knows about Selena, is that her father manufactures tennis balls. As the reader discovers later on, Ginnie doesn't even know that Selena has a sick mother. However, in spite of the fact that Ginnie seems to be intent on anything other than edifying her family, the reader may be edified by her offering. James E. Bryan, in his article "J. D. Salinger: The Fat Lady and the Chicken Sandwich," provides an alternative symbolic interpretation of Ginnie's "vision": he identifies the perfect servant with Christ, and the red liquid and white solid as the bread (body) and wine (blood) of communion, the Eucharist. In this sense, as Bryan argues, Ginnie ironically foreshadows her own edification. The edification that Ginnie moves toward is embodied in the symbol of the Eucharist alluded to in this passage and hints at her eventual epiphany and the high point of her pilgrimage: a blended balance between the spiritual and the physical, and a communion with suffering humanity (the other partakers in communion).

Ginnie's movement toward edification, her pilgrimage, begins on York Avenue. This avenue is not named after James, the Duke of York, as New York City and York Street are (Feirstein 47), but rather after Sgt. Alvin York (Moscow 114). York was a rough Tennessee farmer who renounced his former violent lifestyle after a conversion experience in 1915 (Lee 10). York's new, non-permissive attitude toward violence came into conflict with his patriotism when, in June 1917, he was drafted. Although York applied for conscientious objector status four times, all of them were denied because his church did not have an official pacifist stance contained in its creed ("the Bible being subject to conflicting interpretations"; Lee 17). While York did report for duty, his mind was still uneasy about killing enemy soldiers. After some time spent in training, York was given a ten-day leave to go home during which he reconsidered his ideas about the ethicality of war. After a mountaintop experience, York returned "convinced that God wanted him to fight and would preserve him unharmed in battle" (Lee 20).

Furthermore, the allusion to Sgt. York has at least two layers. While York's exploits occurred in 1918, and York Avenue was named after him in 1928 (Moscow 114), Salinger's readers would be most familiar with York via the 1941 film *Sergeant York*. Released in the summer of 1941, *Sergeant York* was immediately successful, both critically and popularly (Toplin 99). It was also immediately controversial. The film was examined by a subcommittee of the Senate Interstate Commerce Committee for serving as "highly partisan pro-war and anti-Nazi publicity" (Toplin 100). As the story of a reluctant soldier turned war hero, *Sergeant York* would not be considered politically neutral in the years just prior to Pearl Harbor, when the isolationist / interventionist debate was still raging. The producers of *Sergeant York* foresaw some of the potential controversy that could arise concerning the film's subject matter, and endeavored to market it as "an objective, nonpartisan view of the war hero's life" (Toplin 84). Because of the pressure to avoid being labeled "war propaganda," the film is remarkably accurate to York's life aside from a few dramatic flourishes, which are "mild in comparison to those seen in many later Hollywood productions that portray real-life personalities and events" (Toplin 85). **(E3)**

York, like those who accused the film of being an inexcusable example of war-mongering, did not see the film as an entertaining biography. At the gala events proceeding the film's opening, "York said he hoped that the film would contribute to 'national unity in this hour of danger' when 'millions of Americans like myself, must be facing the same question, the same uncertainties, which we faced and I believed resolved some twenty-four years ago'" (Toplin 98). Although in 1941 York hoped that the film would contribute to the war effort, in the mid-1930s he held a quite different position. Like many other Americans during this time, York was disillusioned with U.S. involvement in World War I, even telling a visitor he did not "see that we did any good" by fighting, and arguing that in the future, the United States should let "those fellows fight their own battles and we'll fight ours when the time comes" (Toplin 84). But by the late 1930s, as the situation in Europe began to appear increasingly grim, York's views shifted (Toplin 87). This shift made him ripe for Jesse Lasky's telegram requesting a meeting to "discuss the making of 'a historical document of vital importance to the country in these troubled times'" (Toplin 88). However, even when production for the film was formally announced, York declared, "I don't like war pictures" and that the film "wouldn't be a war picture" ("Cinema: Sergeant York Surrenders"). York's fluctuating stance reveals the complexity of his internal struggles, a seemingly never-ending battle between spiritual ideals and physical realities. More specifically, it is a difficult choice between an isolationism that prevents direct guilt but may result in more blood shed and an interventionism that may save more lives by taking a few (as is argued in the film *Sergeant York*) but is possibly, in spite of good intentions, futile. **(E4)**

York's ethical dilemma contributes to the dynamic force underlying all of the character's interactions in "Eskimo's" and is part of the fire "between" the words that Salinger strove to create (Slawenski 152). When the cab starts down York Avenue, Ginnie decides to confront Selena with the fact that she has not paid her half of the cab fare for the past few weeks. This is the beginning of a petty war between Ginnie and Selena that occurs with the symbolic landscape of York Avenue as a backdrop; it is Ginnie's "way of approach" into the larger, internal battles that are represented by York Avenue. As the skirmish begins, Selena reminds Ginnie that she always supplies the tennis balls, which is something Ginnie had earlier noted about Selena: "she had never known anyone like Selena for bringing fresh cans of tennis balls" (57). Yet, when it is Selena that brings up this point, it makes Ginnie feel "like killing Selena" (59). She self-righteously proclaims that Selena's provision of the tennis balls doesn't matter because "They don't cost *you* anything. I have to pay for every single little-" (59). Ginnie does not recognize the inadequacy of her argument in that the money she has was originally provided by her parents. Just as the tennis balls haven't cost Selena anything, the money that Ginnie has spent on the cab fares hasn't cost *her* anything.

Although both girls are tight-fistedly materialistic and squabble over who has provided what, Ginnie goes one step further and acts as Selena's judge. When Selena asks for a reprieve until Monday, Ginnie decides that "Selena's attitude defied clemency" (59) and refuses her request. In this, there could be an allusion to Jesus' parable of the unforgiving servant found in Matthew 18.23-35. Like the servant in the parable, Ginnie forgets the debt that she has been forgiven (all of her expenses that her parents have paid for), and coldly demands the small amount of money owed to her-a far sight removed from Christ, the symbolic "perfect servant" of Ginnie's vision. Her hardness is further illustrated when Selena reveals that her mother is quite sick and she may have to wake her up in order to get the money; at this revelation Ginnie brusquely says, "I didn't give it to her" (61) and follows Selena into the elevator. Although Ginnie is "slightly put off by this information" (61), for the sake of her pride she cannot back down.

After they enter the apartment, Ginnie begins "mentally rearranging furniture, throwing out table lamps, removing artificial flowers" (62), and comes to the verdict that it is "an altogether hideous room-expensive but cheesy" (62). Ginnie is, at this point, confirming her opinions regarding the Graffs as revealed by her "vision"; they are tastelessly ostentatious. Ginnie is initially unable or unwilling to look beyond the surface. It is only through human contact that Ginnie's vision is transformed, specifically through an honest conversation with Selena's brother, Franklin. Franklin is the key to Ginnie's progression on her pilgrimage; she is significantly influenced by observing and participating in his existential struggles. The crux of this struggle is the isolationist / interventionist debate intimated by the allusion to Sergeant York. Franklin's tension is fueled by the dual nature of his desires: he wants to isolate himself from the absurd world (he has recently quit his job) and at the same time wishes to intervene in its events and remain connected with humanity. During the war, he was assigned 4-F status due to heart problems, excluding him from participation in the war and further isolating him from society. But Franklin's desire to remain connected with those around him is revealed by his hurt and resentment towards Ginnie's older sister Joan for never answering any of his "eight goddam letters" (69), the relationship that he maintains with Eric (one of his former co-workers at the airplane factory), and his interest in establishing a relationship with Ginnie.

The manner in which Franklin's appearance is described gives further indication of his role in the story. After Ginnie is alerted to Franklin's approach, "She crossed her long legs, arranged the hem of her polo coat over her knees, and waited" (62), a formal description that directly contrasts with Franklin's arrival. He "lunged into the room with his mouth open" and is depicted as "a young man wearing glasses and pajamas and no slippers" (62). Franklin is guileless, and actually lunges into the room with his "mouth open," an action and a posture that are both natural and vulnerable. When he realizes that it is Ginnie sitting there, he simply says, "Oh. I thought it was Eric, for Chrissake" and continues across the room "without stopping" (62). Franklin's appearance and demeanor is a strange mixture of adult and youth; Ginnie thinks that "he was the funniest-looking boy, or man-it was hard to tell which he was-she had ever seen" (63). In this line, Franklin's role is revealed: he is a prophet, a truth speaker who hangs suspended between childhood and adulthood, a position which allows him to serve as a guide, a bridge between the two. **(E5)** Slawenski explains that Salinger's "writings evidence the opinion that children are closer to God than adults, allowing them to love more perfectly, oblivious to the divisions created and used by adults to separate themselves from one another" (172). In this story, instead of a wise child, there is a child-man; Franklin contains both the faith of a child and the wise insight into the absurdity of reality appropriate to a man. **(E6)**

The character of Franklin also experiences human suffering, albeit in a largely metaphorical sense. He enters the room cradling a cut finger, and says "Christ, I'm bleedin' to death. Stick around. I may need a goddam transfusion" (63). In addition to its surface appearance as a facetious hyperbole, it could also be reinterpreted as a secular prayer, with Franklin recognizing his inexorable progression toward death and an intense need for new life, a transfusion of the blood of Christ. The way in which Franklin cuts his finger is also a potent image; he "was lookin' for something in the goddam wastebasket and it was fulla razor blades" (63). Seen from a broader perspective, Franklin is looking for something (which isn't specified-perhaps he is not even sure what that "something" is) in a "wastebasket"-a possible metaphor for the world, perhaps alluding to T. S. Eliot's *The Wasteland*. The world, as Franklin discovers, is "fulla razor blades," and he is cut by them. The revelatory nature of Franklin's injured finger is further emphasized by the fact that he keeps it close to his chest and "unveiled it for Ginnie's benefit" (63) so that she too can share in his experience. For him, it is of the utmost importance; his attitude towards it conveys to Ginnie that in his eyes, it is "the true and only focal point in the room" (64).

Later, when Franklin asks Ginnie how to best heal his wound (66), there exists a microcosmic commentary on the problem of pain. Franklin is appalled by suffering, while Ginnie has a more hardened perspective; pain hurts an awful lot, "but it won't kill you or anything" (66). Franklin protests against the pain, claiming that he doesn't "like it." While Franklin is obviously upset by the initial pain of being cut, in this instance, he is protesting against the pain that comes from cleansing. Cleansing pain can also be associated with the pain that accompanies communion with other people. It is only through contact, through relationships, that one can be either harmed or healed. While Ginnie is more hardened to pain, she recognizes that "it won't kill you or anything"-it is possible to be hurt and still live. This realization is a prerequisite for authentic human relationships, for entering into communion. In this, Ginnie plays the role of guide and helps Franklin on his own journey (which simultaneously assists her pilgrimage). Ginnie also attempts to belittle Franklin's complaint but actually lends it more legitimacy by saying that nobody likes it; i.e. Franklin's response to suffering is not all that uncommon; he is thereby connected with the rest of humanity. Ginnie's reminder that Franklin's experience and response to it are not unique to him alone leads into a type of religious experience for Franklin.

Ginnie tells Franklin to stop touching his cut finger; in other words, to stop reminding himself of the pain and quit making it worse. Franklin's reaction to Ginnie's command is surprising: "As though responding to an electric shock, Selena's brother pulled back his uninjured hand. He sat up a trifle straighter-or rather, slumped a trifle less. He looked at some object on the other side of the room. An almost dreamy expression came over his disorderly features" (66-67). This reaction has religious undertones to it, beginning with the jolt of epiphany, and ending with a dreamy contemplation of an "object," which is really only the vehicle for his meditations. Franklin then inquires as to whether Ginnie has eaten lunch yet, a gesture of hospitality. Additionally, the food that he offers to Ginnie is not from his parent's refrigerator, but rather from his own supply; he has "half a chicken sandwich" (67) stored in his room. At this point, Ginnie staves off his attempt at hospitality, and for now, Franklin seems to accept Ginnie's response.

Franklin then moves to embody the difference and the intersection between the physical and the spiritual planes of existence. He advances to the window, places his foot on the window sill, and leans the arm that bears the cut finger on his leg. From above, he observes what he identifies as the absurd movements of humanity. He sees crowds of people scurrying hither and thither who are, in his eyes, rushing to the draft board in order to "fight the Eskimos next" (72), always eager to fight a new enemy. Franklin's injured hand is aligned with the sidewalk below, thereby connecting his wounded body with those on the street and drawing a parallel to Christ. In Franklin's posture (the intersection between the horizontal and the vertical represented by the position of his arm and leg) there is an allusion to the cross, which is simultaneously a symbol for Christ, the God-made-flesh, and for a crossroad, a point where decisions must be made. In Christianity, the cross is, among other things, a symbol of self-sacrifice, based in part on the biblical passage found in Matthew 17.24 when Jesus says to his disciples, "If any man will come after me, let him deny himself, and take up his cross, and follow me." For Franklin and Ginnie, part of taking up the cross is embracing human relationships and the pain that often accompanies them, while simultaneously seeking to abstain from the absurdity of conventional human behavior.

After Franklin physically alludes to the cross, there is another allusion to the Eucharist, which serves as the fulfillment of Ginnie's symbolic vision. Franklin brings Ginnie the half of a chicken sandwich that he had offered earlier. When Ginnie partakes of the chicken sandwich, it is a moment of communion between Franklin and Ginnie, in which they have now eaten of the same bread (it is only half of a chicken sandwich, implying Franklin has already eaten some). This time, Franklin asks her if it's good; Ginnie agrees by saying, "Very" (74), in response to which Franklin nods, a sort of catechism that confirms the goodness of this meal. Their prior conversation has prepared Ginnie for this moment. Franklin also repeats the apparently important information that it's a *chicken* sandwich, connecting it with the bowl of "consecrated chicken soup" (194) of *Franny and Zooey*. However, while Ginnie is ready for this moment, she is still only able to swallow the sandwich with "difficulty" (74), indicating that the pilgrimage is not yet complete. After Franklin exits the room, Ginnie begins to look around "for a good place to throw out or hide the sandwich" (74). Although she has ingested this symbolically consecrated sandwich, she has not yet fully accepted what it symbolizes: her need for communion. Ginnie is only interrupted in her search for a wastebasket by the sound of someone coming through the foyer, which causes her to stash the sandwich into her polo-coat pocket. This "someone" is Eric, the person whom Franklin has been waiting for.

Eric's first action provides another point of allusion. He sits in a "red damask chair" and, "As if he were generally weary, or had just undergone some form of eyestrain, he rubbed his closed eyes with the tips of his extended fingers" (75). The word "damask" points to another "way of approach" in that the word means "originating at, or pertaining to Damascus" ("Damask"). This connection, along with the focus on Eric's closed eyes conjures up the image of Saul/Paul of Tarsus on the road to Damascus (Acts 9). In the story, Christ speaks to Saul and blinds him for three days. When Paul's sight is restored he becomes one of Christ's disciples. Saul, prior to his vision, had been on the road to Damascus to persecute Christians, waging his own private war. The absurd line of division that is the basis for this war is not determined by race but by religious belief. Eric, (like Saul, Ginnie and Franklin), appears in need of epiphany, so that the scales may fall from his eyes, and he can see existence as it really is, an absurd blend of spiritual and physical, in which Salinger portrays even simple things like chicken sandwiches as expressions of the spiritual realm.

The contrast between Eric and Franklin is drawn when Eric stares "vaguely, discontentedly, in the direction of the windows" (75). At this moment, Eric is unable to have the vision that Franklin has, a simile of a God's-eye-view regarding human activity. Neither does Eric's gaze enable him to have a moment of meditation; it only incites him to vague discontentedness. Eric, like Ginnie, is self-righteous and holds a high opinion of himself, even claiming that he is the "*original* Good Samaritan" (76), an oxymoronic statement that is contradicted throughout Eric's dialogue. He describes the person that he, as the Good Samaritan, attempted to rescue, as an "awful little person from Al*toon*a, Pennsylvania" (76). The description of an "awful little person" is enough to contradict the idea that Eric is any kind of a Good Samaritan, original or not, which is ultimately reinforced by investigating the history behind the city's name. While Salinger may not have had this history in mind, the mere fact that he chose this particular town, out of any other town in Pennsylvania or elsewhere, leaves enough room for the idea that perhaps there is more here than at first meets the eye, especially considering that Salinger was at least somewhat familiar with Pennsylvania, having attended two schools in the state (Slawenski 23). The name of Altoona could possibly be derived from the Latin *altus*, meaning "high," due to its location in the Allegheny Mountains. However, another possible source for the name is the town of Altona, which is a suburb of Hamburg in Germany. Altona, in Germany, is "local dialect for 'all too near,' a centuries-old epithet for Hamburg's outcast quarter" (Crane-Engel).

Besides having a long history of being a town of refuge for Jews when tensions in Hamburg became too heated (Rosen), Altona also has a more recent history of violence and persecution. "Bloody Sunday" occurred on July 17, 1932, just weeks before the Nazi Party came to power in Germany (Ahlers 378). Known as the "Red District" of Hamburg, open violence broke out when thousands of Fascists in brown uniform paraded through the streets of Altona, apparently beginning with Communists opening fire on the parade ("Germany: Bloody Sunday"). A year later, four of the leading Communists in this insurrection were beheaded per the order of then Captain Goring, "because of the heinousness of their treacherous attacks and the desirability of setting a deterrent example" ("Germany: Back to the Axe!"). The division between the opponents in this battle is drawn on the basis of political allegiance, another one of the arbitrary adult divisions intended to separate the world into two categories: "us" and "them."

It is also important to note in this allusion that the division is not only political, but is also based on geographic location. It is a battle between Hamburg and Altona, or for Eric, a battle between New York City and Altoona, "or *one* of those places" (76), a battle between the haves and the have-nots, between the somebodies and the nobodies. This realization underscores the absurdity of these battles and the lines of division that categorizes the world and everyone in it. The next allusion goes even further in challenging these lines of division. Eric announces to Ginnie that he and Franklin are going to attend Cocteau's *Beauty and the Beast*, a film which, Eric insists, is "the *one* film where you really *should* get there on time. I mean if you don't, the whole *charm* of it is gone" (79). This film begins with an epigraph that, in Eric's mind, lends the whole story its charm, its magical quality. This epigraph consists of a homily concerning child-like faith scrawled on a chalk board, and begs the audience to have "a little of this childlike simplicity."

Franklin, as the bridge between youth and adulthood, is able to have the faith of a child, and sees with a child's eyes. It is only this vision that allows any truthful glimpse of the magical (spiritual) dimension. Here is the antidote to the persecutions and oppressions based on identities that lead to war: the visionary faith of a child that does not recognize the seemingly undisputable permanence of dividing lines. In the eyes of a child, there is not an impermeable line between the real and the magical, between the physical and the spiritual, the possible and the impossible. The epigraph of *Beauty and the Beast* concludes "to bring us luck let me speak four truly magic words, childhood's open sesame, 'Once upon a time.'" These "four truly magic words" constitute the well-known beginning phrase of many stories intended for children. It implies that the act of storytelling in and of itself, especially when it concerns children or "very young people" is magical. Stories are in their very nature boundary blurring, consisting of lies that convey truth.Beyond its magical or spiritual nature as a story, the content of "Just Before the War with the Eskimos" is also exploring the spiritual and is seeking to say the open sesame that will open the eyes of the reader.

Ginnie must learn to see with the eyes of a child again in order to complete her pilgrimage. From this point on Ginnie seems to have changed and conveys a quite different attitude; she is nearing the end of her pilgrimage. When Selena re-emerges, Ginnie notices that she had changed her clothes, "a fact that ordinarily would have annoyed Ginnie" (80) but now, after her two encounters, it does not. In addition to her change in demeanor, Ginnie has also changed her goals. She says to Selena, "I don't want the money anyway" and keeps her voice down so that "she was heard only by Selena" (80). Ginnie does not want Eric to hear her magnanimous gesture; instead, she is attempting to be kind in a way that does not directly draw attention to herself. Then, Ginnie invites herself to come back later that night, an unprecedented move on her part considering that this is the first day she has come over to the Graffs' home. In doing this, it may be that Ginnie is attempting to continue and build on her relationship with Selena, and particularly with Franklin, whose refreshingly honest existential views have awakened her to the importance of human connections.

After she exits the building, Ginnie begins to walk toward Lexington Avenue to catch a bus, and "Between

Third and Lexington, she reached into her coat pocket for her purse and found the sandwich half" (81-82). It is at this moment that the pilgrimage is brought to a head; she begins to "bring her arm down, to drop the sandwich into the street, but instead she put it back into her pocket" (82). Ginnie's physical location is in tandem with her internal location. Lexington Avenue is named after the Battle of Lexington and Concord, the first battle of the Revolutionary War, the battle where the "shot heard round the world" was fired. This shot was "a fateful action with momentous consequences," though it is unknown whether the shot was fired by the British or the Americans, intentionally or by accident (French 5-6). What is known is that the sound of it was enough to trigger a battle and ignite an entire war. It is also here that Ginnie has her own private revolution, in which she performs a physical act that carries with it a resounding spiritual effect. Ginnie reaches into her pocket in order to find her purse, a symbol of the financial squabbles fueling her "war" with Selena, and instead finds the chicken sandwich. **(E7)**

By keeping Franklin's sandwich, Ginnie is reaffirming the childlike faith and hope that she once had. The concluding sentence reads, "A few years before, it had taken her three days to dispose of the Easter chick she had found dead on the sawdust in the bottom of her wastebasket" (82). The three days that Ginnie kept this Easter chick alludes to the biblical three days Christ lay in his tomb prior to the resurrection, indicating that Ginnie had kept this Easter chick hoping and believing that it would revive, that it too would experience a resurrection. She finds this chick in the bottom of a wastebasket, just as Franklin finds human suffering in there. Presumably, when the chick did not revive she discarded her childlike simplicity and "grew up." Here it seems that, for Ginnie, the failure of the material world to correspond with her conception of the way the spiritual world should work caused her to reject the possibility of miracles. Now Ginnie stands between Third and Lexington, simultaneously experiencing resurrection and revolution. Although life seems to be a never ending "war with the Eskimos," a movement from one absurd battle to the next, Ginnie holds on to the chicken sandwich, choosing to once again believe, even if all appearances seem to preclude the possibility of hope.

Endnotes:

E1: The Fat Lady, as defined by Zooey in *Franny and Zooey*, is both everyone ("there isn't anyone out there who isn't Seymour's Fat Lady"), and "Christ himself" (Salinger 200). This symbol simultaneously expresses the idea that divinity exists within ordinary objects and persons while drawing attention to the humanity of Christ. Instead of a saintly figure dressed in white with a glowing halo, Christ is a Fat Lady, specifically incarnated for Zooey as a cancer ridden woman who is "sitting on this porch all day, swatting flies, with her radio going full-blast from morning til night" (Salinger 199).

E2: Unlike York, Salinger was at first eager to enlist, even prior to Pearl Harbor (Slawenski 37). However, Salinger was unprepared for all of the senseless carnage that he would witness; his unit, the 12th Regiment, endured the highest rate of casualties of all American regiments stationed in Europe during World War II (Slawenski 96). While York largely resolved his concerns with war prior to arriving in Europe, Salinger would wrestle with despair at the pointlessness of war and the evil of humanity both during and after WWII.

E3: In addition to their fears of being considered war propaganda, the filmmakers were motivated by York himself to be as accurate as possible. Like Salinger, York was not willing to sacrifice his ideals to commercialism, and could prove to be a formidable opponent: "York also maintained leverage because of his status as a national hero and his reputation as an individualist who could not be 'bought'" (Toplin 86). Back in 1919 when York had first returned from the war and was received with great acclamation, he turned down numerous opportunities to capitalize on his fame, saying "Uncle Sam's uniform, it ain't for sale" (Toplin 86).

E4: These timeless moral issues may have struck a resonant chord with Salinger. In a *New Yorker* article shortly after Salinger's death, John Seabrook recounts his memory of the first time he met Salinger. He and his girlfriend entered the kitchen in Salinger's Cornish, New Hampshire home to find that "a tall, slender man with a full head of graying hair, wearing a white shirt and a dark vest, was pouring popcorn into a Hamilton Beach popcorn popper" and seemed to be "just as nervous as we were." After making popcorn and rummaging through his selection of old 16-mm. films they decided to watch *Sergeant York* (with captions to prevent missing any of the dialogue). Not only was this film among Salinger's personal collection, Seabrook even notes that "toward the end, he seemed to get choked up." In spite of the fact that Salinger was with strangers and had most likely seen the film before, he was emotionally affected by it, perhaps at least in part due to its exploration of the isolationist / interventionist moral dilemma, not only in its applicability to wars, but to every day life.

E5: In this respect, Franklin is similar to Holden Caulfield of Salinger's *The Catcher in the Rye* (1951), especially when it is remembered that they both share scenes where they condescendingly observe the crowds walking the streets below, while forgetting that they too could be numbered among the phonies.

E6: The erasure of divisions contained in Franklin's role as a man-child is integral to this story; the arbitrary lines of division drawn by adults form the basis for these absurd wars. A "war with the Eskimos" is only possible if there are Eskimos. The first step towards war is identifying and labeling the enemy. For both WWI and WWII, the categorization of race would play a prominent role on both sides of the Atlantic and the Pacific. Salinger experienced first hand the awful effects of this kind of categorization and victimization. After WWII ended, Salinger remained in Germany as a member of the Counter Intelligence Corps. One of the duties of this segment of the military was to investigate reports of concentration camps in their area by heading straight towards its reported location, and "assess the situation, interrogate the inmates, and file a report with headquarters" (Slawenski 132). The territory assigned to Salinger's division contained 123 internment camps that formed the Dachau concentration camp system. The scenes that Salinger witnessed would not soon be forgotten: "'You could live a lifetime,' he mourned, 'and never really get the smell of burning flesh out of your nose'" (Slawenski 133).

Works Cited:

Ahlers, Rolf. "The Confession of Altona." *Harvard Theological Review* 77.3/(1984): 377-394.

"Avenue." *Online Etymology Dictionary.* Douglas Harper, n.d. Web. 31 May 2011.

Bryan, James E. "J.D. Salinger: The Fat Lady and the Chicken Sandwich." *College English* 23.3 (1961): 226-229.

"Cinema: Sergeant York Surrenders." *Time* 1 Apr. 1940: n. pag. *Time*. Web. 31 May 2011.

Cocteau, Jean, dir. *Beauty and the Beast*. 1946. Lopert, 1998. DVD.

Cotter, James Finn. "Religious Symbols in Salinger's Shorter Fiction." *Studies in Short Fiction* 15.2 (1978): 121+.

Crane-Engel, Melinda. "Germany vs. Genocide." *New York Times Magazine* 1994: 56.

"Damask." *Webster's Revised Unabridged Dictionary*. Ed. Noah Porter. Springfield, MA: Merriam, 1998. *The DICT Development Group*. Web. 31 May 2011.

"Edify." Def. 2. *Merriam-Webster Online Dictionary*. N.p., n.d. Web. 31 May 2011.

Feirstein, Sanna. "York Street." *Naming New York: Manhattan Places & How They Got Their Names*. New York: New York UP, 2001. 47.

French, Allen. "The British Expedition to Concord, Massachusetts, in 1775." *The Journal of the American Military History Foundation* 1.1 (1937): 1-17.

"Germany: Back to the Axe!" *Time* 14 Aug. 1933: n. pag. *Time*. Web. 31 May 2011.

"Germany: Bloody Sunday." *Time* 25 July 1932: n. pag. *Time*. Web. 31 May 2011.

The King James Study Bible. Nashville: Nelson, 1988.

Lee, David D. *Sergeant York*. Lexington, KY: Kentucky UP, 1985.

Moscow, Henry. "York Avenue." *The Street Book: An Encyclopedia of Manhattan's Street Names and Their Origins*. Ed. Thomas Tracy. New York: Hagstrom, 1978. 114.

Rosen, Robert S. Introduction. *The Memoirs of Gluckel of Hameln*. By Gluckel Of Hameln. Trans. Marvin Lowenthal. 1977. New York: Shocken, 1978. vii-xviii.

Salinger, J. D. *Franny and Zooey*. 1955. Boston: Little, Brown, 1961.

- --. "Just Before the War with the Eskimos." 1953. *Nine Stories*. By J. D. Salinger. New York: Little, Brown & Co., 1990. 57-82.

Seabrook, John. "A Night at the Movies." *The New Yorker* 8 Feb. 2010: n. pag. *The New Yorker*. Web. 31 May 2011.

Sergeant York. Howard Hawks. 1941. Warner Bros., 2006. DVD.

Slawenski, Kenneth. *J.D. Salinger: A Life*. New York: Random House, 2010.

Toplin, Robert Brent. *History by Hollywood: The Use and Abuse of the American Past*. Chicago: Illinois UP, 1996.

Salinger Criticism and "The Laughing Man": *A Case of Arrested Development* (E1)

Richard Allan Davison
Professor Emeritus
University of Delaware

Published commentary on J. D. Salinger has slowed down considerably during the last fifteen years or so. **(E2)** A kind of depression has followed that remarkable boom of the early sixties. Salinger himself has not published anything since "Hapworth 16, 1924" in the June 19, 1965 *New Yorker*. **(E3)** His only public sign of life has been an irate response to the 1974 pirated edition of his previously uncollected short stories, and that was in a phone call to a San Francisco agent of *The New York Times*. **(E4)** Despite his relative silence, however, the word is that he continues to write. **(E5)** And so do a devoted number of Salinger's commentators, some of whom form the nucleus of a new generation of scholars and critics writing about an author who continues to command a very substantial audience. **(E6)**

Teaching Salinger's Nine Stories

The scholars who have been working quietly during the lull following the plethora of activity produced by the Salinger Industry (the phrase is George Steiner's) went public in Chicago at a special Salinger session at the 1977 Modern Language Association convention which included three panelists who are working on book-length studies of Salinger: Dennis L. O'Connor (Georgetown University), James P. Doyle (Fordham University) and Eberhard Alsen (SUNY Cortland). Another member of the enthusiastic audience (enthusiastic at 8:30 A.M.!), Warren French, has recently revised a book so seminal to Salinger's studies (*J. D. Salinger*). While Doyle's book will be a general introduction to Salinger's writing, O'Connor and Alsen are focusing on Salinger's use of Eastern thought **(E7)** and its impact on our understanding of his later works. With "Teddy" (January 31, 1953) as a possible turning point in Salinger's career, as he allegedly moved from realism to (what was labeled at the Chicago session) a kind of neo-romanticism, their interests seem to be more with that later material signaled by the publication of this, the last of Salinger's *Nine Stories*. The later material includes, of course, "Franny" (1955), "Raise High the Roof Beams, Carpenters" (1955), "Zooey" (1957), "Seymour: An Introduction" (1959), and "Hapworth 16, 1924" (1965). In fact, there is talk of another special Modern Language Association session on Salinger, one devoted wholly to his last published work, the elusive and mind-boggling "Hapworth." No doubt many more critics are lying back quietly waiting for Salinger's next publication. If a Salinger revival is in the offing, and it seems inevitable, it will have to go some to match the volume of output during the late fifties and early sixties. No post WWII writer was more discussed.

By 1962, however, Salinger criticism had peaked. The next year Louis D. Rubin asked "Why is it, one wonders, that the work of J. D. Salinger has attracted the critical attention of so many scholars?" (*American Literary Scholarship [ALS]/1963,* 146). That same year Joseph Blotner voiced hopes "for a moratorium on Salinger criticism" (147). In 1964 William T. Stafford saw even more reason for a respite: "Although studies continue to proliferate in Salinger, many of them are repetitious and unoriginal" (*ALS/1964* 165). He wondered "how long this writing more about less and less in Salinger can continue" (165). Stafford devotes two and a half pages of his section in *American Literary Scholarship* (1965) to Salinger but mainly to praise James E. Miller's *J. D. Salinger* (University of Minnesota Pamphlets on American Writers, No. 51) of that same year. He rates Miller's book as "quite possibly the best word yet written on the fiction of Salinger" (*ALS/1965* 193). Yet while "The Salinger Industry rolls right along" (195) the quality of many of the products has declined. The 1966 *American Literary Scholarship Annual* still devotes a separate section to Salinger but it is only one page long. Disturbed by the inferior criticism, Stafford laments: "Other items on Salinger during the year are hardly better" (*ALS/1966* 180).

Teaching Salinger's Nine Stories

Richard D. Lehan, succeeding Stafford in the 1967 *Annual*, no longer giving Salinger a special section, lumps him with Robert Penn Warren under "Others" and announces that "The Salinger boom seems safely over if the year's scanty amount is any indication" (*ALS/1967* 208). The 1968 *Annual* has James H. Justice returning to a (one page) special section for Salinger but echoing earlier uneasiness: "The year's work confirms an impression some have felt for several years: some day, after a decent interval, this erratic artist must be read with fresh premises and techniques which do not imitate Salinger's own" (*ALS/1968* 213). In 1969 Salinger is all but lost in a section with Saul Bellow and Bernard Malamud. With one paragraph Justice dutifully notes the "only two pieces on Salinger" (*ALS/1969* 243). And in 1970 Salinger is overwhelmed by Malamud (*ALS/1970* 261-62), just as in 1971 Malamud and Bellow again all but squeeze him out (*ALS/1971* 255). Justice's quote from French is anticlimactically appropriate: "Salinger's popularity has declined" (*ALS/1971* 255). In 1972 Salinger is lumped once again with Bellow and Malamud and again given less space, barely two thirds of a page (*ALS/1972* 283-84). By 1973 Flannery O'Connor has her own four and a half page section while Salinger, now housed with Phillip Roth and I. B. Singer, is allotted two sentences (*ALS/1973* 273). Margaret Ann O'Connor takes over as reviewer in 1974 and dispatches Salinger in one short paragraph, discussing two articles (*ALS/1974* 261-62). Nor does she hint of a Salinger revival in the 1975 *Annual*.

What we have had, then, is a relative moratorium on Salinger commentary for almost a decade. It is time for some re-examinations and, if I read the signs rightly, it looks as if the Salinger and Eastern Thought Company will soon be selling stock.

At the risk of running counter to this gathering trend in Salinger scholarship and criticism, I will focus my own remarks on an earlier story, a story that seems to predate Salinger's obsession with Eastern Thought, a story that has been pretty much neglected. For even during the bullish days of the Salinger Industry "The Laughing Man" never received the attention it deserves. Unlike the vastly more popular "A Perfect Day for Bananafish" (January 31, 1948), "For Esmé-with Love and Squalor" (April 8, 1950), and "Teddy" (not to mention "Uncle Wiggily in Connecticut," "Just Before the War with the Eskimos," Pretty Mouth and Green my Eyes," "Down at the Dinghy," and "De Daumier Smith's Blue Period"), **(E8)** "The Laughing Man" does not have a single article devoted exclusively to it. I hope in this essay to fill some of that relative void and perhaps open a fresh discussion of Salinger's "realistic" short stories before they are buried in an avalanche of criticism on the so-called "neo-romantic" works.

To provide a clearer context for my discussion, a brief review of the rather sparse commentary on "The Laughing Man" is in order. One discovers that even the book-length studies of Salinger do not feature "The Laughing Man," although it is in Gwynn and Blotner and French that we find some of the most helpful (albeit brief) discussions of this story, which was first published in *The New Yorker* (March 19, 1949) and later became the fourth collected in *Nine Stories* (1952). Gwynn and Blotner open their two and a half page discussion with high praise: "Apparently simple, it turns out to be one of the most sophisticated and intricate of all Salinger's tales"(24). It is judged "a great improvement over its ridiculous and distant source, Victor Hugo's *L' Homme Qui Rit* (1869)" (25). They correctly see Salinger's story as "the recollection by a mature man of a crucial experience at the age of nine: the end of a hero-worship-laden relationship with an idealized older man" (24); but they wholly ignore the agonizing problems of that "older man," the twenty-two or twenty-three-year-old law student and coach to twenty-five adolescent members of the Comanche Club. George Steiner in "The Salinger Industry" first calls "The Laughing Man" along with "Down at the Dinghy" "fine sketches of the bruised, complicated world of children," but then adds that "neither holds a candle to Joyce's 'Araby' or to the studies of childhood in Dostoevsky"(10). Adult implications are again all but ignored. William Wiegand claims that Salinger is seeking the remedy from banana fever (a central consideration of the adult-centered "A Perfect Day for Bananafish") in "The Laughing Man" through "sublimation in art" (10). Only in "Raise High the Roofbeam" is Salinger "at least able to expose the banana fish. . . . Banana fever no longer seems the shame it did in

'Pretty Mouth,' 'The Laughing Man,' 'For Esmé,' and in 'Perfect Day' . . . itself" (15). In "The Rare Quixotic Gesture" Ihab Hassan treats Gedsudski's story of the Laughing Man (a story within a story) astutely but summarily: "Here the story of the fabulous Laughing Man is itself a quixotic gesture which has the power to influence the youthful audience of the boys, including the narrator of Salinger's story, but is powerless to save Gedsudski" (146). Hassan doesn't explore why Gedsudski is not saved. Most of the remaining critics evidence either diminished concern with the story or a lessened ability to deal with it. This is certainly true of the essays gathered in the seven collections of Salinger criticism.

Henry Antole Grunwald's *Salinger, A Critical and Personal Portrait* contains no reference to "The Laughing Man" outside of the reprinted Steiner essay and the revised Hassan essay. William E. Belcher's and James W. Lee's 1962 *J. D. Salinger and the Critics* includes comments on some twenty **(E9)** of Salinger's short stories (including seven **(E10)** of the *Nine*) but not a word on "The Laughing Man." **(E11)** In Harold P. Simonson's and Philip E. Hagen's 1963 *Salinger's Catcher in the Rye Clamor vs Criticism*, the numerous references to Salinger's stories do not include "The Laughing Man." It is mentioned only once in Malcolm Marsden's *If You Really Want to Know: A Catcher Casebook* and then in another reprint of George Steiner's essay. The only mention of "The Laughing Man" in the *Special Number: Salinger* (Winter, 1963) of *Wisconsin Studies in*

Contemporary Literature is in Donald M. Fiene's Bibliography:. He notes that "The Laughing Man" was "selected by Martha Foley as one of the distinguished short stories published in American magazines in 1949" (113). Nor do Marvin Laser and Norman Fruman, editing *Studies in J. D. Salinger: Reviews, Essays and Critiques of The Catcher in the Rye and Other Fiction* that same year, add anything to our knowledge of "The Laughing Man." Although there are articles in the last book-length study of Salinger, the *J. D. Salinger Special Number of Modern Fiction Studies* (Autumn 1966), dealing with "Esmé" and "Pretty Mouth" at length, "The Laughing Man" is mentioned only once, again in passing. **(E12)**

The best and most extended (although just slightly longer than Gwynn's and Blotner's) discussion of "The Laughing Man" is still found in Warren French's *J. D. Salinger*. He also spends more time on Gedsudski, referring to at least the suggestion of "adult pettiness," his willingness to "sacrifice children's feelings in order to salve his own wounds," and "the inner ruthlessness that motivates the self-made man" (93). French feels, however, that Salinger fails in his portrayal of Gedsudski: "It is finally impossible to tell whether the intention is to exalt or expose Gedsudski" (94). Most of French's focus in on the narrator. He argues that the story "does not concern the romantic break-up [between John Gedsudski and Mary Hudson], but the effects of this break-up on the narrator: he suffers the double disillusionment of seeing the man he idolizes frustrated and of losing a sort of innocent pleasure with the abrupt ending of the story about the Laughing Man" (92-93). French argues well, as far as he goes. If there is an error here it is in his overemphasis on the narrator's emotional experience-his rite of passage.

It has become almost a reflex action in this era of hypersensitive attention to the center of consciousness in literature to read any story told from the first person point of view as being mostly concerned with the spokesman and his self-revelations at the expense of the other characters-even if they be major characters in the story. Certainly Nick Carraway is almost as important as Jay Gatsby, and Jake Barnes is clearly more important than Robert Cohn, as both narrators reveal themselves in even the most minute of their observations. Perhaps it is time to pay more heed to the other main characters so crucial to the narrators' stories. Oliver Evans, for instance, may have been not so wrongheaded when he suggested that Ole Anderson may be the main protagonist in Hemingway's "The Killers" after all. Perhaps the 1946 Burt Lancaster movie was not so fatuous in its greater emphasis on the despairing ex-fighter than on an incredulous Nick Adams.

This plea for a closer look beyond the first person narrator is particularly relevant to a closer scrutiny of Salinger's "The Laughing Man." Although the story, viewed through the center of consciousness of the unnamed nine-year-old and told from the hindsight of this boy as an adult (who is, incidentally, the same age as both

Salinger and Buddy Glass were in 1949), does reveal much about his traumatic rite of passage, it is as much an examination of John Gedsudski, Chief of the Comanche Club, and the reverberations of his ill-fated love affair with Mary Hudson. Certainly "The Laughing Man" is an account of a young boy's initiation into the painful complexities of adult life as clearly as are such stories as Sherwood Anderson's "I Want To Know Why," Hemingway's "My Old Man," and Robert Penn Warren's "Blackberry Winter," but it is also a probing of the older Gedsudski's similar initiation. It is a story of two neophytes (one a physical child, the other an emotional adolescent) who struggle in their initial encounters with the mysteries of sex and adult responsibility. Gedsudski's own fictional creation, the Laughing Man, is, in part, a metaphor for both struggles. Mary Hudson serves as a catalyst for the simultaneous tests of both Gedsudski and his charge. She demands of them a new involvement with which they are powerless to cope.

The worlds of the Comanches and their Chief (and that of the Laughing Man) appear under control and relatively untroubled until Mary's photograph appears above the rearview mirror in Gedsudski's reconverted (and ominously "condemned looking") bus. The male worlds have remained inviolate (while in Gedsudski's story the bandit chief's mother is murdered and the Laughing Man's Eurasian beauty endures unrequited love.) Through her picture **(E13)** Mary is associated with an instrument of measurement, taking on "the unarresting personality of a speedometer" (93). At first the photograph "clashed with the men-only **(E14)** décor of the bus" (93). It is a puzzling complication in the boys' lives. Soon everything during their playtime hours becomes geared to Mary's presence. Mary's picture increasingly insinuates itself into the Comanche routine until Mary herself materializes. Gedsudski disrupts the Comanche schedule (and violates his obligation to their parents), driving one-half mile out of the way and holding up their baseball game to indulge in his selfish concern, his growing infatuation for Mary Hudson. Everything becomes affected by her. Her very presence reveals in the erstwhile unflappable Chief "what had formerly been a well-concealed flair for incompetence" (95). She causes him to pull loose the gearshift knob and makes his usually expert driving at best uncertain as the bus starts "with an amateurlike lurch" (95).

Mary intrudes herself into the all-male passenger bus just as she later intrudes herself into the Comanches' baseball game. The boys, at first hostile, come to accept her, but only after she proves able to meet them on their own terms, at bat **(E15)** on the ballfield. She meets Gedsudski on his own playground, as it were, literally and figuratively. Gedsudski is ecstatic when she hits a triple, handling the bat with surprising control. It seems, at the time, that by blending in with boyish activities she will not disturb his cloistered adolescent world after all. But too much, apparently, has transpired behind the scenes. Her actions remain enigmatic. Seeming at once aggressive and hesitant, she always goes past first base but is never described as reaching home plate. Salinger, in fact, most often associates her with third base, forever in scoring position but never scoring. She waves at the narrator from there: "She happened to be a girl who knew how to wave to somebody from third base" (98). Her final argument with Gedsudski takes place there, and it is from near third base that she bids her final tearful goodbye. Their worlds are to remain apart.

Mary's character, as Salinger presents it, is an ambivalent one. She seems both the epitome of a spoiled rich brat out of a Fitzgerald **(E16)** story and a loving woman who looks for a man and finds instead a slightly overgrown boy scout. It may be that she rejects Gedsudski's attentions just as she rejects the narrator's overtures to her tears. But it is also clear that neither male is prepared to respond with maturity. The narrator admits he did not understand her tears. **(E17)** Gedsudski lets her run from the ballfield. He is not willing to go far enough out of the way to repair their shattered relationship. Salinger further associates Mary with baby carriages, reinforcing her separation from (or closeness to!) Gedsudski and the boy. (One is tempted to trot out the old schoolboy chant: "First comes love, then comes marriage, then comes Gedsudski with a baby carriage," epitomizing his 'aw shucks' adolescent attitude toward matrimony and offspring.) On that last day we see Mary sitting on a bench between two baby carriages. **(E18)** Gedsudski walks over to her and brings her to his game area. After they argue and Gedsudski elects not to follow as she makes her final exit, the puzzled narrator trips over a baby carriage on his way to the bus. Salinger's juxtaposition of the boy's physical obstacle with the man's emotional one is overt. Just as it is never clear that the breakup is Mary's fault, so there is reason to believe that male inadequacy is at least a contributing factor to it.

Throughout the story both the boy and Gedsudski seem to have an adolescent fear of and/or naiveté toward sex and its adult associations. If Gedsudski is balking at such adult responsibility (which, at least in 1928 and 1949, traditionally led to marriage), the boy seems fatefully turned to his chief's emotional vibrations. Gedsudski's apparent reluctance to leave his boyhood environment and fulfill his role as lover/father provokes Mary's tears and alienation more than do their social class differences. This break between the sophisticated young Wellesley graduate with "her Herbert Tareyton cigarettes (cork tipped)" and her beaver coat and the young socially and emotionally retarded first-or second-year law student seems inevitable. Salinger has carefully prepared us for Gedsudski's inability to communicate with the adult world. Rather than being confused about Gedsudski (as others have suggested) Salinger presents him brilliantly in all of his complexities within a world that shares the complexities of its protagonist. The narrator's own feelings **(E19)** about the Chief may be as ambivalent as Holden's are about D. B. and the movies. But the Gedsudski he remembers never comes to positive terms with himself or his world. The creature of Gedsudski's imagination fares no better. The Comanche Chief and the Laughing Man share similar inhibitions. They are also the role models for twenty-five boys.

Gedsudski's complex character is more subtly explored in the interior narrative. Rather than send the reader into a Chinese box succession of reality levels as Albee does in *Tiny Alice*, or into an endless succession of stories within stories as Barth does in "Menelaiad," Salinger establishes more of a one-to-one relationship between John Gedsudski and the Laughing Man. Not merely a wish fulfillment, Gedsudski's creation is a metaphor for the teller's own special vulnerabilities and defenses and for their ultimate failure. The Laughing Man, with his sexual inhibitions and pseudo-Christian overtones **(E20)** (complete with crucifixion), is a more grotesque counterpart of his creator. Although the imaginative creation of the Laughing Man is in part wish fulfillment, Gedsudski's own big-nosed, low-browed squat figure is scarcely compensated for by the noseless, **(E21)** flatheaded, skinny counterpart. This creation is scarcely a physical improvement. He must try to offset even greater handicaps. For Gedsudski's Laughing Man is not so much an escape from his own ugliness, his own sense of immaturity, as an exaggeration of these things. Through the Laughing Man he can plunge more deeply into grotesque disfigurement and alienation only to rise higher in vicarious triumph. It is Gedsudski's way of proving to himself and the Comanches that even a being beyond the limits of acceptable appearance and mature human communion, someone, in other words, immeasurably worse off than Gedsudski, can still command awe, respect and love. The Laughing Man is a logical hero for Gedsudski to create. Like an adolescent fantasy incarnate, the Laughing Man must maintain the invincibility of a Superman who is capable of merciless revenge on those who flout the rules of fair play. But anyone with such a selfish demand for a personal kind of poetic justice is also vulnerable and may crumple like his comic strip counterpart when yesterday's newspaper is discarded.

Both Gedsudski and the Laughing Man have attempted to overcome their ugliness by either a superior ability at sports or a masterful ability to accumulate fortune, by showing off the "unclassifiably" beautiful Mary Hudson or continually outwitting the "internationally famous" DuFarges. While Gedsudski is more overtly athletic, the Laughing Man, who is "as graceful as a cat on his feet" (88), sports "an underground gymnasium and a shooting range" (91) beneath his tiny cottage. Gedsudski's sportsmanship is reflected in the Laughing Man's "singular love of fairplay" (89). Gedsudski thrives on the admiration of the Comanches who see in him a smooth amalgamation of "the most photogenic features of Buck Jones, Ken Maynard and Tom Mix" (86). The Laughing Man, shunned by most humans, befriends all "species of animals" and is adored by four "blindly loyal confederates" (91). "They [do] not think him ugly" (88). He shares with Gedsudski a pleasant voice and speaks to his animals "in their own tongues" (88) as effectively as Gedsudski communicates with his children. Clearly the Chief needs his Comanches, perhaps more than the Laughing Man needs Omba, the dwarf, and his other loyal followers. Downfall in both men involves alienation from their followers. Ultimately Gedsudski's loss of control, beginning with his bad driving, continuing with his swearing and ending with the ego-shattering breakup with Mary, is more nobly reflected in the Laughing Man's final encounter with the DuFarges when, hoping that he can save his beloved timber wolf, Black Wing, he allows himself to be fatally outwitted by these arch enemies.

Both Gedsudski's revenge and the Laughing Man's sacrificial death serve to externalize the boys' reactions to parental neglect or indifference. The Laughing Man himself may be symbolically repudiating his own orphanage upbringing as he sets up the death of the bandit chief's mother. **(E22)** The Comanches' own home environments exude parental rejection. Have the young boys' parents rejected them as the society in Gedsudski's story has rejected the Laughing Man? If not, why do the boys' parents farm them out every day after school and all day on Saturdays and holidays? Why does each boy see himself as the only real ("legitimate") son of the Laughing Man, disavowing his "bogus" parents? Do not the narrator's parents show insensitivity when they send their traumatized child to bed uncomforted? In revising the concluding sentence of the *New Yorker* version of "The Laughing Man" for *Nine Stories*, Salinger placed more onus on the parents by pointing up the absence of any physical contact with the boy. (Compare "I arrived home with my teeth chattering uncontrollably and had to be put to bed" with the more impersonal "I arrived home with my teeth chattering uncontrollably and was told to go right straight to bed.") They seem to be treating an emotional trauma as they would a common chill.

The ability to endure rejection and transcend it is, of course, central to the maturation process. One must cope with rejection and grow because of and/or inspite of the experience. All three main characters are stunned by their encounters and are swallowed up by the resulting void. Unlike Holden Caulfield, they do not allow a Phoebe to ignite their lives with a spark of salvation. While the boy passively accepts the temporary security of his bed, Gedsudski and the Laughing Man actively resist redemption, for acceptance of help involves commitment and obligation. Acceptance of responsibility involves more maturity than they have attained. The physical ugliness of both creator and creation externalizes this absence of mature sexual responsibility that permeates both Gedsudski's real world and his fantasy world.

The fantastic exploits of the Laughing Man reveal the intensity of Gedsudski's attempts to remain impregnable in his tenuous role as hero-counselor-umpire-guide to the Comanches. In his subconscious Gedsudski may be more sensitive to those liabilities exaggerated by the social gap between Mary Hudson (Wellesley, Early American Heritage, Upper Class, Long Island) and himself (New York University, Second Generation American, Lower Class, Staten Island) than Mary is. He tries in vain to close this gap by creating in his fictional serial the distant-closeness of the Chinese-Paris border. In Gedsudski's story, we recall, it is the Eurasian girl-not the Laughing Man-who suffers from unrequited love. He shows her little charity. In fact, Hoang, the giant, and the girl are further from the Laughing Man's favors than the weaker dwarf and the non-human wolf. Those he can most easily dominate pose a lesser challenge to the insularity of his existence. The whole Laughing Man fantasy iterates Gedsudski's need to remain a professional companion of boys, to remain in their eyes an "impartial and unexcitable umpire at all [their] bedlam sporting events, . . . master fire builder and extinguisher, and . . . expert, uncontemptuous first-aid man" (85).

Every detail in Salinger's description of his storyteller's background and accomplishments seems calculated to emphasize Gedsudski's success at boyish games in a boyish world. He is never shown successful in a single adult endeavor. Gedsudski is an Eagle Scout and exudes the youthful tenacity required to pile up dutifully the prerequisite merit badges (including fire building and first aid). Salinger notes that he was *invited* to the New York Giants' baseball camp; there is no evidence that he successfully attended it. He seems to have made no attempt to compete with adults even within the context of his boyhood game. Salinger further notes that he was *almost* All-American tackle. His status at law school is not explored but his tenure is during a time (1928) when most students were neither renowned for their protests nor for their sophisticated involvement in adult activities. In any case, that part of his life remains unexplored.

Perhaps there is more than a hint of a Salinger parody of society's blind worship of the college athlete-hero who is so often a part of the Horatio Alger American success story. F. Scott Fitzgerald (who clearly influenced Salinger) was capable of this kind of semi-parody in such stories as "The Freshest Boy," where Basil Duke Lee's "acceptance" by his peers is tinged with irony. At times the portrait of Mary Hudson is reminiscent of those apparently unattainable society girls sought by the Dexter Greens and Gatsbys and scored by the Anson Hunters. Salinger also may be disclosing Gedsudski's blind adherence to an image of an unattainable girl who may be in reality a warm and responsive woman.

In any case Salinger consistently portrays Gedsudski as balking at adult commitment and suggests his emotional inability to fulfill the role of lover/husband. Gedsudski's refusal to leave the world of children is not unlike Holden's treasuring of childhood innocence and Seymour's attempts to find solace in his communication with the four-year-old Sybil. While Holden strives to resolve his distrust of the adult world by talking to the reader and Seymour dodges into suicide, Gedsudski murders the creature of his imagination, his alter ego. The Laughing Man ultimately has proved as useless in his life struggle as (in "Uncle Wiggily in Connecticut") Jimmy Jimmereeno is to Ramona's. **(E23)** Gedsudski's adolescent hesitation is, of course, no cure for Mary's tears and the subsequent alienation. He engages in what is a symbolic suicide and murder, a murder not only of the Laughing Man but also of the dreams of twenty-five children. That Mary comes near the Chief's territory on that last day may suggest on her part an attempt at reconciliation. Perhaps the narrator's dinner invitation to Mary is an intuitive attempt to compensate for a felt deficiency in his chief. (Or is the invitation the result of an unconscious rivalry prompted by a schoolboy crush of his own?) The boy experiences physically and emotionally (if not intellectually) the agony his chief is enduring but not controlling. After Gedsudski's traumatic parting with Mary climaxes in the death of the Laughing Man, the narrator's teeth chatter "uncontrollably" from his own sense of rejection. The appearance of a facsimile of the Laughing Man's poppy mask exacerbates the boy's emotional upheaval by extending the fictional account beyond the world of fantasy. The "tissue paper" reminder is doubly painful because of its association with the Laughing Man. For to the boy at this moment Gedsudski's creation has become a greater object of sympathy **(E24)** than Gedsudski himself. Certainly to the reader Gedsudski's callous masochistic and/or sadistic murder of the Laughing Man suggests the self-centered peevishness of a child who has not gotten what he may (or may not) have truly wanted.

While the reader is touched by, delights in and then mourns the Laughing Man, he comes gradually to harbor uneasy and uncertain feelings about Gedsudski. The early hints of Gedsudski's failure at adult activities, carrying with it a latent cruelty, serve as a matrix for the ill success in his love affair. As soon as Mary's presence is evident to the Comanches, they also witness in their Chief the beginning of what is to them his transformation, his loss of control. On the day of the final encounter with Mary his wet-combed hair and substitution of an adult's overcoat for a boyish leather windbreaker continue to reflect a superficial and futile attempt to camouflage a deeper absence of mature commitment. The mere doffing of a windbreaker for an overcoat proves no impediment to his ultimate retreat into childish petulance. Gedsudski may emerge from his trials sadder and more aware of adult complexities, but even the ritualistic murder of the Laughing Man which extends beyond the world of imagination does not ensure his putting away all adolescent things. At the end of the story he may be both embittered and relieved: the reader imagines him sitting alone in his emptied bus after the Comanches have stepped out into their far less certain world. That the nine-year-old narrator seems more profoundly affected than his chief pointedly underscores Gedsudski's state of arrested development.

It is a truism that Salinger deals most frequently with the misfit or outsider in society. It is also true that he has become well known largely as a writer about exceptional children. Yet some of his most perceptive revelations (especially in *Nine Stories*) concern either adults or those on the verge of adulthood. "The Laughing Man" is one of many stories that offer more acute insights on adults than on children. Holden, as narrator, is seventeen; Franny and De Daumier Smith are both nineteen. Zooey, Buddy and Seymour are viewed most frequently as adults. "A Perfect Day for Bananafish" centers on Muriel and Seymour: "For Esmé with Love and Squalor" focuses on Sergeant X, not the children, and "Down at the Dinghy" is as much or more about a sensitive mother's understanding of her child than it is about the four-year-old runaway. "Just Before the War with the Eskimos" concerns a teenager *and* a twenty-four-year-old misfit, while "Uncle Wiggily in Connecticut" deals more with the self-absorbed mother than her ill-adjusted daughter. "Pretty Mouth and Green My Eyes" is wholly about adults and the artificiality, sterility, cruelty and pathos in adult relationships. Even "Teddy," which does focus on a ten-year-old, relies heavily on the adult reactions of, notably, the McArdles and Nicolson for a complete portrait of this boy genius. Perhaps Salinger should be viewed as a writer about adults and his canon re-examined in this light.

As he got more concerned with Eastern thought he seems to have translated his views into fiction that increasingly reflects the Mahayana, Zen and Vedanta philosophies. Yet before one can fully comprehend what Salinger is doing in the later works it is crucial to re-examine his concerns in the earlier ones. His preoccupation then, I submit, is largely with adult considerations and adult struggles in which all of the actions of children are judged against a norm that, when not of Christ, is of an adult world with its flaws and imperfections, its phoniness and cruelty, but a world also peopled with the D. B.'s and the Mr. Antolinis, whose hearts may have lost some of the purity but none of the love. If the Gedsudskis of the world do not radiate ultimately positive values, it is because they are doomed to reside in a perennially arrested state where values are not so much childlike as childish.

Endnotes:

E1: This essay originally appeared in *Studies in Short Fiction* 18.1 (1981): 1-15. It is reprinted with the author's permission.

E2: There is only one article on Salinger noted by Margaret Anne O'Connor in *American Literary Scholarship: an Annual/1975*. Hans Galinsky cites one from a German festchrift and Keiko Beppu has discovered an essay from Japan. This is a far cry from the peak years of Salinger criticism. See pages 322, 484 and 496 of *ALS/1975*.

E3: Magazine copies of this story, which features an incredibly precocious seven-year-old Seymour, are becoming rarer each year. Many library copies have been stolen or mutilated.

E4: For an account of Salinger's comments see Lacey Fosburg's "J. D. Salinger Speaks About His Silence," *New York Times*, November 3, 1974: 1, 69.

E5: Brendan Gill, for instance, assures us that Salinger is still hard at work. See *Here At the New Yorker* (New York: Random House, 1975): 228.

E6: Sales of his paperbacks continue to move briskly. College students remain enthusiastic about both *Catcher in the Rye* and *Nine Stories*.

E7: Salinger's interest in the philosophy of the New and Old Testament, Advaita Vedanta and Classical Taoism as well as Mahayana and Zen literature was discussed most recently by Alsen and O'Connor at the 1977 Modern Language Association meeting.

E8: These last five stories were also first published in magazines before being collected in *Nine Stories*. They appeared on the following respective dates: March 20, 1948 (*New Yorker*); June 5, 1948 (*New Yorker*); July 14, 1951 (*New Yorker*); April 1949 (*Harper's*); and May 1952 (*World Review*).

E9: There are some twenty short stories in various magazines that Salinger has chosen not to republish.

E10: "Just Before the War With the Eskimos" is also omitted.

E11: Belcher and Lee do reprint comments on "Bananafish" and "Esmé" from Gwynn and Blotner's *The Fiction of J. D. Salinger*.

E12: The Autumn 1966 issue of *Modern Fiction Studies* is Volume 12, Number 3. In 1965 James E. Miller, Jr. gave a once-over-lightly treatment of "The Laughing Man" along with "Dinghy," "Eskimos," "Wiggily," and "Pretty Mouth," while "Esmé" "De Daumier" "Teddy" and "Bananafish" are dealt with at greater length. See *J. D. Salinger*, University of Minnesota Pamphlets on American Writers, Minneapolis, 1965.

E13: Mary Hudson is shown "dressed in academic cap and gown" (93), a constant reminder of her graduation from undergraduate life.

E14: Although in 1928 as well as 1949 clubs were typically segregated by sex, Salinger seems to be underlining the exclusively male existence of Gedsudski and the Comanches.

E15: No doubt there may be conscious Freudian implications on Salinger's part concerning her expert handling of the bat: "[Gedsudski] told her not to choke the bat too tightly. 'I'm not,' she said" (96). Mary Hudson remains a precarious outfielder, however, as she is as ineffectual on fly balls as Holden Caulfield is in his attempts to prevent the children of his world from plunging off the cliff at the edge of the field of rye.

E16: Among the possible echoes of Fitzgerald are those from "The Diamond as Big as The Ritz." Like Braddock Washington The Laughing Man amasses "the largest personal fortune in the world" (90). While Washington converts his diamonds into radium and places it into bank vaults, The Laughing Man converts his "fortune into diamonds and lowers it into emerald vaults" (90-91). Washington puts his potential enemies in a huge glass bowl in the earth. The Laughing Man incarcerates his in a "deep but pleasantly decorated mausoleum" (89).

E17: In the book version Salinger allows the narrator a glimmer of understanding. The parenthetical statement in the magazine version: "I had no idea what was going on between the Chief and Mary Hudson (and still haven't)"

(31) is changed to "(and still haven't, in any but a fairly low, intuitive sense)" (105).

E18: Salinger initiates the baby carriage motif in this second paragraph of the story: "If we had straight athletics on our minds, we went . . . where the opposing team didn't include a baby carriage or an irate old lady with a cane." Freudian critics would see sexually threatening implications in the "irate old lady with a cane." One could also argue (shades of controversy in *Franny*?) that through the later association of Mary with "nursemaids with baby carriages" (103) Salinger is implying that she is pregnant. Even the hint of such a condition is potential support for my argument concerning Gedsudski's fear of adult responsibility.

E19: Although the question of the narrator's reliability is a difficult one, we must assume a certain objectivity on his part, even though, like Whitman's narrator in "Out of the Cradle Endlessly Rocking" ("A man, yet by these tears a little boy again"), he is moved as he relives the emotions of his childhood.

E20: Salinger remarks early on his "singular love of fair play" (89) and his "compassionate side" (89). The Laughing Man remains chaste and befriends the lowly. He allows his enemy "to tie him with barbed wire to a tree" (101) and suffers and dies there refusing "the vial of eagle's blood" and giving up a "heart-rending gasp of final sorrow" (110) at his death.

E21: Noselessness has been associated quite frequently with lack of virility or impotence. See Rabelais and Sterne.

E22: The hypocrisy of the Laughing Man's parents, a "wealthy missionary couple," is apparent when they refuse "(from a religious conviction) to pay the ransom for their son." The refusal prompts the bandits to place "the little fellow's head in a carpenter's vice," which leads, of course, to his hideous disfigurement (87).

E23: Ramona's pathetic attempt to replace the imaginative Jimmy Jimmereeno (whom she has run over by a car) with the equally unreal Mickey Mickeranno is another escape device no more successful than her mother's attempt to escape the sterile present through memories of the dead Walt Glass.

E24: Certainly the gentleness the Laughing Man exhibits to his friends at his death is in sharp contrast to Gedsudski's cruelty to the boys. Even though their club is named after an Indian tribe noted for its bravery, there is no evidence to suggest he is merely testing them. Nor is there reason to believe that a comic pint of the story may be in the fact that the teller sees the plight of Gedsudski as more tragic than it is, thus revealing his own immaturity.

Bibliography:

American Literary Scholarship: an Annual/1963. Louis D. Rubin Jr. "Fiction: 1930s to the Present: ii. J. D. Salinger." Ed. James Woodress. Durham, NC: Duke UP, 1965. 146-49.

--- *an Annual/1964.* William T. Stafford. "Fiction: The 1930s to the Present: vii. J. D. Salinger." Ed. James Woodress. 1966. 165-66.

---*an Annual/1965.* William T. Stafford. "Fiction: The 1930s to the Present: ix J. D. Salinger." Ed. James Woodress. 1967. 193-95.

---*an Annual/1966.* William T. Stafford "Fiction: The 1930s to the Present: x. J. D. Salinger." Ed. James Woodress. 1968. 180-81.

---*an Annual/1967.* Richard D. Lehan "Fiction: The 1930s to the Present: x. Others." Ed. James Woodress. 1969. 204-209.

---*an Annual/1968.* James H. Justus "Fiction: The 1930s to the Present: vi. J. D. Salinger." Ed. J. Albert Robbins. 1970. 213-214.

---*an Annual/1969.* James H. Justus. "Fiction: The 1930s to the Present: vii. Saul Bellow, Bernard Malamud, J. D. Salinger." Ed. J. Albert Robbins. 1971. 240-43.

---*an Annual/1970.* James H. Justus. "Fiction: The 1930s to the Present: iv. Bernard Malamud and J. D. Salinger." Ed. J. Albert Robbins. 1972. 260-63.

---*an Annual/1971*. James H. Justus "Fiction: The 1930s to the Present: iii. Saul Bellow, Bernard Malamud, J. D. Salinger." Ed. J. Albert Robbins. 1973. 252-56.

---*an Annual/1972*. James H. Justus "Fiction: The 1930s to the Present: iv. Saul Bellow, Bernard Malamud, J. D. Salinger." Ed. J. Albert Robbins. 1974. 279-84.

---*an Annual/1973*. James H. Justus "Fiction: The 1930s to the Present: v. J. D. Salinger, Philip Roth, and I. B. Singer." Ed. James Woodress. 1975. 276-77.

---*an Annual/1974*. Margaret Anne O'Connor. "Fiction: The 1930s to the 1950s: i. Dissenting Voices-'Art For Humanity's Sake.'" Ed. James Woodress. 1976. 254-62.

Blotner, Joseph L. and Gwynn, Frederick L. *The Fiction of J. D. Salinger*. Pittsburgh: Pittsburgh UP, 1958.

Evans, Oliver. "The Protagonist of Hemingway's 'The Killers.'" *Modern Language Notes*. 72 (1958): 589-591.

Fiene, Donald M. "J. D. Salinger: A Bibliography:." *Wisconsin Studies in Contemporary Literature*. 4.1 (1963): 109-149.

French, Warren. *J. D. Salinger*. Boston: G. K. Hall and Co., 1976.

Grunwald. Henry Anatole, ed. *Salinger: A Critical and Personal Portrait*. New York: Harper, 1962.

"J. D. Salinger 'Special Number.'" *Modern Fiction Studies*. 12.3 (1966).

Laser, Marvin and Fruman, Norman. Studies in *J. D. Salinger: Reviews, Essays and Critiques of The Catcher in the Rye and Other Fiction*. New York: Odyssey, 1963.

Marsden, Malcolm, ed. *If You Really Want to Know: A Catcher Casebook*. Chicago: Scotts, Foresman and Co., 1963.

Miller, James E. *J. D. Salinger*. University of Minnesota Pamphlets on American Writers, 51. Minneapolis: Minnesota UP, 1965.

Simonson, Harold P. and Hagan, Philip E. *Salinger's* Catcher in the Rye *Clamor vs Criticism*. Boston: D. C. Heath and Co., 1963.

Steiner, George. "The Salinger Industry." *The Nation*. 189 (1959): 360-63.

Wiegand, William. "J. D. Salinger: Seventy-Eight Bananas." *Chicago Review*. 11.4 (1958): 3-19.

"the old ship is steady again": Empathy and The Divine Comedy in "Down at the Dinghy"

Michael Renganeschi
SUNY New Paltz

"Down at the Dinghy" has received little critical attention since its publication in 1949. Much of the criticism concerning the story of Boo Boo Tannenbaum and her son Lionel focuses on the problem of anti-Semitism in post-WWII America, the treatment of which led Warren French to dismiss the story as "the most contrived in the collection" (74). French goes so far as to argue that "Down at the Dinghy represents "the measure of the limits of [Salinger's] ability to stare unblinkingly at the human condition" (74). However, alongside a story of anti-Semitism and playful scenes between a mother and her son, Salinger crafted a story of miscommunication, misunderstanding, and the struggle to live with empathy. Lionel and Boo Boo's story moves from misunderstanding, reiterated in Sandra and Boo Boo's complaints that no one can "hear" Lionel, towards the deep connection that they share at the end. I want to suggest that by reading the story through the lens of Dante's *Divine Comedy*, we can begin to see Beatrice "Boo Boo" Glass Tannenbaum take on the role of her namesake. She becomes a guide for Lionel, who must, as Dante must, navigate two worlds: one of hellish ignorance and bigotry and one of compassion and love. By the end of the story, Boo Boo helps her son to safely reconcile his innocence with the demands of the adult world and communicate with the people living in it.

As in many other stories in the collection, Salinger uses descriptive details to create a distinct separation between characters, casting them as figures from two different worlds: a material world defined by pretension and a spiritual world defined by sincerity. In Mrs. Snell, and the insistent description of her clothing, we are immediately introduced to the former:

Mrs. Snell had her hat on. It was the same interesting, black felt headpiece she had worn, not just all summer, but for the past three summers-through record heat waves, through change of life, over scores of ironing boards, over the helms of dozens of vacuum cleaners. The Hattie Carnegie label was still inside it, faded but (it might be said) unbowed. (74)

Her handbag bears an equally impressive label. Throughout this first scene, Mrs. Snell lives up to this characterization; she is concerned mainly with her own tea, and she feigns attention to her friend Sandra, who is dealing with an ostensibly traumatic and worrying problem.

In this first scene, Salinger also introduces Sandra, who is characterized mainly through her connection with Mrs. Snell. Sandra is equally self-absorbed and arguably more materialistic, evidenced in her contempt for Mrs. Snell and her condescension to conversation with her. In Sandra's eyes, Mrs. Snell is, despite the labels in her hat and bag, considerably below her: "Sandra stared rancorously at the opposite wall. 'I'll be so gladda get backa the city. I'm not foolin'. I hate this crazy place.' She gave Mrs. Snell a hostile glance. 'It's all right for *you*, you live here all year round. You got your social life here and all. You don't care" (76). Despite her "social life," Mrs. Snell is able to survive in "this crazy place" only through indifference, and Sandra is so unable to connect with the people around her that she insultingly dismisses her friend's life as trivial and banal. The women's conversation is defined by the same sort of indifference and isolation with which Sandra views Mrs. Snell. Rather than working to understand and ameliorate the effect of Sandra's anti-Semitic remark, the solution for these women is to avoid dealing with the situation, to, as it were, *run away* from their problems.

Sandra's refusal to worry about Lionel links her with the young boy. At this point in the story, the characters are completely unable to communicate with each other: Lionel has isolated himself in the boat just as Sandra has isolated herself through her indifference. However, the connection between these two characters reveals one of the most important aspects of Salinger's story. Sandra is repeatedly unable to see or hear Lionel, a problem that is revisited later in the story as Boo Boo struggles to hear the barely audible words of her son: "The last thing I'm gonna do is *worry* about it. Only, it drives ya loony, the way that kid goes pussyfootin' all around the house. Ya can't *hear* him, ya know. I mean nobody can *hear* him, ya know. Just the other day I was shellin' beans-right at this here table-and I almost stepped on his *hand*. He was sittin' right under the table" (75). In this early scene, Sandra's inability to hear Lionel reinforces the lack of communication between the characters' different worlds. Lionel, in his childhood innocence, represents a sort of ideal enlightened figure, reminiscent of Seymour or Teddy, who is often unable or unwilling to communicate with people from Mrs. Snell and Sandra's world. Unlike "A Perfect Day for Bananafish" or "Teddy," "Down at the Dinghy" emphasizes the importance of bridging these two worlds through compassion, care, and understanding: where Seymour and Teddy can find no solution but to escape this world, Boo Boo and Lionel are learning to live in it. **(E1)**

When Beatrice "Boo Boo" Tannenbaum enters the kitchen, she further emphasizes Lionel's separation from the adult world. The women in the room are at first silent-presumably afraid they will reveal what Sandra is trying so hard not to worry about-but Mrs. Snell soon asks Boo

Boo about Lionel: "'I hear Lionel's supposta be runnin' away.' She gave a short laugh" (77). Mrs. Snell's condescension and dismissal of Lionel's actions not only highlights the division between these two worlds, but also stands in ironic contrast to her earlier advice that Sandra run away from her problems. However, Salinger continues to suggest that the ability to understand, or attempt to understand, the actions of children is one of the defining features of compassionate and sincere people. Kenneth Slawenski argues that the "spiritual purity of adult characters" can be measured by their attempts to understand the children around them: "Perhaps the clearest example of this reflection appears in *The Catcher in the Rye* when Holden observes a women and her son in a movie theater. Although the woman cries throughout the film's maudlin plot, she refuses to take the boy to the bathroom, causing Holden to judge her as being 'Kindhearted as a goddam wolf'" (172-3). At this point in the story, the conversation between the three women is both thematically and structurally important: Boo Boo's time in the kitchen links the scene between herself and Lionel with the scene between Sandra and Mrs. Snell in the same way that she links the worlds of adulthood and childhood. It is through this link that she acts as a guide for Lionel, allowing him to maintain his spiritual purity after Sandra's anti-Semitic remark, and also, by luring him out of the boat, teaching him how to reconcile two different worlds. As a guide, Boo Boo fulfills her namesake, and reading Boo Boo alongside Beatrice in *The Divine Comedy*, particularly in the later Cantos of *Purgatory*, suggests an important dimension of an integral story in the collection.

Ruth Prigozy has traced some of the Dantesque motifs of *Nine Stories* and agrees that these motifs "reinforce the primary conflict in the collection between the material world, a modern 'Inferno,' and a spiritual realm" (102). While her analysis provides an important framework for reading the collection, Prigozy limits her critique of Salinger's symbolic allusions to "A Perfect Day for Bananafish," "For Esmé-With Love and Squalor," and "Pretty Mouth and Green My Eyes." **(E2)** However, I want to suggest that a complete understanding of the "Inferno" of *Nine Stories* depends on reading Boo Boo through the lens of Dante's Beatrice. **(E3)** Such a reading allows us to begin to see the importance of reconciling the material world and the spiritual realm: Boo Boo, as Lionel's guide, shows that in Salinger's modern inferno, communication, empathy, and understanding-the cardinal virtues not only of "Down at the Dinghy," but of much of Salinger's later work **(E4)**-are the key to living rightly.

Throughout the story, Salinger repeatedly depicts characters who are unable to communicate with one another. Beginning with Sandra's claim that is impossible to hear Lionel-"nobody can hear him" (75)-we are shown a picture of isolation in the summer house fallen into disuse. Sandra's second complaint reiterates this: "I don't know why they wanna stay up here all October for . . . I mean none of 'em even go anywhere *near* the water. *She* don't go in, *he* don't go it, the *kid* don't go in. *Nobody* goes in now. They don't even take that crazy boat out no more" (76). Through Sandra's repetition of "nobody," Salinger subtly links Lionel's attempt to run away with his family's late season lack of interest in the lake and the boat. Lionel's fear is bigger than Sandra's anti-Semitism and helps account for his misunderstanding of "kike" (86). Lionel appears to be afraid that his father, and thus his family, will continue to move further away from him; he is afraid that the distance between himself, his mother, and his father will continue to grow. Once Boo Boo enters the story, she works to decrease that distance as the momentum of Salinger's story moves toward reconciliation and reunion.

Boo Boo is almost immediately characterized in contrast to Mrs. Snell and Sandra. While Mrs. Snell addresses Lionel's actions with a laugh of dismissal, Boo Boo gives a detailed account of her son's past attempts to run away. When Mrs. Snell asks Boo Boo why Lionel ran away before, Boo Boo responds that a "child in the park that afternoon had come up to him with some dreamy misinformation, 'You stink, kid.'" She then claims, sincerely, that it is "all slightly over [her] head" (79). In her reply, Boo Boo refuses to condescend as Mrs. Snell or Sandra would, and acknowledges her own inability to understand her son. Thus far in the story, Salinger has suggested that Lionel's actions are not far from the course that Mrs. Snell suggests Sandra pursue. Boo Boo, on the other hand, is exemplary not only in her attempts to understand Lionel, to "lure him out of the boat" (77) and back into society, but also in her attempts to communicate with Mrs. Snell and Sandra. Boo Boo, whose "joke of a name" (77) links her with the world of childhood, acts as an intermediary not only between these scenes, but between these two worlds. **(E5)**

In *Purgatory*, immediately after Dante recognizes Beatrice, he describes his vision of her: "my soul, that could not see her perfectly, / still felt, succumbing to her mystery / and power, the strength of its enduring love" (XXX: 37-39). Boo Boo similarly has trouble seeing Lionel: "Boo Boo found it queerly difficult to keep Lionel in steady focus" (80). While the roles are reversed, it is important to note that in both scenes, the pilgrim and his guide are separated by water and are unable to see each other clearly. Following this description, and after Dante notices that his former guide, Virgil, has disappeared, he gives a more detailed description of Beatrice:

> *Just as an admiral, from bow to stern*
>
> *watches his men at work on other ships,*
>
> *encouraging their earnest labors-so,*
>
> *rising above the chariot's left rail . . .*
>
> *... I saw the lady who had first appeared*

beneath the angelic festival of flowers

gazing upon me from beyond the stream.

(XXX: 58-66)

The first encounter between Lionel and Boo Boo plays on similar imagery:

"It is I," Boo Boo said. "Vice-Admiral Tannenbaum Née Glass. Come to inspect the stermaphors."

There was a response.

"You aren't an admiral. You're a lady," Lionel said.

The combination of admiral and lady that Dante sees in Beatrice evokes a sense of shame and repentance. Dante's actions to this point and the sins he sees paid for during his journey into the Inferno have led him to realize his inferiority in the face of Beatrice:

I lowered my head and looked down at the stream,

but, filled with shame at my reflection there,

I quickly fixed my eyes upon the grass.

I was the guilty child facing his mother,

> *abject before her harshness: harsh, indeed,*
>
> *is unripe pity not yet merciful.* (XXX: 76-81)

However, Lionel, unlike Dante, is not immediately moved by Boo Boo's appearance alongside the lake; he is not convinced of her authority.

Although Boo Boo presents herself as both an admiral and a lady, Lionel disagrees. Again his inability to communicate with his mother is reiterated: Lionel answers Boo Boo, but he answers "inaudibly" and must repeat himself (81). His second contention that Boo Boo is not an admiral is similarly inaudible, again forcing Boo Boo to ask him to repeat himself. As he repeats himself for the third time he seems final: "You aren't an admiral. You're a lady all the time" (81). Early in this scene, Lionel is unable to see his mother as Beatrice, as a figure of spiritual authority from the world of adulthood, nor as Boo Boo, the childhood figure her name suggests.

However, Boo Boo persists with her act as an admiral. After she sounds an impressive "kazoo style peculiar amalgamation of 'Taps' and 'Reveille,'" she finally gains Lionel's attention: "Lionel instantly looked up" (81). After Boo Boo gets Lionel's attention, she attempts to enter the boat, but Lionel is quick to block her: "[Boo Boo] started to lower herself into the dinghy. 'Get off!' Lionel ordered, but without giving over to shrillness, and keeping his eyes down. 'Nobody can come in'" (83). After Boo Boo pleads to Lionel to let her into the boat because she has "been all alone in the house all day without anybody to talk to" (83), he repeats his order that "Nobody can come in" (84) and instructs Boo Boo that she "can talk from *there*" (84). Again Boo Boo is unable to understand Lionel, but he repeats his order and she tells him that she cannot follow it: "No I can't. It's too big a distance. I have to get up close" (84). As Lionel echoes Sandra in his repetition of "Nobody," Salinger emphasizes the characters' isolation on the lake: neither Lionel, Boo Boo, Sandra, nor Mrs. Snell have anyone with whom they can communicate. It is not until Lionel goes through a process of repentance similar to the one Dante must go through before entering into Paradise with Beatrice that he is able to truly perceive his mother, communicate with her, and continue his journey to adulthood.

Dante's process of repentance is initiated in Canto XXX, as Beatrice explains why she sent Dante on his journey through Hell: "My purpose is / to make the one who weeps on that far bank / perceive the truth and match his guilt with grief" (106-108). After she upbraids him for straying from the truth that is both her and God's grace, she demands that Dante confess his indiscretions: "speak now, is this not true? Speak! You must seal / with your confession this grave charge I make" (XXXI: 5-6). Dante is, like Lionel, at first unable to speak, but eventually he bursts forth in confession:

My deep fear and chagrin, between them, forced<
out of my mouth a miserable "yes"-
only by ears with eyes could it be heard
... so I was shattered by the intensity
of my emotions: tears and sighs burst forth,
as I released my voice about to fail. (13-21)

Dante's image of "ears with eyes" is evoked in "Down at the Dinghy" as Lionel dismisses Boo Boo's supposed naval rank: "Boo Boo not only listened to his voice, she seemed to watch it" (80). Reading Dante and Beatrice's ability to communicate alongside the understanding that Lionel and Boo Boo achieve reveals the nature of the complex and intimate relationship between mother and son.

In order to achieve this understanding, Lionel must undergo a similar process of confession and purgation. After Dante confesses to Beatrice, he is purged in the Lethe and is able to drink from the Eunoi 乭; only then can he enter into Paradise. I want to suggest that Lionel's actions with the goggles and keys be read in this vein. Frederick Gwynn and Joseph Blotner have argued that Seymour's goggles and Boo Boo's keychain are "objects from the adult world...a world of facts [Lionel] unconsciously does not want to see, whose doors he does not want to open" (26). French calls Lionel's throwing of Boo Boo's keychain into the lake an act of "punishing himself for spitefully throwing away his uncle's goggles" (95).

The goggles and keys are both important symbols of the adult world: they represent both perception-in the ability to see clearly-and understanding-in the symbolic unlocking of knowledge. The goggles hold a special significance in this framework because they once belonged to Seymour, a figure who in other stories-particularly in "A Perfect Day for Bananafish"-seems closest to bridging the worlds of childhood and adulthood. However, the most important aspect of this scene is not the significance of the objects themselves, but Lionel's reaction to his misbehavior: "He then immediately looked up at Boo Boo, his eyes filled not with defiance but tears. In another instant, his mouth was distorted into a horizontal figure-8, and he was crying mightily" (85). Lionel's actions are a catalyst for his confession, and the cathartic force of his actions ultimately enable him to see his mother clearly: importantly, without Seymour's goggles, Lionel's "eyes reflected pure perception" (85). Like Dante, he is able to see Beatrice, accept her, and follow her back into the adult world.

The final scene of "Down at the Dinghy" provides an image of reconciliation not only between mother and son, but between the two conflicting worlds of the story. Boo Boo's response to Lionel demonstrates a level of understanding that was absent earlier in the story. Despite the hurtfulness of Sandra's remark, Boo Boo assures Lionel that it "isn't the *worst* thing that could happen" (86). Once she realizes that Lionel has misunderstood Sandra's anti-Semitic slur, she works to assuage his true fears: "'Tell you what we'll do," she said. "We'll drive to town and get some pickles, and some bread, and we'll eat the pickles in the car, and then we'll go to the station and get Daddy, and then we'll bring Daddy home and make him take us for a ride in the boat. You'll have to help him carry the sails down. O.K.?" (86).

Boo Boo emphasizes the unity of the family through her repetition of "we'll" and reassures Lionel that his father will not move further away from him. Sandra's ignorance, in both her anti-Semitism and her inability to understand Lionel and his family, is overcome through Boo Boo's compassion and engagement with her son, and the story ends on a note of triumph and reunion: "They didn't walk back to the house; they raced. Lionel won" (86). The story reaffirms the importance of empathy and human community, virtues that were crucial to helping Salinger overcome the horrors of WWII **(E6)**; virtues that are equally crucial to a full understanding of not only "Down at the Dinghy," but of *Nine Stories* collectively.

Endnotes:

E1: Ruth Prigozy in an insightful analysis of Salinger's *Nine Stories* argues that language in "Down at the Dinghy," like in many other stories, goes beyond referential meaning to suggest some deeper, emotional truth: "Just as Sybil's three words ['see more glass'] suggest deeper implications, the too-obvious meaning of Mrs. Snell's [sic: "Sandra-told Mrs. Smell" (86)] description of Daddy as a "big-sloppy-kike" (86) which Lionel hears as "kite," suggests an adult world that this intuitive child cannot forever flee" (97). Prigozy's attempts to link the mysteries of *Nine Stories* force her brevity on this very important point. Salinger's stories, when read with a focus beyond their literal meaning, repeatedly transcend what French calls "contrived."

E2: See Ruth Prigozy, "Salinger's Link Mysteries" for more. Also John Hagopian's "'Pretty Mouth and Green My Eyes': Salinger's Paolo and Francesca in New York," *Modern Fiction Studies* 12.3 (1966): 349-354.

E3: Although I think this Hell is best described in this line from Dostoevsky in "For Esmé": "Fathers and teachers, I ponder 'What is Hell?' I maintain that it is the suffering of being unable to love" (105). This quote is perhaps the most important line in *Nine Stories* when considering the importance of compassion and love, arguably the two most important themes in the collection.

E4: Kenneth Slawenski, in a recent biography, reaffirms this point. Slawenski contends that "Down at the Dinghy," and much of Salinger's later work was guided by the a *New Yorker* article detailing the atrocities committed by Nazi soldiers against the children of a small Czech village named Lidice. The article, "The Children of Lidice," details the vast slaughter of these children in gas chambers and crematoriums; however, Slawenski points out that it was a glimpse of hope in the face of despair that ultimately reached Salinger: "The closing paragraph of the sad tale of the children of Lidice directly followed the words that Salinger had written down, and it was the power of those words-and not the despair of Salinger's selection-that would finally take hold and guide his pen: 'I haven't given up hope,' the article proclaimed. 'None of us have given up hope'" (qtd. in Slawenski 173).

E5: Admittedly, Boo Boo is in many regards unlike Dante's Beatrice. Dante's perception of Beatrice throughout *The Divine Comedy* is a complicated mix of the erotic and the spiritual, but in the later Cantos of *Purgatory*, she serves most importantly as a spiritual guide and symbol of salvation. Salinger is quick to point out that Boo Boo does not have the "perfect beauty" (*Purgatory* XXXI.52) of Dante's erotic Beatrice: "She was a small, almost hipless girl of twenty-five, with styleless, colorless, brittle hair pushed back behind her ears . . . her general unprettiness aside, she was-in terms of permanently memorable, immoderately perceptive, small-area faces-a stunning and final girl" (77). Salinger's Beatrice need not be read in a direct correspondence with Dante's. However, considering the interconnected nature of the Glass family stories, as well as the hellish representations of the world of adulthood and the pure, innocent representations of the world of childhood that permeate *Nine Stories*, the allusion to Beatrice seems hard to ignore. Boo Boo is, ultimately, the figure that can bridge these two worlds and offer guidance to her son, the would-be pilgrim.

E6: Slawenski makes this point in detail: "The story… is a reaffirmation of the human connection he had found on the battlefields of France and had nearly lost in the agony of the death camps, a confirmation that began to emerge in 'Just Before the War with the Eskimos' and comes to fruition in 'Down at the Dinghy.' Upon returning home to Connecticut and after three long years of doubting the presence of God in man, Salinger proudly declared to Elizabeth Murray that, spiritually, "the old ship is steady again" (176).

Works Cited:

Alighieri, Dante. *The Portable Dante*. Ed. Mark Musa. New York: Penguin, 2003.

French, Warren. *J. D. Salinger, Revisited*. Swansea: Wales UP, 1988.

Gwynn, Frederick, and Joseph Blotner. *The Fiction of J. D. Salinger.* Pittsburgh: Pittsburgh UP, 1958.

Hagopian, John. "'Pretty Mouth and Green My Eyes': Salinger's Paolo and Francesca in New York," *Modern Fiction Studies* 12.3 (1966): 349-354.

Prigozy, Ruth. "Nine Stories: J.D. Salinger's Linked Mysteries." *Modern American Short Story Sequences.* Ed. J. Gerald Kennedy. Cambridge: Cambridge UP, 1995.

Salinger, J. D. *Nine Stories.* New York: Little, Brown, 1953.

Slawenski, Kenneth. *J. D. Salinger: A Life.* New York: Random House, 2010.

Esmé's Kind of Squalor

Donald Junkins
Professor Emeritus
University of Massachusetts at Amherst

What strikes an old re-reader of J. D. Salinger's short stories **(E1)** is the seemingly effortless movement from his alert but seemingly ordinary opening sentences into immediately deepening, often mock-ironic, human dramas. In the Esmé story, mock-ironic in the sense that an unacknowledged authorial hand, in this case within the voice of the central character, Sergeant X (the anonymous civilian speaker in the first two paragraphs), purveys a narrative that leads the reader seemingly away from but finally into the disported relief of the concluding paragraph.

All but the first page of the twenty-seven page story relates two flashbacks that, aside from the war itself, do not clarify the origins of Sergeant X's breakdown, and only partially clarify the origins of Sergeant X's awarenesses of himself in relation to characters in the three scenes from the six-year span of the story: Esmé and her younger

Teaching Salinger's Nine Stories

brother Charles during Sergeant X's training time in England just prior to the Allied invasion of France; Corporal Z (Clay) in immediate post-war Germany; and his American wife, re-joined after his discharge from the army.

The story unfolds as kind of what might be called a delayed distraction. The narrator, whom we shall call Civilian (formerly Sergeant) X, has presumably recovered from a nervous breakdown near the end of World War II in Germany, yet his "recovery" is still on display within the first page of the story. A wedding invitation has arrived from a young English girl named Esmé (now nineteen), to whom he promised five years earlier, at the end of his pre-invasion WW II training in England, a written story containing "squalor."

"Delayed" in the above phrase "delayed distraction" is meant to focus exactly on the original psychological territory that the serious writer enters when pursuing whatever occurs in the journey into plot, partially remembered or imagined. The "distraction" is the writing of the story itself. What is being distracted from is whatever precedes the unknown mental condition of the story's narrator as he currently tells the story, whether or not the objective story itself is wholly or partially invented. The creative gifts of the writer arm him against the disclosure of the undisclosed information, as his creative intuitions focus exactly the information necessary for the reader's comprehension. Such undisclosed information lurks behind all creative activity to produce that sublimated or partially manifested truth of art itself, the greater the art the greater the profound transcendent energy that is produced or created in the process. The "how" of getting there, which is the work itself, defines the validity or reality of what "there" becomes in the journey.

Whatever rehabilitative progress X has achieved in his civilian life, the tone of the opening section of the story, in addition to what it creates plot-wise or stylistically, pinpoints, to use non-Salingerian terms, the human struggle to survive the deepest human sensitivities and consequent frailties. The story in its inception is originally intended as a gift to a thirteen year old girl, precocious in both her manner and expression, but years later conceptualizes as a wedding gift to a now unknown, but remembered, nineteen year old stranger, estranged Esmé, recollected from her wit and her charming and precocious assertiveness during wartime England when she distracted Sergeant X for part of an afternoon from himself. His return to that afternoon, as a prelude to the "squalor" he promised to include in a short story he would write especially for her, leads him to a re-visitation of events that followed, and includes the promised "squalor."

In the "For Esmé" story, we are immediately working backwards, from a kind of post-war controlled distress in the form of irony, described on the opening page (and set in the States), into a heightened wartime environment that in fourteen and a half pages cleverly masks an oddity in

Teaching Salinger's Nine Stories

the second scene, set in Devon, England where the narrator goes for a walk on a rainy Saturday afternoon at the end of a three week pre-invasion training exercise. The oddity is nothing more than the narrator's self-detainment before a church bulletin board and subsequent entry into the church-clearly normal behavior, perhaps. Yet the details of the first two-and-a-half pages suggest otherwise.

Our man Salinger has known all along that the short story devil lurks in the details because the details shape tone, and although the devil may be a shape-shifter, he is not a tone-shifter: tone not plot tells the story. The opening one page scene not only establishes the tone of the story, it provides all the information necessary for an ending. Whoever said that the ending is in the beginning knew, among other things, about short stories.

Let's begin with the mock irony in the two paragraphs of scene one. We know by the fourth line that Civilian X cannot go to "the" wedding, "It happens to be a wedding I'd give a lot to be able to get to. ... I thought it might just be possible for me to make the trip abroad, expenses be hanged" (87). Why can't he fly to England for the wedding? The answer he gives is because his mother-in-law is coming to visit, which is obvious baloney. So, he says, he jots down a few "revealing notes" (87) that he hopes will not upset the groom. (There isn't anything in the story itself that could possibly upset the groom, but the seemingly throwaway comment reveals a hint of the strong feelings that the narrator has retained for the imminent bride.)

One of the charming things about Salinger is that nothing is a throwaway, especially seemingly innocent asides, and the imagery of these opening two paragraphs shows us how he works (the words "a Poem Means" in the title of John Ciardi's book, *How a Poem Means*" could easily be replaced by "Short Stories Mean"). Note two phrases: "expenses be hanged," and "a breathtakingly levelheaded girl" (the latter referring to his wife who has already convinced him that he should stay home because her mother is coming to visit). Both phrases put into context crucial literary mechanisms that function throughout the recapitulated story to follow: the deadly nature of the details and the mock ironic tone that encompasses them.

Scene two: a rainy afternoon on the last day before Sergeant X's intelligence-group departs for London and the consequent invasion of France. After two paragraphs describing the members of his special training force as letter-writing non-mixers, and adding the details that he had thrown his gas mask out a porthole during his Atlantic crossing and now wore his overseas cap "slightly down over both ears" (89), he now stands in the rain studying a church bulletin board, noting each name of a children's choir, then enters the church to witness choir practice.

At the conclusion of choir practice he enters a civilian tearoom where he meets Esmé, whom he noted in the choir, and her little brother Charles, and promises to write a story especially for her. Scene three focuses on the mid-distress mental breakdown of Sergeant X in the post-war occupation zone in Germany.

The "oddity" mentioned above, glossed over quickly in the narration of the story itself, centers on Sergeant X's entering the church to attend as a spectator the children's choir practice. Salinger has created previously in the first two-and-a-quarter pages a character who is slightly fishy, but compelling, and in so doing has literarily dodged the rational question of why in the world would an American soldier in an intelligence unit enter a British church to listen to a children's choir practice on a rainy afternoon. Certainly on a whim is the answer, but there are in fiction prepared-for whims. So the answer to the oddity question is that this particular oddity is in the eye, or mind, of the reader who has not carefully read the first two pages of the story where the narrator has already leveled with the careful reader. This "leveling" comes to the reader, however, not in the facts of the story, but in the asides, the tone; in other words, the crucial details.

Before we get to Esmé and Charles and then Corporal Z, let's return to Sergeant X's wife in the opening page. Well into the middle section of the story, Esmé bluntly, and quite obtrusively, asks Sergeant X if he is "very deeply in love with his wife" (95), a question that seems out of her range except that she has already been presented as precociously forthright. We, however, never get to know what prompted the question, and it remains part of Esmé's complex character. We also never get to know the answer to the question, and it, in an equally poignant way, remains part of Sergeant X's character by enhancing his own complex state of mind as partially revealed on the first page of the story.

The details of the opening paragraph are impeccably precise. "It happens to be a wedding I'd give a lot to be able to get to" (87). By this third line we know that we've arrived at the begging point, as in begging the question, but not haphazardly; all doubt about anything coincidental has been removed. "I'd give a lot" immediately introduces a shadow on his ability to go to the wedding. "To be able" states immediately that something serious, if not looms, then unmistakably blocks his path to the wedding. He'd "give a lot," but not enough to change plans, or not enough to sidestep something else. Which is what? Expense is not the preventing agent.

He has discussed his making the trip to England for the wedding "rather extensively" with his wife, so we know that he has belabored the possibility. Yet just before we hear of his belaboring, he says "expenses be hanged," a seemingly neutral colloquialism except for its death image. Something is hanging over his decision, and he is almost forthright about it, as he notes that he has discussed the matter with his "breathtakingly levelheaded" wife, whom he calls a "girl," fondly dismissing the "reason." What immediately follows in a tone of double-displaced seriousness, prepares the reader for the psychological ambiguity in his decision to stay home. He ostensibly defers to his wife's (the girl) over-riding concern about her mother's upcoming visit, one of the reasons being that she, his mother-in-law, is "looking forward" to the visit.

But Salinger is not through with the first paragraph, and he semi-explains: "She's fifty-eight. (As she'd be the first to admit)" (87). He has just said that "she's not getting any younger," and the number fifty-eight adds a little more ironic salt to his attitude toward her, because the number indicates that Mother Grencher is arguably of prime age for mothers-in-law, and it will not be her last visit. In the sentence before, he has named her "Mother Grencher," calling into play (which is the right word for more than one reason), the female fictional character, Grendel's mother, in the Anglo-Saxon epic *Beowulf*, the family he married into. Later, when Esmé asks him if he is "very deeply in love with his wife," the question resonates with the overtones of the opening page of the story.

Other reasons, obviously more serious ones, why our hero and his wife decide against his traveling to the wedding, lurk behind their decision. The evasions beneath the surface of the text, even though we don't know what they are, tell us much more than the jokey, diversionary commentary about the mother-in-law, followed by the flip, even more diversionary self-analysis of the second paragraph. In a strange but telling double negative sentence that indicates a kind of psychological suppression, "I don't think I'm the type that doesn't even lift a finger to prevent a wedding from flatting" (87), he pries open the beginning of the two scenes that follow, seemingly almost unable to leave the satiric gloss of his current mood. He tells the reader directly that he knows more about the bride than her current groom can possibly know, but he's not "aiming" to please the groom, but "really to edify, to instruct" (87) the reader. In other words he's sticking to his story.

Not a consecutive story in actual time, but a sequential story in which the narrator evolves from his being stationed as intelligence enlisted personnel in April of 1944 in Devonshire, England where he describes himself as a loner preoccupied with non-military mental diversions, to a battle-fatigued post-war mental case in occupied Germany, to a married wise-cracking American back in the States who is subjected to the accouterments of marriage, such as an upcoming visit of his mother-in-law and the singular reasonableness of his young wife.

Salinger's management of aesthetic distance is one key to the ingenuity of the story, another is how he rides the overtones of what he leaves out. The answer to the first is his humor; what I mean by 'riding the overtones' is simply the "how" of why the story works its ways.

The transition back six years begins, "In April of 1944," and as noted above we are back in England, about to enter a war story, though as we discover, J. D. leaves out the war. Esmé, remember, for those of you who have read the story, after their meeting in the tearoom, mails Sergeant X her father's watch, and it arrives after the war is over, during Sergeant X's mental breakdown. We discover at the end, in the third section of the story, that the crystal of the watch has been broken in transit. Time for both of them has not only stopped, it has ceased to be a factor in their relationship. The watch was sent shortly after their tearoom meeting, on June 7, 1944, the day of the invasion. Esmé's final comment to him as they parted in the tearoom had been, "I hope that you return from the war with all your faculties intact" (103). This is one of the two key points in the story, the other being when Esmé asks Sergeant X whether he is "very deeply in love with his wife" (95).

The second scene, however, on the rainy afternoon in the tearoom, gives us not only Esmé herself, but her younger brother Charles, for whom she has become the parent after the demise of their own parents, the mother in a bombing raid and the father in North Africa. Charles is sort of an odd little duck himself. On his introduction to Sergeant X, he asks X why people kiss sideways in the movies. He's also covetous of the answer to his one riddle that features the question, "What did one wall say to the other wall?" and when he repeats his first success with it, accesses his first-quality temper when Sergeant X prematurely, from Charles' point of view, supplies the answer, "Meetcha at the corner" (100). Charles stalks back to his original table, fuming. Yet like Esmé, whose interest in Sergeant X has been piqued by his visit to the choir rehearsal in the church, and who responds to his proximity in the tearoom with her complex and formal intimacy, Charles insists, we discover near the end of the story when Sergeant X reads the letter in the package from Esmé with her father's watch broken in transit, on adding his two cents worth to the letter:

HELLO HELLO HELLO HELLO HELLO
HELLO HELLO HELLO HELLO HELLO
LOVE AND KISSES CHALES. (113)

These loving hellos appear eleven lines before the end of the story, four lines before Sergeant X realizes that the crystal of the watch had been broken in transit. He wonders if any other part of the watch is broken "but he hadn't the courage to wind it and find out" (114). Suddenly he feels almost ecstatically sleepy, and the final lines are addressed directly to Esmé:

> You take a really sleepy man, Esmé, and he always stands a chance of again becoming a man with all his fac-with all his f-a-c-u-l-t-i-e-s intact. (114)

The wedding invitation has arrived five years after time has been stopped in Sergeant X's relationship with Esmé, whether the rest of the watch has been broken or not, because watches in 1945 stopped ticking if not wound frequently. The key damage has been done to the crystal, (the crust of the earth or the moon), that which one sees through, to the face of time.

Previously, in the last sentence of the middle scene, Esmé leaves the British tearoom "testing the ends of her hair for dryness" (103), much as the third scene opens in the following paragraph with Sergeant X, in occupied Bavaria, testing his gums with his tongue, causing them to bleed. In their pre-invasion departure scene, Esmé, as noted above, hoped out-loud that Sergeant X would come through the war with all his faculties intact, and then asked Sergeant X if he was familiar with squalor. He replies that he is "getting better acquainted with it" (103), and within a paragraph of the third scene, the reader knows that Sergeant X is immersed in it.

The reader also knows immediately that the scene transition from Devon, England to Gaufurt, Germany is merely an accommodation of the psychological transition, from Sergeant X's pre-invasion state of mind in England to his occupation force state of mind in Germany.

He is seated at night under a hanging light bulb on a folding chair before a small writing desk messy with unopened letters and packages on the second floor of a civilian German home that was requisitioned before the end of the war to house ten American soldiers. It is reminiscent of a prison scene. He is trying to read a novel but for an hour has been triple-reading, first paragraphs and now sentences.

Salinger's details indicate that Sergeant X recently, without textual explanation, had completed a two week hitch in an army hospital in Frankfurt, obviously, to the careful reader, with a mental, not a physical disability; that his fingers trembled together when he tried to light his cigarettes; that he sometimes sat by the hour provoking his raw gums to bleed at the touch of his tongue. He picks up and re-reads a hand-written sentence, on the inside cover of a book written by the Nazi propaganda minister Goebbels, *A Time Without Comparison*, by a young woman whom Sergeant X himself had arrested because she was a low level Nazi party official. Her inscription reads, "Dear God, life is hell" (105). Under the inscription, Sergeant X adds, "Fathers and teachers, I ponder, 'What is hell?' I maintain that it is the suffering of being unable to love" (105). He had started to write Dostoevsky's name as the author and then realized that what he had written was "almost entirely illegible" (105).

Into this last scene appears Corporal Z, also referred to later as "Clay," and the five-and-a-half pages that follow, preliminary to Sergeant X's discovery of Esmé's letter written thirty-eight days after the tearoom encounter with him in England, picture Corporal Z as an accommodating, mindless army buddy who points out to Sergeant X that his girlfriend back in the States who's majoring in psychology wrote to him that "nobody gets a nervous breakdown from the war and all. She says you probably were unstable like, your whole goddam life" (109). When Sergeant X comments that "Loretta's insights into things were always a joy," Clay fires back, "Listen ya bastard, she knows a goddam sight more psychology than you do" (109). Clay then urges Sergeant X to "C'mon down and listen to [Bob] Hope on the radio, hey. ... It'll do ya good, I mean it" (111).

Clay's acceptance of Sergeant X's mental state with the same tonal placidity he seemingly accepted the war itself marks the gulf between their sensibilities. When Clay begins to reminisce about an incident during the war when they were pinned down by shelling next to their jeep in Valognes and he shot a cat that jumped suddenly onto the jeep, Sergeant X says, "Don't start that business with the cat again, Clay, God damn it. I don't want to hear about it" (110). Clay persists and tells X that his girlfriend explained that he was temporarily insane, and X says, "No, that cat was a spy. . . a very clever German midget dressed up in a fur coat" (110). When Clay asks him if he can't ever be "sincere," X vomits in the waste basket.

Finally, Esmé herself, the little girl in the church choir, the one on the end of the row who had the sweetest voice and whose "wide nostril wings" (90) gave away her closed mouth yawn. She's the archetypal Salinger heroine, alert, insightful, wary of being weak and thus sometimes cautiously brazen. She tells X that he's "the eleventh American I've met" (93), noting that he seemed "quite intelligent for an American" (94). Her penchant for squalor corroborates her realistic outlook, yet she bites her fingernails. Her conversational agility sometimes leads to probing questions that test the boundary of what might be considered a wise-ass, but her seemingly humorless straight-forward conversation not only attracts Sergeant X but carries considerable weight with her younger brother Charles. Her talk and manner are extremely advanced and compelling, and she projects a quality of formal, if not wholly rational empathy, even a decent caring that transcends its own formalism. She doesn't fool around, and her endearing gestures cut through her own potential brittleness. When she asks X if he's "very deeply in love with [his] wife," before he answers she immediately follows with the question whether she's being "too personal" (95). He doesn't answer except to say that when she "was," he'd speak up.

The written story in the final two scenes has become the story that the American soldier promised to write for the teenage British girl, but it is preceded by an opening scene six years later in time, after the former American soldier has received a wedding invitation from the girl, now nineteen.

At the conclusion of the published story, Sergeant X still owes Esmé both the story itself, which he has written for her, and her father's watch that she sent him to keep for the "duration of the conflict" (113). The published story allows the reader to ponder the newly created context of the word "conflict," and this post-story aesthetic puzzle is part of the genius of the story, that everything depends on how the reader views, in light of the story, the meaning, now, of the word "conflict," whether it refers to the literal and now concluded war, or to Civilian X's inner, ongoing war.

That the narrator addresses Esmé directly in the final three lines, switching from the third to first person, enhances, if nothing else, the restrained intensity of feeling that the narrator feels for his/the heroine.

At the end, what we do know in the light, or darkness, of the opening one page scene incorporating the intervention of his wife, is that Civilian X will now keep Esmé's father's watch with the broken crystal, and that the once stopped time of World War II will remain stopped forever.

Endnotes:

E1: This essay was the co-keynote address (along with an abbreviated version of Richard Davison's essay "Salinger Criticism and The Laughing Man"-which included an *inspired* reading from the story "The Laughing Man") at the 2009 South Atlantic Modern Language Association Convention for three panels of papers on Salinger entitled "Rediscovering J. D. Salinger's *Nine Stories.*"

Bibliography:

Ciardi, John. *How Does a Poem Mean ?* Boston: Houghton Mifflin, 1975.

Salinger, J. D. *Nine Stories*. New York: Little Brown, 1981 (1953).

The Necessity of Art in "Pretty Mouth and Green My Eyes"

Holland Whiteburch
Baylor University

Most of Salinger's stories in *Nine Stories* seem to be both inscrutable and charged with several layers of meaning. "Pretty Mouth and Green My Eyes" seems to be the most impenetrable of them all; unlike several others, the story excludes precocious children and sympathetic eccentrics. Instead, Salinger presents callous adults who seem incapable of redemption. "Pretty Mouth," originally published in 1951 in *The New Yorker*, reveals the hollow relationships between three people in the city: Joanie, Arthur, and Lee. Only two critical essays exploring the intricacies of the story have been published. John Hagopian's article, "Salinger's Paolo and Francesca in New York," admits that the story "has never been carefully explicated" (349); Hagopian's thesis is summed up with the fact that "the story has more than sociological implications. The fire and ashes symbolism suggests that Lee and Joanie are in a Dantean inferno" (353).

Along with Kenneth Hamilton's "Hell in New York," however, the essays mostly focus on the religious implications of the story's ending. These essays build an argument to explain burning cigarettes and God-filled expletives, but they overlook the full scope of the story. Authors like Warren French and John Wenke also include the story in their comprehensive books on Salinger, but they, too, mostly focus on the "moral collapse" (French 130) of the characters. However, the style of "Pretty Mouth" sets the story apart from others in the *Nine Stories* collection: the story covers a much briefer length of time, and it reads like a carefully scripted scene of a movie. Therefore, the more overt features of "Pretty Mouth" must be taken into account: the meticulous attention to surface details, constant storytelling (of memories and of lies), and miniscule glimpses of honesty.

Just as the title implies, "Pretty Mouth" focuses on disembodied depictions, and the story hinges on a phone conversation that serves to obfuscate the true interactions between the characters. The most explicit aspect of the story seems to be the perpetuation of lies; therefore, this trope of deceit should be the starting point for a different kind of critical explication of the text focusing on the characters' use of art, or more specifically, artifice, in order to survive the pain of daily interaction.

The characters in "Pretty Mouth" are the perfect examples of Salinger's "phonies." In addition to the characters' struggle between surface versus substance and true art versus artifice, Salinger presents the story itself as a study in surfaces, which is emblematic of the *New Yorker* story of the 1950s. The following explication of the text will investigate each character's use of art and artifice, the story's slightly postmodern take on itself as artifice, and the story's connection to *New Yorker* style; these aspects of the story can also be seen as emblematic of Salinger's entire short fiction oeuvre.

The ringing of a phone initiates the action of "Pretty Mouth." Arthur, who calls Lee, is looking for his wife, Joanie, who left a party without him. Lee attempts to reassure Arthur that his wife is probably with friends, and Arthur spends most of the phone call questioning his wife and their marriage. The inevitable Salingerian twist occurs when the reader realizes that the unnamed woman in bed with Lee at the beginning of the story is, in fact, Arthur's wife. When Arthur calls back a second time, he announces to Lee that his wife returned home and invents a complicated story to explain her disappearance.

Obviously, Joanie is still in bed with Lee, but Arthur tries to save face in front of his law firm associate. Arthur utilizes art and artifice within the story in two different ways. First, he uses artifice to attempt to shield his broken marriage from his friend. Whereas in the first phone call Arthur honestly confesses his inability to relate to his wife and his vacillating love for her, the second phone call completely undermines the honesty of their interaction. Arthur loses his struggle against phoniness, and his second phone call to Lee becomes a performance of marital bliss rather than the truth of discord. Even more humiliating, his performance fails since his audience knows the sad truth of his wife's location. His attempt at artifice hides nothing.

Arthur's second use of art occurs in his first conversation with Lee, when he recalls a poem he wrote for his wife when they were dating. As repeated in the title, the poem mentions the physical characteristics of Joanie, including her green eyes, but Arthur exclaims: "Christ, it's embarrassing-it used to remind me of her. She doesn't have green eyes-she has eyes like goddam sea shells, for Chrissake-but it reminded me anyway" (125). Perhaps the point of the poem was an honest representation of the subject, not the actual color of her eyes. Still, this poem seems to represent the most beautiful and true moment of Arthur's artificial relationship with his wife, though this beauty is precisely because of the poem's artifice.

Arthur cannot escape the struggle against artifice; he has no way out of it, except for the art of the poem, which is simply artifice on a higher level. "Phone" in Greek means both "sound" and "voice," so perhaps Salinger's "phonies" are people whose voice is no more than sound, who do not express a "logos" of truth or meaning or beauty within them. The poem in "Pretty Mouth" could be an attempt to turn "phone" into "logos," but it ultimately fails. Arthur needs artifice in order to survive his relationships; he keeps declaring his weakness to Lee as the source of his marital problems in the first phone call, so the lies of the second phone call create a sense of strength for Arthur.

Lee utilizes artifice through his insistence on "helping" Arthur deal with his relationship with Joanie. His artifice is perhaps the most dangerous, since he appears to be offering guidance to his friend. He creates a scenario for Joanie's disappearance to assuage Arthur's nerves, and he also advises Arthur against becoming deconstructive in his relationship with his wife. Lee calmly explains to the irrational Arthur: "What I would like to do, though, if it's at all humanly possible, I'd like to help you, boy" (126). Lee performs like a dutiful friend and even a concerned father figure; in reality, he lies (physically and metaphorically) in bed with Arthur's wife.

Lee's artifice is also present in his relationship with Joanie. The description of their movements in bed is altogether sexless. When Lee reaches for the phone, he holds Joanie with one hand and the phone with the other: "[he] slipped his hand under the girl's supporting arm, above the elbow, working his fingers up, making room for them between the warm surfaces of her upper arm and chest wall" (115). Later, he takes his hand out from between her upper arm and chest wall. In this position, Lee would be touching her breast, which would seemingly be an enjoyable experience for him.

Instead, he seems to be absently touching an object beside him. The only point at which the couple in bed actually looks at each other occurs when Arthur proposes coming over to Lee's place to talk, and even then, the look is only glancing. In conversation, Lee and Joanie constantly interrupt each other, and they distract themselves with cigarettes and ashtrays. At the end of the story, Lee and Joanie are together in bed but are still disconnected as Salinger significantly ends with the phrase, "she pulled back her hand" (129). The artifice portrayed in relationships affects the adulterous couple as well as the married couple in "Pretty Mouth." Lee must force himself to perform for Arthur and for Joanie in order to retain any semblance of dignity and false empathy he has created.

Joanie has the empty countenance and reactions of a soap opera actress. Her entire character seems artificial, and her words to Lee sound like rehearsed lines. After he hangs up with Arthur the first time, Joanie applauds Lee's performance: "You were wonderful. Absolutely marvellous" (127). She praises Lee for his playacting abilities, and even seems like a star-struck movie fan in reaction to his performance: "I'm *limp*. I'm absolutely *limp*. Look at me!" (127). As evinced by her repeated praise, Joanie also seems to perform through her exaggerated remarks to Lee. She tries to bring attention to herself through her dramatics; even when she merely brushes cigarette ashes from Lee's arm, she informs him, "I think you're on *fire*" (127). Joanie keeps swearing, "God, I feel like a dog!" (127).

Although Joanie has few speaking parts in the story, her lines sound overly emphatic, almost as if she must prove to herself and to Lee that she actually feels bad about her adultery. The story's description of her expressions indicates her vacuous nature; her eyes, "more just open than alert or speculative," belie an absence of concern for the situation (127). Arthur lambastes her for her love of television and psychoanalysis, and he even tells Lee that she hasn't got any brains. To Lee, Joanie becomes merely hands, as she constantly brushes away ashes and picks up cigarettes. Although the pretty mouth and the eyes from the story's title seem like inaccurately disembodied representations of Joanie, they actually prove to be evocative of her entire character. Therefore, she must hold fast to her artificial devices of playacting in order to hold on to the men in her life.

In addition to the characters' focuses on surfaces, the structure of "Pretty Mouth" functions to emphasize the role of artifice. The story forces the reader to perceive only superficial details in its exacting depiction of the characters' movements. The brief moments not spent on the phone reveal few substantial details about the characters; instead, Salinger prevents the reader from knowing anything other than what the character in the story has constructed to perform. Every action is meticulously described, down to the exactness of hand movement: "He reached for the phone with his right hand. To reach it without groping, he had to raise himself somewhat higher, which caused the back of his head to graze a corner of the lampshade" (115). The precise nature of these details creates an uncomfortable setting for the characters, and they lend the story a directive script-like quality, highlighting the performance-obsessed artifice of the characters.

In addition to the story's details as tools for emphasizing the role of artifice, the entire premise of "Pretty Mouth" centers around two telephone calls. Phone calls allow for a disembodied relationship between people; rather than experiencing the physicality of face-to-face interactions with eye contact and body signals, the phone call presents a voice that can be disconnected from truth and reality. In "A Perfect Day for Bananafish," the phone call between Muriel and her mother operates in this same way. Although they mention Seymour's apparent psychological problems they attempt to talk around the issue with talk of dresses and sunburns.

In "Uncle Wiggily in Connecticut," Eloise pokes fun at her daughter and her husband while talking to her friend Mary Jane, and she acts the part of a bored, sarcastic housewife in her initial interactions with Mary Jane and during her conversation on the phone with her husband. When her husband calls Eloise to get a ride home in the snow, she unconcernedly remarks, "Well, that's tough, kid.

Why don't you boys form a platoon and march home?" (35).

In "Pretty Mouth," the phone calls between Arthur and Lee allow Salinger to recreate the futility of phoniness acted out by Muriel and her mother as well as Eloise and her husband by letting the actors in "Pretty Mouth" speak for themselves without the benefit of giving the reader background information. The style of dialogue between Arthur and Lee on the phone also emphasizes their artificial relationship. Neither man hears the other, as they constantly interrupt each other. Instead of communicating, the interruptions on the phone portray the men as voices shouting into a receiver in vain without a listener on the other end. The story itself is an example of artifice on a higher level, much like Arthur's poem. Therefore, the truth in Salinger's art lies in the story's honest portrayal of marriage and infidelity.

Interestingly, the premise of "Pretty Mouth" as a story that is about its own surfaces relates to a *New Yorker* style typical of the time period. Generally, these stories lacked major events in plot, focused on nuances of conversation, and emphasized character development. Thomas Leitch's article on the history of *New Yorker* short story style posits that the history of this magazine's stories is important to the evolution of the American short story because the magazine "provided a forum for authors and readers alike to tenure in the conventions of the modern short story by denying . . . that what they are producing and consuming are short stories at all" (149).

In other words, what we call a "typical" *New Yorker* story actually plays with the rules of the short story to engage readers in a more significant way than merely providing a short form of narrative entertainment. In Salinger's case, he produces a short story that appears to merely chronicle infidelity in the city, but he also playfully exploits his own story to make it appear almost artificially soap opera-like. He also points a self-reflexive finger at his *New Yorker* audience through the characters in the story, who seem like they could be a part of the magazine's readership.

In his second phone call to Lee, Arthur comments, "What a rat race. Honest to God, I think it's this goddam New York" (128). Even the mythical New York becomes the stuff of play in the story. Although the aforementioned critical articles by Hagopian and Hamilton look at New York as being Salinger's hell in the story, his love for the city seems too strong to warrant a stern warning against city life. Even after he moves to Cornish, Salinger continues to set his stories in the city; while he could be issuing a cautionary tale to city dwellers of the dangers of fakery, he also pokes fun at others' misconceptions of the city. Obviously, Arthur and Joanie's marriage will not be saved through a move to the country as suggested by "Uncle Wiggily."

Instead, Arthur's attempt to place blame on the city is another example of artifice. The most important aspect of Salinger's style in the story that relates to *New Yorker* style is the author's use of conventions to present an unconventional idea: the characters in his story actually need artifice to survive in their relationships with each other, and they resist redemption from their vice. Except for Lee at the end of the story, none of the characters in the story even express discomfort with their phony behavior. Though the reader intuits Arthur and Lee's discomfort with the situation that they have created, the men refuse to acknowledge their discomfort, thereby resisting redemption through willful ignorance.

Although "Pretty Mouth" presents the role of art in daily life in a different manner than the other stories in the collection, the characters' pretense relates to a kind of artfulness inherent throughout *Nine Stories*. Many stories revolve around the importance of art in daily life: "The Laughing Man" and "De Daumier-Smith's Blue Period," with their focuses on storytelling and the creation of art, are the most explicit examples of this theme. Perhaps "Uncle Wiggily" relates most closely to the depiction of phony adult interactions shown in "Pretty Mouth," but even Eloise appears to come to a point of drunken realization of her folly.

The characters in "Pretty Mouth," however, cling to the corrupting artifice in their relationships and choose to ignore their phoniness to some degree. Whereas the role of art in other stories allows for transcendent moments for characters, art in "Pretty Mouth" becomes base. In light of the struggle between surface versus substance and true art versus artifice, the battle against phoniness in "Pretty Mouth" sheds a new light on the struggle within the entirety of *Nine Stories*: this story shows that maybe there is a point at which one cannot escape artifice in the modern world. The misery shown in "Pretty Mouth" could relate more to the characters' resistance to redemption from their flaws rather than their embrace of the inevitability of artifice; their true problems result from their need to act out parts that they have falsely created for themselves.

Interestingly, in the same month that "Pretty Mouth" appeared in the *New Yorker*, *The Catcher in the Rye*, the ultimate manifesto of the struggle against the phony, was released. Even Holden Caulfield falls prey to the allure of the phony, and his narrative also shows his constant struggle against falsehoods. Still, the end of *Catcher*, with Holden's admission of missing everyone, seems much more positive than the end of "Pretty Mouth"; perhaps Salinger shows that phoniness can only be prevented by beginning the process of awareness and resistance at a young age. Most importantly, in all of Salinger's works involving the role of art, he emphasizes the necessity of honest interactions rather than faked relationships. In this way, we can augment the Salinger canon by viewing his works in light of the search for the art of being with others.

Works Cited:

French, Warren. *J. D. Salinger*. Boston: Twayne, 1976.

Hagopian, John. "'Pretty Mouth and Green My Eyes': Salinger's Paolo and Francesca in New York." *Modern Fiction Studies* 12.3 (1966): 349-354.

Hamilton, Kenneth. "Hell in New York: J. D. Salinger's 'Pretty Mouth and Green My Eyes.'" *Dalhousie Review* 47 (1967): 394-399.

Leitch, Thomas. "The *New Yorker* School." *Creative and Critical Approaches to the Short Story*. Ed. Noel Harold Kaylor, Jr. Lewiston: Mellen, 1997. 123-149.

Salinger, J. D. *Nine Stories*. Boston: Little, Brown, 1953.

Wenke, John. *J. D. Salinger: A Study of the Short Fiction*. Boston: Twayne, 1991.

Salinger and Sincerity: "De Daumier-Smith's Blue Period"

Alex Shakespeare
Boston College

When we hear [the word "sincerity"], we are conscious of the anachronism which touches it with quaintness. If we speak it, we are likely to do so with either discomfort or irony. In its commonest employment it has sunk to the level of a mere intensive, in which capacity it has an effect that negates its literal intention-"I sincerely believe" has less weight than "I believe" ... To praise a work of literature by calling it sincere is now at best a way of saying that although it need be given no aesthetic or intellectual admiration, it was at least conceived in innocence of heart. **- Lionel Trilling, *Sincerity and Authenticity***

I did not really mean to steal your purse. I just took it because I love you. **- J. D. Salinger, "The Heart of a Broken Story"**

In September 1941, *Esquire* published the twenty-four year old Salinger's "The Heart of a Broken Story." The editors ran the first few paragraphs on page 32 and printed the rest of the text in the issue's back pages. The story was thus broken in two. Appropriate, not only given the story's title, but given that the narrative divides itself neatly in two parts: first, a false start to a New York love story, then Salinger's rollicking commentary on the kind of slick urban love stories that were frequently published in magazines (like *Esquire*) in the 40s. "The Heart of a Broken Story" is pre-War Salinger-a piece of juvenilia really-not one of his profounder efforts. But it remains entertaining in no small part because the figure of the desperately lonely, romantically yearning New York citizen that he depicts in Justin Horgenschlag (the heartbroken protagonist) has lost none of its currency. **(E1)**

Horgenschlag, a "thirty-dollar-a-week printer's assistant," has seen "about 75,120 different women" in his life but "with only 1" does he "fall in love at first sight" (32). This is a girl named Shirley Lester, and all because her mouth is "open in a peculiar way," Horgenschlag is a dead duck. As Salinger puts it:

> *Shirley was reading a cosmetic advertisement in the wall panel of the bus; and when Shirley read, Shirley relaxed slightly at the jaw. And in that short moment while Shirley's mouth was open, lips were parted, Shirley was probably the most fatal one*

in all Manhattan. Horgenschlag saw in her a positive cure-all for a gigantic monster of loneliness which had been stalking around his heart since he had come to New York. Oh, the agony of it! The agony of standing over Shirley Lester and not being able to bend down and kiss Shirley's parted lips! The inexpressible agony of it! (32)

In the midst of this shticky sequence of events, Salinger interrupts himself: "That was the beginning of the story I started to write for *Collier's*" (131). The problem he had finishing it, he confesses, was his realization that in a boy-meets-girl story the writer must "unfortunately, go about the business of having the boy meet the girl" (131). The rest of the text is a list of failed scenarios, abandoned plotlines, and absurd wiseguy humor. For instance: even Horgenschlag, a bumpkin from Seattle, cannot lean over and beg Shirley's pardon, saying "Gosh, how I love you. Are you busy tonight?," for Horgenschlag may be a "goof," Salinger says, "but not that big a goof" (131). Likewise, Horgenschlag cannot suddenly make himself suave; he cannot pretend he mistakes Shirley for a girl named Wilma Pritchard he knew back home; he cannot faint and in doing so grab for support, "the support being Shirley's ankle," and accidentally-on-purpose tear her stocking, offer to repay her for the damage, and get her address to boot. Indeed, the only resolution that Salinger can come up with is the "more logical" possibility that Horgenschlag might have got desperate:

Teaching Salinger's Nine Stories

There are still a few men who love desperately. Maybe Horgenschlag was one . . . He might have snatched Shirley's handbag and run with it toward the rear exit door. Shirley would have screamed. Men would have heard her, and remembered the Alamo or something. Horgenschlag's flight, let's say, is now arrested. The bus is stopped. Patrolman Wilson, who hasn't made a good arrest in a long time, reports on the scene. What's going on here? (132)

Salinger follows the thread of this absurd love-narrative straight down the line. Horgenschlag is "hauled into court"; in court, he learns Shirley's address. The judge sentences Horgenschlag to a year in jail, where, having memorized Shirley's address, he writes her a letter. Salinger decides, however, that this scenario can only end with Shirley rejecting Horgenschlag by mail (Horgenschlag, "what a name"), the poor young inmate being mistaken by his cellmates for Ratface Ferrero, a man who ratted them out in Chicago, and eventually getting shot-again, mistakenly-during a prisonbreak in which one of his cellmates captures the warden's eight-year-old niece. "And, thus," Salinger writes, "my plan to write a boy-meets-girl story for *Collier*'s, a tender, memorable love story, is thwarted by the death of my hero" (132).

But that's not the end of Salinger's "Broken Story." Horgenschlag may be a schlemiel (and a shlamazel), but what if-the story is told almost entirely in the realm of *if-*

what if Horgenschlag could have written Shirley a letter from prison:

> *I loved the way your lips were so slightly parted. You represented the answer to everything to me. I haven't been unhappy since I came to New York four years ago, but neither have I been happy. Rather, I can best describe myself as having been one of the thousands of young men in New York who simply exist. ... Loving you is the important thing, Miss Lester. There are some people who think love is sex and marriage and six o'clock-kisses and children, and perhaps it is, Miss Lester. But do you know what I think? I think love is a touch and not a touch.* (133)

Horgenschlag-in this letter that he does not write, and which Salinger composes for him-is at his most nakedly romantic. Horgenschlag here is seeking *connection*, some authentic contact with another human being in the loneliness of a city in which he simply exists. He is seeking after that quality of love that is at once physical and metaphysical, flesh and more than the mere touch of flesh. **(E2)**

If it makes any real sense, and it may not even begin to, I want to propose "The Heart of a Broken Story" as a touchstone in Salinger's oeuvre. It offers us an early model, if nothing else, of the narrator who turns on himself, who can't stop turning on himself, mid-sentence-in other words, a model of the endless self-deprecation that inflects (or infects) so many of Salinger's first-person narrators. In "Broken Story," the narrator's self-deprecating attitude is meant to balance the narrative's sentimental premise-the "inexpressible agony" of falling in love with a stranger on a Third Avenue Bus. And I think similar deflections of sentiment, similar efforts to keep *sincere* affection from turning into blasé affectation, are at the heart of Salinger's more mature stories as well.

"De Daumier-Smith's Blue Period," though it was written and published relatively late (1952) in the composition of what would become *Nine Stories*, is in its loose narrative construction and talky manner, the most reminiscent of pre-War Salinger of his post-War period. Perhaps this is because the story returns to a historical moment a few years before America entered the war (1939), and offers Salinger an opportunity to reflect on his own former youth and innocence. De Daumier-Smith's facility with visual art may also easily be coupled with Salinger's youthful facility with literature. Perhaps Salinger wrote the story, in part, as a fond farewell to an earlier self-as an apologia for the early work which was at least *sincere*, in Trilling's debased sense, at least "conceived in innocence of heart" (Trilling 6).

But such a strictly autobiographical approach to Salinger leads to an unsurprising dead end. Probably it is more useful to think of "De Daumier-Smith's Blue Period" as a story in which Salinger has gathered together themes and character traits from earlier work only to rework them within the elaborately constructed short story cycle of *Nine Stories*. In 1941, Salinger got stuck on the bus with Horgenschlag because he had imagined himself into an unsolvable fictional problem-how to get the boy to meet the girl. But Horgenschlag's story is shlock, the man himself has no character, only a sociological description; and his story can only be saved from its own predictable mechanics by Salinger's wit. In "De Daumier-Smith's Blue Period," on the other hand, we are immediately presented with a fully drawn character-thanks to a narrator who is humorously recalling the exploits of his younger self-and De Daumier-Smith's experience on a New York City bus offers us immediate insight to his character and his situation in life, "a significant incident" as he calls it:

> *I was standing up in a very crowded Lexington Avenue bus, holding on to the enamel pole near the driver's seat, buttocks to buttocks with the chap behind me. For a number of blocks the driver had repeatedly given those of us bunched up near the front door a curt order to 'step to the rear of the vehicle.' Some of us had tried to oblige him. Some of us hadn't.* (131)

We can guess which group the narrator belongs to when the bus driver turns to him and says: "All right, buddy ... let's move that ass" (131). Informing the driver, "in French, that he was a rude, stupid, overbearing imbecile, and that he'd never know how much I detested him," the narrator then, finally, steps to the rear of the vehicle.

Unlike Horgenschlag, this young man has no apparent interest in connecting with others (even girls his own age go unmentioned until the end of the story): he wants only to be alone. His failure to find a seat on the crowded bus leads to a fantastical vision of absolute loneliness where "all the seats from all the buses in New York had been unscrewed and set up in the street, where a monstrous game of Musical Chairs was in full swing" (132). "I prayed for the city to be cleared of people," he tells us, "for the gift of being alone-a-l-o-n-e: which is the one New York prayer that rarely gets lost or delayed in channels, and in no time at all everything I touched turned to solid loneliness" (132).

As most readers note, Jean's desire for a *seat* is a major concern of the story. First the seat on the bus, then the fantastical game of musical chairs, and later, after Jean has moved to Montreal and begun work at the Les Amis des Vieux Maîtres Correspondence Art School, the lack of a chair in his room. The only time that Jean finds a seat in New York is in a dentist chair where he has "eight teeth extracted, three of them front ones" (133). And the only time he finds a seat in Montreal is when he drags one upstairs himself.

The critic Mike Tierce claims this as Salinger's "final key reference to a chair" because it designates Jean's "new sense of security" at the story's end (57). Having expelled four of his students from the correspondence art school in a fit of self-aggrandizing adolescent rancor, Jean has now had his "Experience," and is back in his room writing letters reinstating those students:

> *I said a mistake had been made in the administration department. Actually, the letters seemed to write themselves. It may have had something to do with the fact that, before sitting down to write, I'd brought up a chair from downstairs.* (Nine Stories 164)

The chair is certainly a symbol of Jean's newfound sense of security and self. But the question of finding a seat-a place to sit in-is equally connected to Jean's sincerity (or lack thereof). On the Lexington Avenue bus, he is a poseur par excellence: he speaks rudely to the New York bus driver in French. In the fantasy of musical chairs, he wants "special dispensation from the Church of Manhattan guaranteeing that all other players would remain respectfully standing till I was seated" (132). And at Les Amis des Vieux Maîtres, his very presence is based on a series of lies, which he feels increasingly threatened to maintain despite-or, more likely, because of-the Yoshotos' silence and inscrutability.

Jean De Daumier-Smith is, in short, one of the most insincere characters in Salinger's fiction. From his made-up moniker on down to his dandy appearance, he is an expert fabricator of complicated, ridiculous lies. Yet the *narrator* of De Daumier-Smith, whatever his name may be, is one of the sincerest narrators in *Nine Stories*. Along with the tellers of "The Laughing Man" and "For Esmé-With Love and Squalor," the elder "Jean" has a wonderful way of making fun of and exposing the inner workings of his younger self simply by telling the truth about himself (or what passes as truth in fiction).

Even as the details of Jean's lying exploits seem almost-almost-exaggerated (the seventeen self-portraits he paints in New York, his proclamation of kinship with Honoré de Daumier, his friendship with Picasso, and his wife dead from stomach cancer), together this record of fibs stack up to a portrait of a teenager driven so wild by the will to deceive *everyone*, including himself, that his identity threatens to topple over and break at any second. And so it does.

The trouble begins with the boy's grief over his mother's death, a grief which is only aggravated by his stepfather Bobby's necessary move (it is 1939; Hitler has or is about to invade Poland; Europe is about to be at total war) back to New York, where, to add insult to injury as far as Jean is concerned, Bobby begins seeing another woman, a Mrs. X. The job at Les Deux Amis in Montréal offers Jean an escape from his stepfather-from their "ghastly little after-*you*-Alphonse relationship" (133)-and from New York itself. But the one thing the journey to Montreal cannot offer him is an escape from his grief.

On the contrary, his solitary existence in Montreal and the lies which got him there require that he live on insincerity from the very beginning. When M. Yoshoto picks him up from Windsor Station, Jean, seated but seated very awkwardly, feels compelled to talk, "with my legs crossed, ankle on knee, and constantly using my sock as an absorber for the perspiration on my palm" (139). He finds himself in the Dostoyevskian throes of compulsive insincerity:

It seemed to me urgent not only to reiterate my earlier lies-about my kinship with Daumier, about my deceased wife, about my small estate in the South of France-but to elaborate on them. At length, in effect to spare myself from dwelling on these painful reminiscences (and they were beginning to feel a little painful), I swung over to the subject of my parents' oldest and dearest friend: Pablo Picasso. (139)

Jean is in a daze of dissemblance. The narrator repeats the phrases "at some length" and "I said," in particular, to give an idea of his fibbing frenzy. At the school, for instance, at a loss what he should do, Jean runs through various possible Picasso anecdotes before praising a "goose-in-flight picture hanging over Mme. Yoshoto... lavishly at some length" (145), and then: "I said I knew a man in Paris-a very wealthy paralytic, I said-who would pay M. Yoshoto any price at all for the picture" (145). Luckily, M. Yoshoto "said the picture belonged to his cousin" (145). "Then, before I could express my regret," the narrative begins to turn, "he asked me-addressing me as M. Daumier-Smith-if I would kindly correct a few lessons" (145). After this exchange, the narrative becomes less concerned with Jean's outrageous stories about himself and more concerned with Jean's developing relationship-filtered largely through questions of art and what it means to be an artist-with the world at large.

That relationship begins on a small scale, with Bambi Kramer, R. Howard Ridgefield, and most of all Sister Irma. Sister Irma's answers to the school's standard questionnaire-"filled out as perhaps no questionnaire in *this* world deserves to be filled out" (148)-suggest a pure and sincere person. Her hobbies are "loving her Lord and the Word of her Lord and 'collecting leaves but only when they are laying right on the ground'" (148). Irma's painting of Christ's Burial moves him first because of its "major figure": "a woman in the left foreground, *facing* the viewer" who with her right hand raised over her head is "frantically signaling to someone-her child, perhaps, or her husband, or possibly the viewer-to drop everything and hurry over" (149). The second figure in the painting that moves him is Mary Magdalene, or a woman he takes to be

Mary Magdalene, who "was in the middle-foreground, walking apparently self-detached from the crowd, her arms down at her sides" (149). Jean is moved by what he takes to be her stoic grief. "She wore no part of her grief, so to speak, on her sleeve," he says; "in fact, there were no outward signs at all of her late, enviable connections with the Deceased" (150). "It was, in any conclusive sense, an artist's picture," he says, "steeped in high, high, organized talent and God knows how many hours of hard work" (150).

There are a number of possible reasons why Sister Irma's picture should affect Jean so profoundly. There is, foremost, the grief that he perceives in the figure of Mary Magdalene, which offers him a mirror of his own grieving for his mother. In Sister Irma, he may indeed see a surrogate mother-a motherly image of ideal purity and sincerity that would redeem him of his own confused identity.

Then there is the religious faith that apparently imbues Irma's picture with "high, high, organized talent and God knows how many hours of hard work." Certainly, Jean's "Experience" in front of the orthopedic appliances shop window inspires a number of viable religious interpretations. It's not at all out of the question to understand the faceless wooden dummy as God, and the "hefty girl of about thirty, in a green, yellow and lavender chiffon dress" changing the rupture truss on the wooden dummy as a Magdalene tending to the wounded Christ (it is a rupture truss). Sister Irma's sincerity is rooted in her Christian faith, which is quite different from Jean's layman's interest in religious mysticism; to leapfrog the literal and actual facts of the story risks smoothing over the deliberate rough edges of Salinger's narrative here.

Thus a third reason why Jean may be so moved by Sister Irma's picture has to do with the *lack* of information that Irma provides about herself-no age, no photograph of herself, a painting full of vague or faceless entities-a lack which allows Jean to project onto her a slew of sympathetic traits, and a lack which also allows him to express himself about something besides *himself*: "You paint slightly the way [St. Francis of Assisi] spoke," he writes her, "in many pleasant ways, in my opinion" (153), and later "I think you are greatly talented and would not even be slightly startled if you developed into a genius before many years have gone by" (153). Jean desperately wants to talk to her about her "spiritual path" (as Teddy will have it) as well as her path toward artistic "genius," but he goes about this inquiry by means that Sister Irma is more than likely not prepared for:

If it is not overstepping myself, I would greatly appreciate your telling me if you find being a nun very satisfactory, in a spiritual way, of course. Frankly, I have been studying various religions as a hobby ever since I read volumes 36, 44, 45 of the Harvard Classics, which you may be acquainted with. I am especially delighted with Martin Luther, who was a Protestant, of course. Please do not be offended by this. I advocate no doctrine; it is not my nature to do so. (154)

Sister Irma has probably not read the *Harvard Classics*. But the volumes Jean refers to tell us something about his own omnivorous forays into comparative religion. Volume 36 (which includes Martin Luther, as well as Sir Thomas More and Machiavelli) along with volumes 44 and 45 (selections from Confucian, Hebrew, Christian, Buddhist, Hindu, and Mohammedan scriptures and psalms) represent the core of the *Harvard Classics*' secular-humanist attention to religious texts (that there are 43 volumes *before* scripture is a good indication of the *Classics*' emphasis on religion). And while there is every reason to question Jean's motives for convincing Sister Irma to become an artist-and, possibly, not quite consciously, to give up the habit-there is little reason to doubt Jean's sincere interest in religions or his poorly articulated admiration for St. Francis.

But what does the reader make of the narrator's "Experience"? William Wiegand, in a 1963 article titled "Salinger, from Daumier to Smith," claims that Jean, in front of the shop-window, has "a frankly mystical Experience," adding: "Salinger himself, only half ironically, uses the capital "e" [sic] to describe it, perhaps to indicate that it takes a momentary union with God in order to achieve a real insight into a man's relationship with his fellows" (13). If so, why does the narrator insist that he would "like, if possible, to avoid seeming to pass [the experience] off as a case, or even a borderline case, of genuine mysticism" (*Nine Stories* 163)? (This is the narrator talking, after all, not the unreliable young Jean, and we have no reason to doubt him.)

It's most telling to look closely at the incident in the text before jumping to extratextual conclusions. As the girl is dressing the dummy in the shop-window, she turns and sees Jean looking at her, blushes, steps backward, and slips "on a stack of irrigation basins":

I reached out to her instantly, hitting the tips of my fingers on the glass. She landed heavily on her bottom, like a skater. She immediately got to her feet without looking at me. Her face still flushed, she pushed her hair back with one hand, and resumed lacing up the truss on the dummy. It was just then that I had my Experience. Suddenly (and I say this, I believe, with all due self-consciousness), the sun came up and sped toward the bridge of my nose at the rate of ninety-three million miles a second. Blinded and very frightened—I had to put my hand on the glass to keep my balance. (163-164)

When Jean recovers from this sudden burst of light, "the girl had gone from the window, leaving behind her a shimmering field of exquisite, twice-blessed, enamel flowers" (164). This passage contains yet another in a long series of glass imagery in *Nine Stories*, with the glass of the shop-window harking back to "See More Glass" in "Perfect Day for Bananafish" and, more distantly, to 1 Corinthians 13.11-12. And indeed the narrator is about to put away "childish things" by several means: by writing letters reinstating the art-school students he has unfairly dismissed, by giving up his false identity as Jean De Daumier-Smith and rejoining his stepfather Bobby in Rhode Island "investigating that most interesting of all summer-active animals, the American girl in shorts" (164-165), and by giving Sister Irma "'her freedom to follow her own destiny. Everybody is a nun.' (*Tout le monde est une nonne.*)" (164).

All of this-at least until we get to the postscript-like ending and "the American girl in shorts"-is very tempting to interpret against the narrator's own warning that his is *not* "a case, or even a borderline case, of genuine mysticism." But Jean's "Experience" has far more to do with grieving over his mother than St. John of the Cross' *via negativa* or the gentle orders of St. Francis.

In his interaction with the woman who falls on the stack of irrigation basins, and whom he reaches out to through the glass, he is beginning to reach out to the world beyond himself. He is beginning to embrace his involvement with the rest of humanity-to break out of a youthful solipsism into a more mature view of the world, in which he will have gravity, visibility, and culpability for the lies he tells. On the most basic level, "Everybody is a nun" means that *everybody* is worthy of Jean's sympathy-not only the ideal, and idealized, Sister Irma. **(E3)** "In a burst of light," as Kenneth Slawenski writes, "Smith experiences the revelation that beauty and value are inherent in all things, even the most lowly and untalented" (226).

This is not to deny the religious symbolism that surrounds nearly every detail in this part of the text (as Slawenski adds, the beauty inherent in all things proclaims for Salinger "the presence of God" [226]). The twice-blessed flowers clearly allude to *The Flowers of St. Francis* (the patron saint of this story); the burst of light, figured as "the sun," which sends Jean reeling, drives home the allusion to Corinthians both in its suggestion that for a moment he does not see through the glass darkly and that it is the sun/son-that age-old Christian pun-that lights his way. But the burst of light may also recall Zen "satori"-a sudden flash of enlightenment, "individual and intuitive and the opposite of intellectual knowledge" (227). These multiple symbolisms are, however, implicit in the language, and unless one proposes to interpret the text allegorically, there's no rational basis for arguing that Jean has "seen the light" and is now going on down a recognizable mystical path, whether Christian, Buddhist, or otherwise.

Rather, the story concludes in an affirmation of Jean's newfound comfort in being "John Smith" (the underlying

American identity of Jean De Daumier) and his spiritual *sortie* will be that of an artist. He has brought a chair down from upstairs, and taken a seat, and he has, in light of his crisis of grief and faith, begun to see that he is only one person among many in the world. If he is going to live in the world, he is going to have try his hand at being sincere rather than smart. He is, in other words, going to have to embrace sincerity even though he recognizes (with Salinger himself) "the anachronism which touches ['sincerity'] with quaintness," the anachronism that makes us speak it "with either discomfort or irony" (Trilling 6).

In the stories leading up to "De Daumier-Smith," Salinger has signaled the word "sincerity" in two key senses-on the one hand, in its root sense (the sincere sense of "sincere") as it appears in "For Esmé" when Sergeant X is reassuring Clay he was right to shoot the cat that jumped on the hood of their jeep when the two of them under heavy fire at Valognes:

"That cat was a spy. You had *to take a pot shot at it. It was a clever German midget dressed up in a cheap fur coat. So there was absolutely nothing brutal, or cruel, or dirty, or even-"*

"God damn it!" Clay said, his lips thinned. "Can't you ever be sincere?" (110).

At this, "X suddenly felt sick, and he swung around in his chair and grabbed the wastebasket-just in time" (110). In the midst of wartime trauma, the idea of sincerity is nauseating to X.; it may indeed be his recognition of the impossibility of his own sincerity-his own total discomfort with it-that he finds so nauseating.

Then, in "Pretty Mouth and Green My Eyes," the gray-haired man reassures the friend with whose wife he's having an affair:

> "I'd like to beat some sense into that head of yours, boy, that's what I'd like to do . . . For a helluvan-For a supposedly intelligent guy, you talk like an absolute child. And I say that in all sincerity." (123)

Here "sincerity" is being used in its most devalued sense, spoken by a man who is lying to his friend by omitting that *he* is the man sleeping with his wife. Here Salinger's reader has to understand the deep irony of the gray-haired man pretending to have any kind of sincerity at all.

In "De Daumier-Smith's Blue Period," Jean is insincere in every aspect of his life except his letters or at least parts of his letters to Sister Irma (one of which he conventionally signs "Sincerely yours"). **(E4)** Only in these "long, almost endless" letters does he discover a medium to record not only his inward transactions but also his transactions with another, with the world beyond himself. Of course, he never receives an answer from Sister Irma and the result of his frankness, his blunt naked adolescent sincerity, is that Irma-a nun, after all-must resign from the school. Jean's letters provide him a means of confession, even if that confession is primarily to and for himself (and, finally, we the readers).

Almost the only way to understand Jean-to figure out where he stands (or sits)-is to look closely at his lies, his insincerities. The title itself here provides a key. "De Daumier-Smith's Blue Period" draws on Jean's fabricated kinship with Honoré de Daumier as much as to Picasso's Blue Period, when Picasso, still in his twenties, painted many of his paintings in cool blue tones. The overly simplistic textbook analysis of the period is that these blue tones "established a melancholic mood and stressed the isolation of many of his works' subjects" (Kerr 206). But the word "period" assures us that De Daumier-Smith's blues are just a passing phase. As Picasso's Blue Period was followed by the Rose Period (when, Kerr too simplistically informs us, "his art became lighter and less bleak" [206]), Jean also turns to a rosier view of life (those "American girls in shorts" again).

But this is only a superficial reading of Jean's "Blue Period." If we turn back to his ride from Windsor Station with M. Yoshoto-when he finds it "urgent not only to reiterate my earlier lies...but to elaborate on them"-we remember one of Jean's biggest whoppers about *le pauvre Picasso*:

> For M. Yoshoto's benefit, I recalled, with a showy amount of natural compassion for a fallen giant, how many times I had said to him, "M. Picasso oi ᴨ allez vous?" and how, in response to this all-penetrating question, the master had never failed to walk slowly, leadenly, across his studio to look at a small reproduction of his "Les Saltimbanques" and the glory, long forfeited, that had been his. The trouble with Picasso, I explained to M. Yoshoto as we got out of the bus, was that he never listened to anybody-even his closest friends. (139)

This must be one of Jean's most revealing lies. In his portrait of Picasso Jean makes something close to a self-portrait. Jean never listens to anybody, even his stepfather. And Jean's Picasso is very much unlike the artist himself in that this fictive Picasso gazes longingly back to his more *realistic* early work, the work that preceded the complex experiments of Cubism and all that followed. Jean is the one who values draftsmanship above all else, the miniaturized perfection of a realistic scene suffused with figures of isolation and melancholy over the fractal and fractured work of the post-1909 Picasso. **(E5)**

In Jean's letters, and in the windy construction of "De Daumier-Smith's Blue Period" as a whole, the reader finds one of the first instances of Salinger's own more fractal and fractured post-Cubist style-a style in which the neat endings, which maddened Salinger as early as 1941, were no longer of the essence. This is why William Wiegand writes that "De Daumier-Smith's Blue Period" "is Salinger's last 'shaped' story; for in earlier stories, regardless of what may have been implied, nobody ever said that everyone was a nun" (71). In later stories, narrators and protagonists "*are* to be found saying such things and consequently speaking in defense of non-discrimination...and of garrulousness" (71, my italics). Even as "De Daumier-Smith's Blue Period" looks back to Salinger's talky wiseguy beginnings-to "The Heart of a Broken Story"-it also looks forward to the mystically-laced, deliberately broken ramblings of *Seymour* and *Raise High the Roof Beam, Carpenters*, and, maybe, to whatever new forms of expression Salinger found thereafter. (**E6**)

It is in their effort to be sincere that the "late" Salinger (everything from *Franny* and *Zooey* onward) stand or fall. Beginning with "De Daumier-Smith's Blue Period," Salinger seems to have banked heavily on the importance of his narrator's recognizing their own phoniness, their own insincerity, perhaps as a means of better understanding the transience and illusory nature of the material world-"this splendid planet where (please don't shut me up) Kilroy, Christ, and Shakespeare all stopped" (*Seymour* 98). He sought to reach out to readers not through the artifice of fictional construction, of which *Nine*

Stories proves him a master, but through an elaborately direct address to the reader himself, as he does near the beginning of *Seymour: An Introduction*: "I privately say to you, old friend (unto you, really, I'm afraid), please accept from me this unpretentious bouquet of very early-blooming parentheses (((( ))))" (98). The question that remains in my mind (and, I have no doubt, in the minds of others) is *if* Salinger continued to find paper and ink a suitable medium for the sincere address of unknown others, whether its extreme privacy has not made his very intentions forbidding.

Endnotes:

E1: Having thought for years, stupidly, that I was alone in admiring "The Heart of a Broken Story," I was flabbergasted and floored when I read the following passage in the Spanish writer Enrique Vila-Matas's novel *Bartleby & Co.* in which the narrator spots Salinger on a bus "on New York's Fifth Avenue" at the same time that he falls in love with a girl sitting next to him:

> *I was suddenly reminded of a story by Salinger, 'The Heart of a Broken Story,' in which someone on a bus, on seeing the girl of his dreams, planned a question to the one I had secretly formulated. ["Gosh, how I love you. Are you free tonight?] ... It occurred to me to approach Salinger and say to him, "Gosh, how*

I love you Salinger. Would you mind telling me why you have not published anything in so many years? Is there an essential reason why one should stop writing? (79-80).

Bartleby & Co. is itself an inquiry into silence and literature, into why some writers decide to stop writing, or to never write at all. Salinger's chapter takes up a significant section of the (very funny) book.

E2: The curious fact that Salinger is only rarely grouped with his contemporaries encourages many readers to think about him too purely on his own terms. Salinger's Horgenschlag (even more than the young De Daumier-Smith) is among the ranks of mid-century urban characters of American Fiction, who yearn for spiritual contact (and who also get the spiritual mixed up with the carnal). Bellow's *Dangling Man*, whose narrator is perplexed by "the common, neutral matter of an existence" would be one good example. Salinger and the early Bellow may have more in common than critics (or Bellow, for that matter) have cared to admit:

There was a time when people were in the habit of addressing themselves frequently and felt no shame at making a record of their inward transactions. But to keep a journal nowadays is considered a kind of self-indulgence, a weakness, and in poor taste. For this is an era of hardboiled-dom.... Do you have feelings? There are correct and incorrect ways of indicating them. Do you have an inner life? It is nobody's business but your own. Do you have emotions? Strangle them.... If you have difficulties, grapple with them silently, goes one of their commandments. To hell with that! I intend to talk about mine, and if I had as many mouths as Siva has arms and kept them going all the time, I could not do myself justice. (7)

E3: There is also bilingual punning in Salinger's inclusion of "*Tout le monde est une nonne,*" which suggests a pervading *non*-a recognition of the material world's nothingness, as written about in St. John of the Cross or in Buddhism. But this reading is only hinted at, never brought to the forefront as it would be in later works like *Zooey* or *Seymour*. The all-important chair is also hinted to be "the mercy seat"-the lid of the Ark of the Covenant, which is the sign of concord between God and man that is the basis of the Jewish religion. And Jean's upper room recalls the upper chamber to which the disciples retire in *Acts*.

E4: Only young children are truly sincere in Salinger's fiction-Sybil in "Perfect Day for Bananafish," or Lionel in "Down at the Dinghy." Teddy is an absolutely sincere character who is both a child and a wise old sage.

E5: Picasso's *Les Saltimbanques* (1905) is a painting of the Rose Period, not the Blue Period (whether a mistake of Jean's or Salinger's, I don't know); and other than its pinkish color there is very little reason to file the painting under the heading of a "lighter and less bleak" artistic vision. A desert landscape dominated by six traveling circus performers ("saltimbanque" literally means *acrobat* or *street performer*, and these were Picasso's favorite subjects at the time), each of the six figures looks in opposing directions. Every one of these performers is isolated from the others' gazes. And in fact, the performers are very likely stand-ins for Picasso's own band of outsiders (Apollinaire, Max Jacob, Andre Salmon, his lover Fernande Olivier, and the main figure, furthest to the left, who seems either to be a taller version of Picasso himself or a combination of his profile and that of his old friend Casamegas whose suicide prompted him, in part, into the melancholy tones of the Blue Period (see Blum and Blum). How much of this would have been known by Salinger is unclear.

A footnote to this footnote: Rilke's fifth *Duino Elegy* takes up *Les Saltimbanques*, and if Rilke is in fact the "German poet" that Seymour insists Muriel should read in "A Perfect Day for Bananafish," perhaps the allusion to Rilke is indirectly continued and deepened here.

E6: Many readers-in fact, some of Salinger's most committed readers-tend to interpret Salinger's early work with information gained in the late work. Salinger himself encourages this in the fiction by creating a Yoknapatawpha-esque world where everything (or nearly everything) meshes together.

But it's important to note that Leslie Fiedler's disgust with Seymour Glass ("J. D. Salinger's insufferable Seymour Glass, whose death by his own hand-presumably for all of our sins..." [65]), for instance, has its basis, *in part*, in the faulty idea that Seymour is redeeming anyone by blowing his brains out on a bed across from his wife. Either Salinger has a very weak understanding (which seems unlikely) of suicide and its effects on others, or he hadn't fully worked out the significance of Seymour's suicide when writing "A Perfect Day for Bananafish." If Seymour were as Christly as some critics say, he should be able to see that Muriel, too, "is a nun." Only in the later works do we get the idea of Seymour (most explicitly in "Seymour: An Introduction" [106]) as a guru or a kind of savior. In fact, it may be Salinger's urgent attempt to clear Seymour's name and justify his action that he focuses so intently upon him in the later fiction.

Works Cited:

Bellow, Saul. *Dangling Man*. NY: Vanguard, 1944.

Blum, Elsa and Harold. "The Models of Picasso's Rose Period: The Family of Saltimbanques." *The American Journal of Psychoanalysis* 67 (2007): 181-196.

Fiedler, Leslie. *Fiedler on the Roof: Essays on Literature and Jewish Identity*. NY: Godine, 1991.

Kerr, Christine. *Bloom's How to Write About J.D. Salinger*. NY: Bloom's Literary Criticism, 2008.

Salinger, J. D. "The Heart of a Broken Story." *Esquire* XVI Sep. 1941: 32, 131-133.

---. *Nine Stories*. Boston: Little, Brown, 1953.

---. *Raise High the Roof Beam, Carpenters and Seymour: An Introduction*. Boston: Little, Brown, 1963.

Tierce, Mike. "Salinger's 'De Daumier-Smith's Blue Period." *The Explicator* 42.1 (1983): 56.

Trilling, Lionel. *Sincerity and Authenticity*. Cambridge, MA: Harvard UP, 1978.

Vila-Matas, Enrique. *Bartleby & Co*. NY: New Directions, 2005.

Wiegand, William. "Salinger, from Daumier to Smith." *Contemporary Literature* 4 (1963): 70-87.

One Little Genius Among the Missing:
Loss, Human Communion, and the Negative Way in "Teddy"

William Boyle
University of Mississippi

In "A Reading of Salinger's 'Teddy,'" James Bryan writes: "Coming at the end of *Nine Stories*, 'Teddy,' with its optimism and serenity provides a satisfying closing bracket for the collection" (366). Bryan argues that its connections with the other stories can be seen in Salinger's use of symbolic imagery in the story: pair/twin imagery, broken head imagery, the empty pool on E deck. Most importantly, he notes: "The opening of 'A Perfect Day for Bananafish' ends tragically with Seymour Glass's suicide, while 'Teddy' ends with a death that signifies, Teddy insists, that no tragedy is possible to the mind that thinks rightly" (367). Of course this flies in the face of most critics' reactions to "Teddy," a story often designated as the weak link in an otherwise classic collection. Even Salinger himself-via Buddy Glass in "Seymour: An Introduction" describes it as an "exceptionally Haunting, Memorable, unpleasantly controversial, and thoroughly unsuccessful short story about a 'gifted' little boy aboard a transatlantic liner" (176). Still, Salinger-or Buddy, or whoever-must have held the story in high regard at some point to give it such a prominent place in the collection. This is, after all, not a baseball lineup. "Teddy" was intended to be *something big,* Salinger's "Big Two-Hearted River," a story meant to leave us with a great feeling of hopefulness.

Yet, as I have said, it has been a sort of whipping boy story for critics of Salinger. Frederick Gywnn and Joseph Blotner note the "growing diffuseness of the story and the ambiguity of the conclusion" (40). James Lundquist argues that the story "does not move," saying "its static quality is the consequence of contrast without conflict" (108). Laurence Perrine concedes that the story is "vivid" and "brilliantly written" but argues that its "focus is uncertain and its conclusion mystifying" (223). Perrine continues: "the ambiguity of the conclusion suggests that the author either was unclear in his aims or lacked the courage of his conviction" (223). Anthony Kaufman's "'Along this road goes no one': Salinger's 'Teddy' and the Failure of Love," one of the most recent pieces of criticism on the story, comes to Salinger's defense, arguing that "Teddy" is "highly successful-indeed deeply moving-when we understand that [it] is the story not of a cool and detached mystical prodigy, but of an unloved, frightened ten year old" (129). Both Kaufman and James Bryan draw a link between "A Perfect Day for Bananafish" and "Teddy," arguing, in fact, that Teddy *is* Seymour, and that "Teddy" is the logical conclusion to a collection that begins with "Bananafish."

To support their arguments, Kaufman and Bryan draw on the testimony of Buddy Glass, who admits, in "Seymour: An Introduction," that some of the Glass family members accused him of trying to make Teddy a sort of disguised version of a young Seymour (there are many similarities between the young Seymour we see in "Hapworth 16, 1924," Salinger's last published story, and Teddy, not the least of which is that they are both compulsive letter-writers). In fact, Buddy tells us, a lot of people insist that all of his stories are about Seymour and Seymour only. Buddy says that Seymour was the Glass family's "blue-striped unicorn, or double-lensed burning glass, our consultant genius, or portable conscience, our supercargo and our one full poet" (*Raise High* 106). Kaufman and Bryan draw out these connections, and Kaufman is at his best when he talks about "Teddy" as an "interesting and credible study of the way in which a ten year old has intuitively defended himself against the ego, anger, and indifference that his parents and the adult world have inflicted upon him" (130). Kaufman continues: "In its portrayal of the underloved child, 'Teddy' embodies the Salinger masterplot as seen in *Catcher* and the other stories of *Nine Stories*" (130). I lose track of his argument, however, when he suggests that Teddy's death is a suicide. Though he means to draw a further connection between Teddy and Seymour, he is wrong in suggesting that Teddy has committed suicide. We are meant, on the other hand, to consider Seymour's suicide in a much different light after witnessing Teddy's relaxed approached to death. (Kaufman is wrong about another thing, by the way. Teddy is detached, though not in the angsty way that Kaufman's language implies. Teddy's detachment, instead, is of the spiritual variety.) In his conversation with Nicholson, Teddy says of death: "All you do is get the heck out of your body when you die. My gosh, everybody's done it thousands and thousands of times. Just because they don't remember it doesn't mean they haven't done it. It's so silly" (Salinger 193).

Teddy goes on to essentially predict his death-his sister pushing him into the empty pool on E deck, Teddy fracturing his skull and dying instantaneously-and he continues: "That could happen, all right. What would be so tragic about it, though? What's there to be afraid of, I mean? I'd just be doing what I was supposed to do, that's all, wouldn't I?" (193). Nicholson replies: "It might not be a tragedy from your point of view, but it would certainly be a sad event for your mother and dad. Ever consider that?" (193). Teddy says, "Yes, of course, I have. But that's only because they have names and emotions for everything that happens" (194). Viewed in this light, the suicide-Seymour's suicide-that opens the book and informs so much of Salinger's, of Buddy Glass's, fiction, is NOT tragic. Seymour is doing what he is supposed to do: merely leaving his body. Teddy continues to explain that the goal of humans concerned with spiritual advancement should be to forget the way "all the other apple-eaters look at things" (196). Seymour is doing this in "Bananafish," trying to retreat to an innocent view of the world. His encounter with Sybil reveals his disassociation from a world of nail lacquer and false morality, fashionable codes and spiritual trampdom. Seymour, after all, was the one who said that "all we do our whole lives is go from one little piece of Holy Ground to the next" (*Raise High* 213). Teddy, in a way, explains and *justifies* Seymour's death, his choice to move on.

If Teddy, then, seems too didactic, a character whose only function is to talk to us about how to live and die, we are looking at him the wrong way. Remember: he answers questions only when prompted by the nagging Nicholson. He is not attempting to convert, only recounting what he has learned, what he feels. Teddy is the real hero of this story, of this collection, because he is humble, because of his mystical understanding of loss and human communion, because of his sense that enlightenment can only be achieved through nothingness, because of his *detachment*. On that note, much has been made of Teddy's penchant for Eastern religion, but little has been said about his relationship to Catholic mysticism. In *The Way of Perfection*, St Teresa of Avila writes:

> *If this be perfect it will include everything else. I say "it will include everything else" because, if we cling to our Creator alone and care nothing for created things, His Majesty will infuse the virtues into us, so that, doing by degrees all that is in our power, we shall have little left with which to struggle, for our Lord will defend us against the devils and the whole world as well.* (52)

And then there is St. John of the Cross's theory of *via negativa*–that the only way to possess everything is to possess and desire nothing–which Teddy seems to know well. He tells Nicholson: "You know that apple Adam ate in the Garden of Eden, referred to in the Bible? You know what was in that apple? Logic. Logic and intellectual stuff. That was all that was in it. So-this is my point-what you have to do is vomit it up if you want to see things as they really are. I mean if you vomit it up, then you won't have any more trouble with blocks of wood and stuff. You won't see everything stopping *off* all the time" (Salinger 191). Teddy, following St. John of the Cross's example, knows that when you finally feel the presence of nothing, when you have expelled the food of humankind's first sin, that you must cultivate nothingness, and that a sense of nothingness prepares you to truly believe.

Teddy's dismissal of poets, who take "the weather so personally," who are "always sticking their emotions in things that have no emotions," is followed fast by his admiration of two Japanese poems that lack "a lot of emotional stuff," that exemplify the way of detachment (185). Teddy recites these poems to Nicholson: "Nothing in the voice of the cicada intimates how soon it will die" and "Along this road goes no one, this autumn eve" (185). After reciting the poems, Teddy claps his right ear with his hand in an attempt to get water from yesterday's swimming lesson out of his ear, essentially answering the Zen *koan* that serves as the epigraph to *Nine Stories*: "We know the sound of two hands clapping. But what is the sound of one hand clapping?" Teddy claps his ear two more times, sits back, and puts his arms up on both armrests of the chair he's sitting in. Salinger writes: "It was, of course, a normal adult-size deck chair, and he looked distinctly small in it, but at the same time, he looked perfectly relaxed, even serene" (186). James Bryan makes much of this, writing that Teddy "has emptied his head of the last of the distractions and, perfectly voided, is ready to become one with the 'Void.' Hence, all the main symbols-ocean, water, pool, empty pool, and the emptying of heads-come together in this ostensibly casual description" (367).

When I speak of Teddy's sense of loss and human communion, I am commenting on the "outsider" role he has been relegated to as resident pint-sized mystic. He tells Nicholson: "I mean it's very hard to meditate and live a spiritual life in America. People think you're a freak if you try to. My father thinks I'm a freak, in a way. And my mother-well, she doesn't think it's good for me to think about God all the time. She thinks it's bad for my health" (Salinger 188-89). Teddy, of course, learned-at six-that "everything was God" (189). He also learned, over time, that God was not meant to be loved sentimentally. When Nicholson asks Teddy if he loves his parents-who we've only seen bickering, his mother peppering Teddy with inappropriate attention, his father making empty threats-Teddy responds: "Yes, I do-very much. But you want me to use that word to mean what you want it to mean, I can tell" (187). Teddy decides that "affinity" (187) is a much better word for what he feels toward his parents. His understanding of love as humility, of human communion as a product of selflessness, informs a deep understanding of a world where there is no loss, no tragedy. Teddy says: "Everybody just *thinks* things keep stopping off somewhere. They don't. The reason things *seem* to stop off somewhere is because that's the only way most people know how to look at things. But that doesn't mean they do" (189-90) Thomas Kranidas tells us that the major message of "Teddy" and "one we have been approving almost to the very end is transcendence" (91). Addressing the lack of resolution that many readers and critics feel at the end of the story, Kranidas writes: "Our concern for the temporary ambiguity convicts us of the same misunderstanding of Teddy which Nicholson demonstrates when he hurries down to the swimming pool. The ambiguity is a brilliantly contrived obstacle to the easy resolution of the story. It prolongs our concern for

Teddy to the point where we see that that concern is wrong: like Nicholson, our ignorance and this-worldly misemphasis has caused the concern" (91). And that concern, as Kranidas suggests, is wrong.

To call Teddy a Christ figure would probably be overdoing it. But Teddy's vision of life and death is certainly meant to serve others. When we last see Teddy, calm, raising Nicholson's hand to shake it, he is headed toward a death he knows may be coming. Earlier in the story, he tells us in his notebook: "It [my death] will either happen today or February 14, 1958 when I am sixteen. It is ridiculous to even mention" (Salinger 182). Teddy's mystical union with God and the world-what Benedicta Ward called the "center of wholeness"-allows him to approach death stoically, serenely. "Salinger's use of child as seer," Bryan writes, "is a functional device for the author to show by contrast what he feels most deeply is wrong with contemporary life and to present a consoling religious optimism" (369).

In that way, Teddy's death-and the story itself-leaves us with a sort of prayerful hope and makes a quiet protest against a world where values have been so far mixed up that someone like Seymour Glass could be driven to kill himself. Only through *emptying out* can we begin to *see* like Teddy. Perhaps characters like Mr. and Mrs. McArdle, Nicholson, and Booper will consider Teddy's death a tragedy (Booper's piercing scream is the first evidence of this) and will gain no enlightenment from it. What matters is that Teddy has transcended at story's end, and that he has moved one step closer to attaining conscious knowledge.

In "The Holy Refusal: A Vedantic Interpretation of J. D. Salinger's Silence," Dipti R. Pattanaik argues that "Salinger's regression into silence may be a reminder of the primacy of self-realization in this clamorous age of ideologies, revolutions, and upheavals whose effect is as temporary as their promises lofty" (126). Teddy's death stands against this, a hushed act of redemption, and "Teddy" is a sharp, precise, and powerful story that seeks to recover nothingness, to bring us into our own presence, that asks us to pause and consider what we think we know about living and dying, what we think we believe.

Works Cited:

Bryan, James. "A Reading of Salinger's 'Teddy.'" *American Literature* 40:3 (November) 352-369.

Gwynn, Frederick L. and Joseph Blotner. *The Fiction of J.D. Salinger*. Pittsburgh: University of Pittsburgh Press, 1958.

Kaufman, Anthony. "'Along this road goes no one': Salinger's 'Teddy' and the Failure of Love." *Studies in Short Fiction* 35.2 (Spring 1998): 129-140.

Kranidas, Thomas. "Point of View in Salinger's 'Teddy.'" *Studies in Short Fiction* 2 (1964): 91.

Lundquist, James. *J.D. Salinger*. New York: Ungar, 1979.

Pattanaik, Dipti R. "The Holy Refusal: A Vedantic Interpretation of J.D. Salinger's Silence." *MELUS* 23.2 (Summer 1998): 113-127.

Perrine, Laurence. "Teddy? Booper? Or Blooper?" *Studies in Short Fiction* 4 (1967): 217-24.

Saint Teresa of Avila. *The Way of Perfection*. Trans. Benedictines of Stanbrook. New York: Cosimo, 2007.

Salinger, J. D. *Nine Stories*. Boston: Little, Brown, 1981 (1953).

----. *Raise High the Roof Beam, Carpenters and Seymour: An Introduction*. Boston: Little, Brown, 1971 (1963).

Additional Copyright Details

The View from the Shore: Seymour Glass in *The Waste Land*. © 2011 by Joseph A. Thompson.

Uncle Wiggily's Haunted House. © 2011 by Olivia Carr Edenfield.

From York to Lexington: A Pilgrimage Through Allusions in "Just Before the War with the Eskimos." © 2011 by Sarah Marshall.

Salinger Criticism and "The Laughing Man": A Case of Arrested Development. © 1981 and 2011 by Richard Allan Davison.

"The old ship is steady again": Empathy and *The Divine Comedy* "Down at the Dinghy." © 2011 by Michael Renganeschi.

Esmé's Kind of Squalor. © 2011 by Donald Junkins.

The Necessity of Art in "Pretty Mouth and Green My Eyes." © 2011 by Holland Whiteburch.

Salinger and Sincerity: "De Daumier-Smith's Blue Period." © 2011 by Alex Shakespeare.

"One Little Genius Among the Missing": Loss, Human Communion, and the Negative Way in "Teddy." © 2011 by William Boyle.

About the Author

Brad McDuffie teaches at Nyack College. His work has been published in various journals including *The South Carolina Review*, *Aethlon* and *North Dakota Quarterly*. His article, "For Ernest, With Love and Squalor: The Influence of Ernest Hemingway on the Life and Work of J. D. Salinger," was excerpted by the *Kansas City Star* in July 2011 and appeared in the spring 2011 edition of *The Hemingway Review*. He has also published articles in several books and journals on Elizabeth Madox Roberts and Richard Aldington. He published his first book of poems, *And the West Was Not So Far Away*, in 2009 and a chapbook of poetry, *Seven Hymns From The West*, in 2010. He received his MA from SUNY New Paltz in 2005 and is currently (2011) finishing his PhD at Indiana University of Pennsylvania.

Also of Interest
from New Street

Hemingway's Paris: Our Paris?
by H.R. Stoneback
"Stoneback's lyrical prose takes the reader inside the soul of Hemingway's Paris, penetrating the surface of guide-books to reveal tantalizing secrets." - A.E. Hotchner

Hemingway's Dark Night: Catholic Influences and Intertextualities in the Work of Ernest Hemingway
By Matthew Nickel
"Matthew Nickel is a thorough and careful scholar. He has delved beneath the surface and found a treasure trove of meaning. This book will enrich every reader's understanding of Hemingway … ." - Valerie Hemingway

On Hemingway and Spain: Essays & Reviews, 1979-2013
by Allen Josephs
" … a deeply felt record of literary criticism at its best as authentically incarnational experience." - H.R. Stoneback

www.ingramcontent.com/pod-product-compliance
Lightning Source LLC
Chambersburg PA
CBHW050546160426
43199CB00015B/2561